As the lead singer and songwriter of Savage Garden and solo artist, Darren Hayes has sold over 35 million albums, achieved two US Billboard number one singles, won 14 ARIAs, 10 APRA songwriting awards and in 2019 received an award in the Order of Australia by the late Her Majesty Queen Elizabeth II for services to the music industry.

Darren has performed at the Royal Albert Hall, Sydney Opera House and Radio City Music Hall. He has duetted with Pavarotti, appeared at the closing ceremony of the Sydney 2000 Olympic Games and twice headlined the Sydney Gay and Lesbian Mardi Gras.

He has studied improv at the renowned Los Angeles theatre The Groundlings, co-hosted numerous episodes of his film podcast 'We Paid To See This' and spent the past five years recording and releasing his most recent album, *Homosexual*.

DARREN HAYES

UNLOVABLE

PENGUIN BOOKS

UK | USA | Canada | Ireland | Australia
India | New Zealand | South Africa | China

Penguin Books is part of the Penguin Random House group of companies
whose addresses can be found at global.penguinrandomhouse.com

Penguin
Random House
Australia

First published by Penguin Books in 2024

Cover photography by Andrew Huebscher
Back cover photograph by Willie Williams
Cover design by Adam Laszczuk © Penguin Random House Australia Pty Ltd
Typeset in 12/17 pt Adobe Garamond Pro by Midland Typesetters, Australia

Printed and bound in Australia by Griffin Press, an accredited
ISO AS/NZS 14001 Environmental Management Systems printer

A catalogue record for this
book is available from the
NATIONAL LIBRARY OF AUSTRALIA   National Library of Australia

ISBN 978 1 76134 191 5

penguin.com.au

MIX
Paper | Supporting
responsible forestry
FSC® C018684

We at Penguin Random House Australia acknowledge that Aboriginal and Torres Strait Islander
peoples are the Traditional Custodians and the first storytellers of the lands on
which we live and work. We honour Aboriginal and Torres Strait Islander peoples'
continuous connection to Country, waters, skies and communities. We celebrate
Aboriginal and Torres Strait Islander stories, traditions and living cultures;
and we pay our respects to Elders past and present.

This book is dedicated to my mother, Judy, who somehow in the midst of a lifetime of challenges filled with sadness, violence and abuse found it within herself to make me feel like the most magical little boy who ever lived. Thank you for loving me and protecting the part of me that was most fragile yet so essential to who I am as a man today. You are and always will be the person I want to be when I grow up.

The Secret

I think I'm psychic. I've suspected it for quite some time, but now that I'm eight years old I'm convinced of it. There are just too many examples for this to be coincidence. The emergence of my powers always follows the same pattern: it starts with a fluttery feeling in my tummy, like butterflies, but not the exciting kind. Rather, it's like there's a nest of wasps in my belly, buzzing and swarming about and occasionally piercing my insides with their sharp needle stingers to warn me that danger is approaching. They hurt if I don't pay attention to them, so I've learned to listen when they're active. Sometimes I think of that book from kindergarten, about the old lady who swallowed a fly. She swallowed a spider to catch the fly and I don't know about you but I don't want to die, so I'm just going to let these wasps live here inside me and listen to them whenever they're annoyed about something, because if I ignore them, bad things happen. Trust me.

Sometimes it's not wasps. Sometimes the feeling is like something from a horror movie. One time when I couldn't sleep my mother let me stay up late to watch *The Blob*. She told me I shouldn't really be watching it because it was for adults only, but since there were no nude scenes in it she supposed it was okay. I promised to close my eyes if anything got too scary. But I'll never forget the scene when the boyfriend and girlfriend got stuck in the meat locker with nowhere to go and the Blob came oozing underneath the door. That's sort of how the feeling of wasps shows up sometimes. It is as if there's something deep within, something alive, stirring and wriggling around making me feel nauseous. This giant, toxic, black, sludge of darkness expands inside me. The feeling intensifies until it spreads, first to my chest where it transforms into a heavy pressure like an actual giant, stepping on my rib cage. Then it becomes an emotion I can only describe as dread. I have this feeling now. It consumes me and fills the bedroom I share with my big brother, Peter, who has long since fallen asleep.

It's way past my bedtime but I'm wide awake. I'm on high alert. I'm waiting for the bad thing to happen, just like I predicted it would.

Earlier this evening my father finally came home from the pub, hours late. When he walked in the door, he was . . . different. His speech was slurred and louder than usual. The words he spoke had a tone like he was joking, but not the friendly kind of joke. And his energy was different. Before the pub, he was his usual quiet, grumpy and serious self. But now? Have you ever seen that TV show *The Incredible Hulk*? With Bill Bixby? One minute he's Bruce Banner and the next? You don't wanna know.

My father sent my big sister, Tracey, and me to bed as soon as he walked in the door. He told my sister she was in trouble because she was a 'smart-arse'. In fact, as soon as he got home, he singled her out. He often does. She was just sitting on the couch watching *The Streets of San Francisco* – it's her favourite TV show at the moment – and he jeered at her, 'What's your problem?'

She didn't have a problem.

'Have you got the shits or something?' he pressed.

'I'm just watching TV,' she replied.

He turned the volume down. He often does this to annoy her. He did this during Wimbledon when she was watching the tennis last season. He knows she loves watching the games but often he'll walk up to the TV and either turn the volume down or just switch it off for no reason other than to make her cry. Then he turned to my mother with a similar line of questioning, trying to get her to react to the fact that he was very late for dinner and very, very drunk. He called her some awful swear words that I am not allowed to say. Tracey pleaded with him to leave our mother alone. That's when he sent us to bed.

I knew this would happen. The wasps in my tummy told me. I wish, when I first had this feeling, I had just told my mother because then none of what is about to happen, would have happened. But I'm scared to get involved and I don't quite believe in my powers yet. I'm only eight years old.

I'm lying awake in my bedroom already feeling guilty I've done nothing to protect my mother from what's about to happen. I look up at the walls, stained with scuff marks and a yellow tinge. Years of my parents' smoking have turned the once-white paint to a kind of caramel. I never want friends to come over. The whole house looks like a version of this bedroom: neglected and sad. I'm so embarrassed by it.

I've put some posters up in my corner of the room, next to the window, which is next to the alley. There's Wonder Woman that I got from *TV Week*, a picture of Mork and Mindy that I pulled from the Sunday newspaper and some stickers that I've been collecting from cartons of Sunny Queen Eggs my mother buys. I've plastered them all over the walls, on my bedhead and on the back of the door. On Peter's side of the room, the four faces of the members of the rock band KISS look down upon me with sympathy. I wish they could help.

I hear my father's voice and it has an edge to it. I look out through the crack in the door. I can see into the hallway from my bed, which I must specify is a child's bed. It might have a cool new 1970s bedspread but I'm not stupid. It's not a 'big boy' bed. I can't remember when we bought it – that's how old it is. I think it used to be a bunk bed, stacked on top of my brother's. Now they sit side by side. It's another reason I don't let anyone inside my bedroom. I am not a child.

There's movement through the sliver of light in the crack in the door. I can't make out exactly what is being said but I hear the tone of my mother's voice and she is frightened.

For a moment I wish what is happening was a musical. That the two people arguing outside are dancers in a music video like the kind they play on Saturday morning TV. I imagine that instead of my father being truly dangerous, he's just pretending like those dancers in an Elvis movie when they fight. I pretend what is happening outside my bedroom is an elaborate dance sequence on a Friday night variety show. I look up at my posters and project myself onto them – or them onto me. Soon, the bedroom window will open and a troupe of dancers will climb in from the alley and fog will roll in across the floor.

I let my mind wander. It has to. If I leave this bedroom I'm going to get a spanking but the thought of my mother being in danger is too painful to think about. So I think about something else: a musical sequence involving the two of them. I've watched enough Sunday afternoon musicals to take all the information I'm receiving and rearrange it into something not just different from the truth, but comforting and familiar. Instead of the sound of a hand slapping a face, it's a percussive instrument. In place of the flash of my mother's dress rushing past my partially closed door, it's a burst of colour from a rainbow-patterned umbrella, one of many opening on the lido deck of the *Pacific Princess* – the luxury ocean liner from *The Love Boat*. There's a cast of hundreds all in formation, twirling their umbrellas towards the camera as they pan off screen alternatively left and right, left and right, each one smiling at me before they disappear. They are about to reveal something. The conga line eventually ends with my beautiful mother, elegantly reclined on the brown and yellow banana lounge that she so often sits on outside, tanning herself.

But not today.

Today there's a sparkling blue sky with glitter raining down behind her, while artificial waves made of translucent blue fibreglass spin in a gloriously fake ocean below the boat deck, turned by stagehands just off camera. Her dress is moving, tickled by a fan off stage, which gently caresses her blonde hair against her forehead. The camera lens has a star glow filter on it which makes her shimmering blue eyeshadow sparkle as she winks at me, confidently sipping one of those cold frozen adult drinks with a paper umbrella, the same colour as her mango summer dress. She looks up to my father who enters, arm outstretched, to slow dance with her.

Then I hear the *sound* and the illusion is shattered. It's the worst sound in the world. My mother, crying, pleading, screaming his name, begging for him to stop hitting her. 'Robert, you're hurting me!'

I immediately jump out of bed. I look over at Peter but he's still asleep. I wish I were able to go to bed when my parents told me but I have never been able to relax until my mother is in bed. I think about shaking Peter awake but he looks so peaceful. I decide to venture out on my own. I know I'll see Tracey in the hallway.

The sudden change of light from the darkness of my bedroom to the brightly lit kitchen makes me squint but I see everything

I fear clearly enough. My father has gripped her by the hair with one huge fist. His sunburned biceps flex in a show of dominance. My mother is horrified that I am witnessing this. My father is indifferent. Defiant even. 'Go to bed,' he says firmly. I look at my sister. She's hidden from his view in the hallway. She gives me the 'shhhh' signal.

'I can't,' I say, disobeying my father.

Then my sister appears. With a hockey stick. She plays hockey at high school and she's good at it.

'Leave her alone,' she threatens.

My mother tells us everything is okay. She is saying this while my father still has her hair clenched in his dirty fist. The next moments are a slow-motion blur. Maybe it's because this is the only way I can remember things without being re-traumatised by them. Maybe it's because I'd just seen the movie *2001: A Space Odyssey*, but the famous classical music 'The Blue Danube' by Johann Strauss begins to play.

Tracey takes a massive swing of her hockey stick at my father's chunky legs. *Thwack!* He doubles over in agony. My mother takes the opportunity to escape his clutches and mouths instructions to me. 'Run!' I don't know where I am running to but I know I am running away from this house. I am first in line, followed by Tracey, then Peter, who is now up and awake, and then my mother. We make the slowest, most desperate escape. Every lurch forward feels like I'm stuck in quicksand. Do you ever have those anxiety dreams where no matter how hard you try you just can't get away from the monster? It's like your arms and legs are made of spaghetti – all floppy and useless. That's how this feels.

I'm making my way to the front door; I'm so desperate to get outside, the force of my opening it almost pulls it off its hinges. As I run, I make the mistake of looking behind me. My feet make it past the front patio onto the brick pavement when I see it. Tracey has also turned her head. She sees it too.

6

It's not good. My mother has made it to the concrete patio but so has my father. He lunges forward and tackles her. As 'The Blue Danube' continues to play in my head, my mother's cheekbone delicately slams into the concrete and her face seems to bounce as though the floor were made of rubber. *Crack!* Blood shoots from her nose. As if attempting to shout through a wall of treacle, her desperate message to me is reduced to three whispered words: 'Call the police.'

I know what this means.

I run across the street to my friend's house. I am about to break the seal on a forbidden secret. I am about to feel ashamed. Here, in this moment, I will not only destroy any semblance of normality I ever had at Lake Road, the suburban Brisbane street I grew up on, but I will also never be able to talk to my friend again. Because she and her family are about to learn 'the secret'.

Time passes without me noticing.

It must be around 11 p.m. by the time I register where I am. I don't recall the scenes between when my mother's face hit the ground and when the blanket was placed around my shoulders. I don't remember where Tracey and Peter went or what happened to my mother. I don't remember when the police arrived. I just know I'm in a high-set house, looking down at my own low-set brick home across the street. I'm no longer in my body. I'm floating above it, observing. There are blue and red lights flashing outside and my friend's parents have given me a hot chocolate. The police officer is asking me if my father has ever hurt me.

'No,' I lie. I am consumed with embarrassment.

My friend is nowhere to be seen. Why would she be? She's fast asleep and probably has been since 8 p.m. I don't know anyone my age who stays up this late on a school night. Tomorrow my teacher will tell me I look tired. She'll ask if I'm getting enough sleep. She'll ask if there's anything going on at home that I need to talk about. I will lie to her about all of it. I will lie to everyone for the next decade.

Weeks will go by without incident and without any explanation. My father will continue his nightly habit of bringing six large bottles of beer, or 'tallies' as he calls them, home from the pub drive-through and sitting at the kitchen counter drinking them, one after the other, until he falls asleep at the bench. Smoking cigarettes that burn notches into the laminated countertop or fall dangerously to the dark green carpet below. That's on a good night. On a good night he will want to talk about himself for hours and boast about his adventures in life. About how he once charged other students at primary school to watch baby chickens 'dance' on a burning hot plate. Or how he sold condoms at high school to the other kids. Or vent about how his father would beat him if he stayed out too late with my mother on a date. He'll be overly affectionate and will want to hug my mother and force me to kiss him goodnight but he stinks of sweat and dirt and beer.

That's on a good night.

On a bad night he will torment my mother verbally for hours until she's in tears and eventually hit her again. If the evidence of his abuse is visible the next day we are shipped off to a motel for a few days. It's something he does whenever my mother has noticeable marks or bruises on her body inflicted by his hand.

Tonight he's given her a black eye so tomorrow we're going away without him.

The next day we check into our new temporary home while my mother heals. This particular motel is a fancy one. I know it well because we've stayed here a lot. It's far from where we live, right near the beach at a place called the Gold Coast. I like it because there's an in-ground swimming pool and lots of kids to play with. Our room has two beds, a colour TV and a coffee machine. Tracey sleeps in the same bed as my mother and I have to share a bed with my brother. I hate that part. In some weird space-saving and non-gay way, my brother makes us sleep head to toe so our faces don't touch the same pillow.

In the morning we're all spending time by the pool. My mother looks like a movie star in her bikini and with her hair cut short in that wavy Lady Diana way that everyone is copying; only it actually suits my mother. She's reading a Stephen King novel and hiding behind glamorous sunglasses, so big they cover her entire face. They also cover the bruise that's beginning to blacken under her left eye.

It's a busy day at the pool. There are kids of different ages, all splashing about in the kidney-shaped oasis when I decide to make my way to the edge and see what all the fuss is about. I can't really swim. Well, who am I kidding. I can't swim at all. I'm supposed keep these floaties on but I'm too old for that and don't want the other kids to see, so I discreetly slip out of them and allow my body to fall, unnoticed, into the icy-cold embrace of the water.

The feeling is heavenly, breathtaking. And I do mean breath-taking. I've forgotten to hold my breath and watch the world above me rapidly disappear as I sink to the bottom of the concrete pool. It happens so fast I don't have time to panic. I just watch the once perfectly circular hot midday sun turn into this wobbly, blobby liquid smear in the watery ceiling above me, as all the swimmers' legs thrash and move, creating carpets of bubbles and trails of movement captured in translucent tubes of trapped air. It's so beautiful!

Without anyone noticing, suddenly I'm sitting on the bottom, cross-legged, looking up at the surface. There's no air left in my lungs.

I know I should be in a state of sheer terror but all I feel is peace. I can't get over how stunning the world looks from below. My moment of zen is shattered by a break in the surface of the water. With a massive splash a body dives in, perfectly and elegantly aimed towards me. It could be an Olympic diver for all I know. That's how determined and confident this swimmer appears. The next thing I know I'm being pulled to the surface. Two strong arms are underneath mine and *whoosh* we ascend. With a powerful kick I'm thrown over the side of the pool and onto the deck.

I look up at the person who has relocated me from my brief Atlantis and it is, of course, my saviour and guardian angel, my sister, Tracey.

'Are you okay?' she asks sternly.

I splutter chlorinated water and apologetic words onto the warm safety of the pool deck. It doesn't matter that I've defied the 'no swimming without floaties' rule, Tracey is just glad I'm okay. And the weird thing is, I knew I would be because she is always there to protect me.

You Must Be an Angel

In the early 1980s there are no ATMs in the suburbs of Brisbane. Banks operate on regular business hours and there is this thing called cash and if you don't have enough on a Friday afternoon you are broke all weekend. This means that people have to go into the bank to withdraw money or cash their wages if they stand a chance of paying for anything from 4 p.m. Friday until 9 a.m. Monday.

One particularly humid Friday my mother is desperate to get to the bank. She needs to pick up some groceries to get us through the weekend, but she is out of money and my father is holding the car keys as ransom. I came home from school and instantly noticed the tension that has probably been brewing for hours. Like most Friday afternoons, my father has spent most of the day at the pub and is taunting my mother by refusing to give her the keys, completely aware of the clock ticking down towards bank closing time.

As it nears 4 p.m., he agrees to allow my mother to go to the bank on one condition: that he drives. This is, of course, a ridiculous notion given his inebriated state, but my anxious mother has no choice. She is about to agree to this lunacy when he tosses the keys at her and says, 'Alright, you can have the keys. But I want to come for a ride.' The ominous feeling in my stomach immediately arrives. A bad thing is going to happen.

11

Even though we all know this is going to end terribly, we pile into the Ford F100 pick-up truck – my mother, my sister and me all on the one long bench seat – and begin what should be a ten-minute trip to the bank. We're barely out of our driveway when the verbal abuse begins. My mother, according to my father, is a 'smart bitch' and a 'cunt'. The next moments happen in a flash. We pull out onto Wembley Road, the busy two-lane main road that leads to the shopping centre, and he backhands her, hard. Her hands instinctively reach up to protect her face, leaving the steering wheel, and she slams on the brakes. We lurch forward. Then, without saying a word, my mother, sister and I jump out of the truck, while it is still running.

The three of us hold hands as we make our way to the traffic island that divides the lanes. I'm crying. Somehow my mother and Tracey get us to the other side of the road and we head towards the massive shopping centre affectionately known as Kmart, even though the complex contains many other small stores. I'm struck by the horror of this moment. The shopping centre is the mecca of many of my dreams. It's the place I walk to with Tracey to look at *Star Wars* toys and dream of owning them. It's the location of the record store, Woody's, where we put vinyl albums on lay-by, sometimes taking up to twelve weeks to pay for them, counting down the minutes until they will belong to us.

Now it's just a backdrop to another nightmare.

I look back and see my father has taken control of the truck and is driving towards the traffic lights, about to make a U-turn. We start waving down traffic, hoping someone will stop for us. It's the sort of behaviour you might see if you were hailing a taxi, only there are no taxis. This is a desperate plea for help. Nobody is stopping. We look like crazy people. But then, something miraculous occurs. Seemingly out of nowhere a van appears and the driver stops.

Up until this point in my life, I've never seen a member of the church or a priest or whoever this is, up close, let alone hitched a ride from one driving a *Scooby-Doo* van, but that's who pulls over. He sticks his head out the window. This is both fascinating and scary. The priest is different to what I've seen on television shows. He's wearing a brown gown, like something a Jedi Knight would wear. There's a massive rosary around his neck, a wooden one. I recognise it immediately because although my mother says she's a 'lapsed' Catholic, we have various remnants of her faith at home. This man has an aura of calm about him that I can't describe. He's not scary or old. He's younger and round. He has a long wiry beard and wears a crocheted hat. My mother refers to these types of people as 'hippies'. He seems really cool to me, like some of the older kids who hang out at the Argonaut shopping centre playing arcade games like Asteroids, drinking Coca-Cola and smoking cigarettes. 'Get in!' he says as he reaches behind him and opens the van's sliding door.

I notice he has a rosary hanging from the rear-view mirror too.

I feel instantly safe. There are no windows in the van apart from the ones in the rear doors, so nobody can see in. We are safe from my father. The bad feeling in my tummy instantly abates. It just . . . vanishes.

We drive for a few minutes and the van pulls up to a stop. The priest opens the side door and we get out. We're parked in front of a typical two-storey, high-set suburban house, not far from where many of my friends live, in the streets behind Kmart. The priest invites us upstairs for a glass of water.

We sit down in his living room. It's not a church, like I expected. I don't know why I thought we were being taken to a church, but this is just a regular home. There aren't even any pictures of Jesus on the walls.

The priest listens while my mother apologises for what he has just witnessed. All the while he remains calm, sympathetic. That's the thing that keeps playing over and over in my mind. His face is full of love and compassion. There is no judgement. If this were a neighbour or a bystander, I would feel that burning sensation in my ears as embarrassment drowning out all sound. But not with him. He shows no pity, but rather, he simply nods and listens. There's actual love in his eyes. Before I have a chance to notice he has handed me a Burger King glass. Printed on it is Luke Skywalker with his blue lightsaber from *The Empire Strikes Back*. How did this man know I loved *Star Wars*? I look up in wonder. Is he Jesus? Is he an angel sent from God?

He makes my mother a cup of coffee and listens as she cries and explains that she had to get out of the truck because she was trapped in the driver's seat. 'You must think I'm a terrible mother,' she says. 'I didn't mean to stop in the middle of the road, but he hit me.'

'You did the right thing,' the priest reassures her.

I want this Jesus man to be my dad.

My mother says we should probably go, but the priest looks out the window and asks, 'Is that your husband?'

We peer through the venetian blinds and sure enough, we see my father pacing up and down outside, near the house we have found refuge in. He doesn't know where we are, but he must suspect we're hiding somewhere on this street. A few houses down, Tracey spots the F100 pick-up truck.

He's stalking us.

'Stay here for a while longer,' the priest suggests gently. We accept.

It's best to take my father's vengeful threats seriously.

A similarly explosive argument had erupted last summer. The four of us, my mother, Tracey, Peter and I, had fled the house with the car keys. Tracey reversed the truck out of the driveway at breakneck speed, hollering for my mother to jump in. My father ran after us and we all screamed in terror, frantically locking the doors. We managed to lose him and drove to a family friend's house to give him time to sleep it off. When we returned to Lake Road hours later, all the lights were off. My mother assured us that my father would be sleeping by now, as that was what usually happened when he got very drunk. Tracey, however, was convinced something sinister was afoot.

'Mum! In the front garden!' she warned.

My mother was certain that my father hiding in the garden was impossible given the near paralytic state he'd been in just before the incident. 'Don't be silly, sweetheart,' she reassured. 'He'll be passed out by now.'

There was an ominous silence as we walked up the brick-paved pathway.

'See, he's already in bed,' my mother said.

She confidently stepped up to the concrete landing where the front door was framed by two perfectly symmetrical back-lit orange 1970s glass panels.

My sister grabbed her arm and yell-whispered, 'Stop!'

We all stopped.

'I just heard a branch break. He's hiding in the bushes!' Tracey said.

That's impossible. He couldn't be. Could he?

Again, my mother gave the sensible reassurance. 'He's not, sweet-heart. You're just imagining things.'

Tracey, however, was adamant. 'Mum. I heard a sound. I swear, he's hiding in the bushes.'

We stopped again, frozen in our tracks. The four of us looked at the black silhouette of Lake Road dimly outlined against the Queensland sunset as the last remnants of another humid summer's day slipped into twilight. Shrubs, bushes and plants surrounded our home, providing privacy when we were inside. But now, looking at the home from this perspective, they also provided a hiding place for anyone who might want to surprise someone approaching.

We didn't have a choice. It was late, we'd already been gone for hours, and it was a school night. We had to go inside.

That's when it happened.

With the swiftness of the foreboding creature I fear lives underneath my bed, gnashing its claws at a leg carelessly fallen over the side, my father lurched out of the darkness from his hiding place in the bushes. He pounced on my mother, all sweaty and full of rage, smelling putrid and dank and soiled from the hours spent in his secret lair. The night ended all too familiarly, with her receiving some superficial but painful wounds, us children screaming and the police becoming involved.

Back at the priest's house we decide on a different tactic. We call my mother's friend, Lenore, who is one of the few people who knows about 'the secret'. Lenore often helps my mother if we need to borrow $20 or if we need a safe place to hide. A plan is hatched that we'll be dropped at Lenore's house, borrow some money and stay in a motel overnight. The only problem is, we can't leave until my father does.

We wait until sunset before it's clear that my father and his truck are nowhere to be seen. Only then do we leave the priest's house. It's a short, five-minute drive to Lenore's but our journey ends abruptly when we see the F100 truck parked on a side street, near Lenore's low-set brick house. He has anticipated our every move. The priest reverses his van slowly and takes us to a corner shop, where there's a phone booth. My mother calls Lenore, explains the situation and we wait for her to come meet us.

I have so many happy memories of this corner shop; getting an ice block on a blisteringly hot summer's day, and waiting around for fish and chips before heading back to Lenore's to play with her children and the other kids in the neighbourhood. But not tonight. Tonight there is no happiness. Tonight feels dangerous. What if he follows her?

Lenore arrives, thankfully without being followed, and hands my mother some money and some much-needed hugs. The priest takes us to a motel behind my father's favourite pub in Waterford, not too far from where we live. The whole time we are driving we're terrified of being followed. Getting out of the van and checking into the motel, it feels like we're criminals on the run from the police. I look down at my bare, dirty feet. This was just supposed to be a quick trip to the bank, not an overnight stay. I feel embarrassed for how we are dressed. I wonder what the priest thinks of us. I feel poor and dirty. He must think that of us too. I peer into his eyes and am quickly reminded that he thinks nothing of the sort. He is kindness personified.

Inside the motel room there are the obligatory twin beds, a coffee machine and a black-and-white TV. I feel safe. These four wood-panelled walls are like a sanctuary. For the first time today I don't have a worried feeling in my tummy and I know I'll get at least one full night's sleep, near my mother, where I feel safe. And next to my sister, who is my guardian angel. That feeling is so fleeting in my life, when I get to hold onto it, I don't want to let go. Calm. Stillness inside. Safe and protected from danger. I think that's the most beautiful feeling in the whole wide world.

EXTERIOR: Suburban street, Santa Monica, April 2023. A black sports car is parked outside an apartment building

Brake lights cast an eerie red glow upon the black street below. They're the only lights on this otherwise moonlit street. Inside the car, a man, recently turned fifty, blond curly hair, sits in the driver's seat. The engine purrs. The song 'Little Did I Know' by Julia Michaels plays on the car stereo.

I'd make the most beautiful corpse. Think about it. I'm dressed in my stage clothing, I'm the thinnest I've been in years. I don't take drugs, I rarely drink, there's not a drop of alcohol in my system. I've barely eaten tonight, I'm a vegan. All I'd have to do is drive the car into my garage, leave the engine running and . . . sleep. Just let the exhaust fumes finally put me to rest.

To understand how I could have come to the conclusion that being dead was a better option than being alive, my fixation about what my body might look like, and what the coroner might find upon inspecting the contents of my stomach under autopsy, I have to take you back a few years.

This is not the first time I've felt suicidal within the space of the past decade. The most recent instance lasted a long period but eased up somewhat the day I asked my husband for a divorce. Out of a deep respect for the many years we spent together, I won't dissect our relationship here; suffice it to say that when it began I thought it was one of the most beautiful things in the world until one day our once-perfect union had devolved into us being just roommates. We spent a majority of our years together living caring and loving lives as companions, with something missing. It broke my heart. The pressure to stay together was so great, leaving seemed unthinkable, the concept of hurting the one I loved seemed so cruel, that I had thought ending my life was a more appealing option. That conundrum left me feeling utterly trapped and depressed for a long, long time.

It took ten years of therapy in California to even accept that there might be life after marriage. The concept of leaving seemed like the most emotionally horrible and violent thing I could do to someone I cared about. So, rather than end the marriage, I had decided to end my life, but not before leaving behind a musical legacy. I slowly and methodically wrote a musical and then wrote and recorded an album. It was to be my final. Once those two pieces of work were in the vault, I concocted a plan to leave this earth by my own hand, knowing that with those two works to publish and exploit, my husband would be okay financially without me.

Complete lunacy, of course, but that's what a suicidal thought is. It's a moment of psychosis. A moment so disconnected from any rational thought that there is no logic. It's a moment where the emotional pain is so great, the mind would conceive of anything to relieve the body of it.

I'm grateful for the concern of a dear friend, Maddy, who upon seeing the despair on my face one night was somehow able to prise out of me what was wrong. Somehow I told her. That act itself, just talking to anyone other than my husband about my marriage, felt like betrayal. Partly because of advice given to me by a therapist I'd been seeing for a decade who had told me to keep my marital problems between just me and my spouse. I took this advice extremely literally; perhaps that's my fault, but in doing so I cut that subject off from the closest people in my life. My sister, for one, who was really my best friend, someone I would normally talk to about anything. I never once told her there were any problems. My mother too. Not a hint of it. My close friends. Not one person I knew. Media. Fans. Colleagues. Everyone thought we were the perfect couple. I didn't and couldn't confide in a single soul how deeply unhappy I was. Worse still, I felt guilty for being unhappy.

In the years that I'd been married to Richard, I had never once divulged anything private about the inner workings of our relationship to anyone outside of the marriage, let alone uttered a negative word about him. I was old-fashioned about that. I felt we were a team who stuck up for one another.

Having such a strict code of secrecy meant I felt incredibly isolated. Now I understand that, because of the secrets I had to gatekeep about my family as a child, and even later on about how I viewed my sexuality, I had become an expert at internalising things I felt ashamed of.

Sadly, this meant I never once in the almost seventeen years we'd been together gave anyone even the slightest clue there were any problems in our union. It was a combination of misplaced loyalty, a fear of judgement and placing too much power in the hands of a therapist. I think the advice was meant to shield the relationship from the outside opinions of well-meaning but ultimately biased friends and family members. The reality was it created a feeling of isolation and abandonment. The only person I could talk to about the slow disintegration of my marriage was the one person who rarely wanted to talk about it. So I blamed myself – my depression, my mental health, my childhood trauma, all of it – for why I was so sad all of the time and why our marriage had become a friendship. The truth is, our marriage was dying and we were unable to save it, let alone talk about it.

In 2019 I eventually confessed to Richard about the desperation and loneliness that had led me to thoughts of suicide. Thankfully he agreed to go to couples therapy but by the time we went, the damage was done. Our problems were deeply embedded and after many sessions even the therapist felt although we'd had an amazing run, it might be time to call it quits.

I'd been writing songs about the state of the marriage for years, and the latest song I'd finished summed it up perfectly.

It feels like it's over but nobody's leaving, there's so much love left so why I am grieving? You go to bed first, I stay up reading, you have your back turned you're already dreaming, dancing in circles avoiding the inevitable, it's so polite and that's what's breaking my heart. Because we don't even fight for it, we don't even break a sweat. We don't even scream or cry but baby there was a time when baby, you and I we would have died defending this love.

– 'Feels Like It's Over'

We both knew the relationship had run its course but we genuinely cared so much about each other we found it near impossible to admit it. Therefore we let it linger in a state of inertia for a couple of years, neither of us acting upon or discussing the real heart of the matter. All the while, it was tearing me apart.

I worked up the courage, a few days after Valentine's Day, in 2023 to suggest we get a divorce. I had come back from the Australian leg of the Do You Remember? tour and with the time apart it was obvious that if I didn't make a decision now, we'd be in the same patterns of behaviour for another ten years. I realised I had a window of opportunity to make a drastic life change, or else wake up a decade later blaming my spouse. I didn't want to do that. I wanted to leave on good terms. It was an incredibly sad period and we thankfully had time to sit with the grief, together, for weeks. I cried myself to sleep every single night and I woke up with that same grief every single morning but it was good to have each other to lean on.

I only had a month at home before it was time to get on a plane again. It was devastating to leave but at the same time, the pressure of living in a constant state of sadness was something we both needed a break from. The idea of pouring my emotions out onto the stage was just what I needed.

When I left for Europe things felt a little better. I got my head around the hope I would be able to survive this huge change in my life. It seemed easy to do that when I was on the road because being on tour is a suspended reality. On top of that, the shows were going really well. The audiences were enthusiastic and the band and crew were a combination of a reunion of players I first met in the early Savage Garden days, the brilliant bass player Lee Novak and the incredible drummer Karl Lewis. I had my dear friend Maddy with me and my childhood friend Claire. I felt like I was wrapped in cotton wool. It was a false sense of security but it worked to get me through, knowing I was about to go through a divorce. The European dates merged without any time off into the final North American leg of the tour.

It was the best I'd sung in years, and I'd put on my most creative shows ever, in spite of the fact that I'd been put into venues that were either too big or had a production that was too expensive to scale back. But the end result was I left the North American leg and had to write my company a personal a check for six figures just to pay the debt. I didn't care though. I was artistically thriving. I still felt sick in the stomach about returning home to the grief and after-math of the divorce decision, but a happy distraction appeared on the horizon. An indie pop artist was performing in Los Angeles and because someone in my crew knew someone in their crew, I was invited to join them on stage. Apparently one of their recent songs was inspired by one of my old classics.

There I was, exhausted backstage in Boston, smiling with a new boost of confidence that an artist I admired and a very, very cool one at that, wanted *me* to perform a duet at their show in LA. I had just crawled out of a decade of self-isolation from the music industry to make my latest album. My self-esteem in the public eye had been close to zero. But the reviews for the album were great, the reactions from the audiences were great and now a new, hip artist was inviting me on stage! Were things actually about to turn around? My God, what would I wear? The fantasy started taking shape. Emails flew back and forth between the two management teams. The end of my tour wasn't going to be this miserable return home as a divorcing, in-debt has-been. Nope, I was going to be celebrated on stage with a contemporary artist. If I were to believe some of the supportive and encouraging words of my team, this was a *sign*. A precursor to things only getting better.

Until they started slowly going in the opposite direction.

We suddenly heard from the artist's people that they weren't sure they were going to have any featured guests at the show. But we were still welcome to attend. 'If we wanted.'

If we wanted? I thought they wanted *me?*

I felt like a fool. I was so humiliated. My depressive thoughts escalated. It's easy to be rational and explain the situation away when you're in a sound state of mind. But to me, in my depressed state, I felt rejected. I got home and spiralled into a very dark, depressive state. My friends were worried about my mental health and convinced me to go to the show anyway, to 'cheer me up'. In the end I agreed because my dear friend Trevor, my musical director and just all-round amazing guy, promised to be my plus one.

So we turned up. I wore my tour outfit – black lace long-sleeve shirt, eighteen-hole Doc Martens, vintage Gucci leather jacket. I felt like a star. We walked up to the box office and . . . our names weren't on the guest list. Trevor called the mutual friend who had started the whole fiasco and after being forced to witness some excruciatingly cringeworthy problem-solving in real-time, some seats and after-show passes were eventually found for us. But the damage was done. I started spiralling again.

We watched the show, the show that was supposed to have no guests. I counted five special guest vocalists who appeared on stage with the artist. As each new featured guest appeared my self-esteem plummeted lower. Because of my state of mind, I took it very personally. It was me. I was too uncool to be invited on stage. My inner voice, the intrusive thoughts that were so cruel, wouldn't stop. I was a loser. A has-been. I was nothing.

We left the show and got a cab to the after-show party which was a twenty-minute drive away in downtown Los Angeles. Our names were not on the after-show guest list either . . . I wanted to go home but Trevor suggested we stay. So we waited in line for about forty minutes until Trevor finally put me out of my misery by taking me to dinner.

Later that night I'd sit in my car, a few streets away from my home, and wonder how difficult it would be to rig a pipe from the exhaust to the car window.

I would make a beautiful corpse.

That one sentence kept running through my mind. I knew it was irrational but I'd grown up in the era of seeing River Phoenix in an open coffin, and those horrible autopsy photos of Marilyn Monroe. I was weirdly obsessed with the fact that on that particular night, I was in the best shape of my life. I could die pretty.

I sat in my car and cried so deeply, I don't think I've ever cried so much. A guttural moan passed through me, like someone had taken a microphone to my soul and my body was merely a freeway underpass through which this sound was travelling. The pain shook my entire body. I had nothing to live for anymore. I thought about the situation with Richard. The guilt of the hurt I was causing him by leaving. I thought of the shame I felt from being a flop. An artist so uncool that even a supposed fan didn't want me on stage. I don't know if that was true or if it was just my irrational, depressive thoughts, but that's what I felt in that moment of temporary insanity. I thought about my screaming arguments with CAA, my agents, who told me that, despite me having no manager and funding the entire tour myself and attending every single Zoom meeting and responding to every email, I was a huge part of the reason tickets hadn't sold well in parts of the US. Apparently I'd missed one call and in the absence of a manager, 'the buck stops with you' they'd yelled. The reason I hadn't been on the call? I was in Australia, in another time zone, doing a production rehearsal.

It was all too much. If there'd been a power switch to my body I would have reached for it and powered down. But there wasn't.

But then I thought about my eighteen-year-old nephew, Ben, who had died from suicide just five years earlier. I thought about the endless river of grief and suffering his passing had caused us all. I thought about what my leaving might do to my mother, to my sister, to Richard, even. I believe that's what stopped me. Knowing how much of a legacy of grief my actions would leave behind for those still living.

So I paused.

I went home and I peeled off the lace shirt from my perfectly starved abs, shaped to Hollywood's over-exercised, under-nourished and impossibly perfect standards. I ripped off my skinny jeans – revealing legs that looked like they belonged to a man ten years my junior. I slowly unpicked the laces of my Doc Martens and I curled into a ball in the guest bedroom of my own home and cried and cried and cried . . .

I felt so alone. So empty. So desperate for love. So deprived of affection. So starved of approval. Begging for an end to my suffering while simultaneously trapped by a contract I'd made with my family and my audience. I felt like a failure.

> And it's not that I don't want to live. It's the pain that I wish I could kill. All the times that I wanted to die. I made a promise I was gonna survive. Every day's a decision to stay with my poison blood.
>
> – 'Poison Blood'

I was bound by my lyrical promise to stay. Poisoned by my own DNA. This pain inside me felt ancient. Yes, I was going through a divorce. But this pain had been lurking for decades.

Depression

INTERIOR: Psychiatrist's office, San Francisco, 1999

A young man in his mid-twenties, dyed black hair, trim, dressed in a navy Bonds T-shirt and Levi's 501s paired with colourful Reeboks, sits in a wicker-backed chair. Opposite him, an older man in his mid-fifties, long wavy grey hair, linen shirt, grills the young man about his childhood . . .

I can't believe this is happening to me. I'm not crazy. I'm not one of those people who complain about their 'terrible childhoods'. Sure, I had it rough. But I survived. No, I fucking *thrived*. I'm a popstar. I'm rich. I'm successful. I own my own home, I paid the mortgage off on my siblings' homes and my mother and father's house. I probably won't ever have to work again if I don't want to. In three months' time I'll release the second Savage Garden album – that's the name of my band with Daniel Jones – and it's destined to be another massive hit. Our first album sold ten million copies and had a US Billboard number one single, 'Truly Madly Deeply', that became a hit all around the world. This new album, I've been assured by all the arse kissers at Columbia Records, will do exactly the same thing. It too has a future number one single on it, 'I Knew I Loved You'.

Life is great.

Life is perfect.

26

I'm just a little bit suicidal.

Okay, so life is not *entirely* perfect. Maybe there are a few things that could be better.

I've been sleeping my days away so much that Leonie, my assistant, has been checking every morning to see if I'm alive. Yeah, that's not great. I've had some, I guess you'd call them, dark moments. It's complicated.

I recently came out (God I hate that phrase) to friends and family and the record label, as gay, and I thought that was going to be liberating and put an end to all of this suffering I've been experiencing but actually I've just experienced nothing but non-stop heartbreak ever since.

I guess I always knew there was something different about me but then what does knowing really mean? I was five years old when I kissed Noah, the boy who lived around the corner. The shame of knowing I was different seemed to pre-exist all thought, all feeling. It was as though I knew there was something terrible, something rotten and disgusting about me from before I could even verbalise it. Perhaps it was the subtle way other people treated me, or the distance I felt from my father, or this instinct to hide the most gentle, fragile parts of myself from the world. Somewhere in my earliest moments I received messages that who I was, deep in my core, was intrinsically bad and should be hidden.

Hindsight has given me clues that explain where much of this shame developed. Children, as we all know, are born pure of heart. They do not judge. They do not censor themselves. They act out of pure instinct and gravitate towards joy and pleasure, love and the need for safety. A child doesn't decide to be attracted to a gender; in the same way a child doesn't choose to love ice cream. Everything is instinct. You're either drawn towards something or you aren't. As a very young child I remember being subtly redirected away from being attracted to boys. It started off with my language being corrected.

I might be watching a television show and say that an actor was 'cute' and a sibling would say, 'Boys can't say boys are cute!' I don't blame my siblings for doing this, it's how children behave, especially in a world where parents and caregivers naturally reinforce gender norms. As a result, children mimic this policing of behaviours.

I was once a pre-school teacher. Sitting here in this therapist's office, in my fancy San Francisco neighbourhood, it's hard to imagine that well before all this popstar bullshit, I was forced to get a 'real job' by my father. Not many people know this, but the perks of having a father who never believed in you is that his complete and utter lack of faith in my talent as a musician resulted in a pep talk where he threatened to throw me out of the house unless I got a university degree. He taunted me, saying 'You'll end up living in the gutter' if I pursued music. I eventually got a teaching degree and spent time working with young children in order to keep a roof above my head. While doing so I witnessed firsthand how children love rules, boundaries, consistency and the safety of a belief system that their peers have demonstrated for them. I can't tell you the amount of times I had to stifle laughter when an extremely concerned four year old would raise her hand and exclaim in an anxious, life-threatening tone that a fellow classmate was not following 'the rules'. Usually this meant the person next to her was not sitting on the mat during story time.

From my siblings, to my parents, to kids at school, I was constantly corrected and redirected away from my natural instincts so that I stayed within the lines of what was considered to be normal and acceptable; whether that was to prevent me playing with dolls, or to steer me away from spending more time with girls, to shut down any expression of an attraction to the same sex, or to stifle any hint of emotion more typically expected from the opposite gender.

There was also a real-life Grimms fairy tale in our family that had a profound effect on how I viewed homosexuality: the tragedy of Aunt Vivienne.

The Shame Monster

Once upon a time there lived a little boy who was so full of love. It has been said that when he came into this world, his being was so pure and full of light, it had never seen hatred, never passed by the doorway of disgust and never, ever spent any time under the shadow of the monster you know and call shame. Somewhere there exist photos of this little boy as an infant, laughing with such reckless joyful abandon, his mouth so wide his siblings called him a fly trap, for his grin was so huge as to engulf his entire face. At least, that's how he entered this world. Before the shame monster found him. Before the wasp laid eggs in his tummy.

This boy was the youngest of three children. Peter, his older brother by almost three years, was anxious, angry and desperately in need of a father's love. Tracey, almost three years older still, was a strong maternal figure made that way out of necessity rather than choice. A young girl who never really had a chance to experience childhood because it had been shattered by violence and then burdened with protecting her baby brothers and of course her mother, who was sometimes more like a best friend and a sister. This was not the fault of her mother. She had no-one to confide in and so her anxiety and need for comfort were offloaded and subsequently soothed by the calm, stoic nature of a daughter wise beyond her years.

29

My mother, Judy Hannon, born in the tiny country town of Werris Creek, NSW, had grown up in poverty without realising it in a family so full of love that it didn't matter that her father worked on the railway lines in the tent city railway town of Hornsby. They felt rich because they were surrounded by love. There were five Hannon children: Vivienne, Judy, Dianne, Robbie and Jenny. Sometimes their father, Clarry, would come home from work with little inexpensive gifts for his children and leave them on their pillows with a note that said, 'Just because'. He was tender and loving and sentimental. His meagre wage fixing coal train lines was all that kept five children fed and warm in a makeshift and often mobile home lovingly cared for by his wife, Jean.

Judy was much like the youngest of the three children she would one day give birth to – a dreamer. She had a wonderful sense of humour and a natural curiosity that sometimes got her into trouble. For example, although she knew the soft-top roof of the family car was not a trampoline, and was warned many times not to use it as one, it wasn't until both of her legs pierced the vinyl that she finally understood why her father had been so stern about playing on top of the car. Boy did she get into trouble for that one! But still, she had a soft heart and a natural affinity to win over her father's affections and Clarry found it near impossible to be too stern with 'Hattie', the nickname he'd given her at birth.

Clarry was a gentle giant while Jean was a sensitive, emotional and extraordinary woman. But they struggled financially and with so many children they barely made ends meet. Judy started working at the age of fifteen. She hated school and begged her parents for an escape from the very strict Catholic school where she had been physically punished so much for being left-handed that the constant whips from the cane made her ambidextrous. The extra help around the house was useful and she assisted her mother raising the younger babies, Robbie and Jenny. By that point, her sister Vivienne had already left home to marry, and her mother had begun experiencing symptoms of depression and anxiety.

For a while, Judy worked in a fancy department store in Sydney, then known as Grace Bros. She held a position in the accounts department where she did basic filing and fulfilment of orders and would occasionally regale the family with tales of local celebrity visits to the store where she proudly proclaimed she treated every customer the same 'no matter who they were'.

By the time Judy was sixteen, she had met a handsome drummer named Robert Hayes at a birthday party. His family came from the very well-to-do suburb of Windsor, near the Hawkesbury River, but when Robert met my mother, his family had moved to Hornsby too. This boy was told the Hannons – who lived in the wrong part of town – were not good enough for a Hayes boy to associate with. Robert didn't care. He pursued Judy anyway.

Robert's parents were strict and the complete opposite of Judy's. There were four Hayes children: Robert, Philip, Jeanette and ironi-cally also a Judy. Their father, Harry, was stern, allegedly verbally and physically abusive, especially to his son Robert and his wife, Alma. He was obsessed with the notion that Robert should become a police officer, as this was considered a respectable career. Robert's mother was cold, emotionless and very formal. She always dressed immac-ulately and presented like royalty, but hid an ocean of sadness and anger and rage just beneath the surface.

Robert was a natural rebel. He had the IQ to study higher educa-tion but he was desperate to escape his father's grip, so as soon as he was able to leave school he pursued an apprenticeship as a fitter and turner – a career which disgusted his father because it was manual labour.

His romance with Judy began with a spark but soon Robert dis-played jealous behaviours and violent tendencies. He hit Judy one night and her father told his daughter to stay away from the Hayes boy; he was bad news. But young love is untamed and can rarely be negotiated with. Their relationship was a fiery one but marriage became necessary when Judy fell pregnant, and so they were married at the age of nineteen. In 1966 they welcomed my sister, Tracey, to the world.

I'm told my father beat my mother up on their wedding night. At the time, she was too ashamed to tell anybody, and there was always the implied threat from his family that gossip and 'bad news' about him would affect his career because he was now a police officer, as his father had wanted him to be. Judy's father was a pacifist and a harmless lightweight while her mother was already struggling with her mental health. Ultimately they could not afford to take in a mother and child. What was she to do? There were no programs for single mothers, no government assistance, and domestic violence wasn't a crime. It wasn't until the *Family Law Act* of 1975 that physically assaulting a wife was considered a crime.

Consequently, Judy suffered, often in silence. Soon she was a mother of two, with the addition of my brother, Peter. She also had her own two very much younger siblings, Jenny and Robbie, to worry about. Leaving Robert Hayes was not an option.

INTERIOR: Living room, Lake Road, 1985

My two school friends are coming over to my house today to watch a video. Not just any video. It's Madonna, live in concert, the Virgin tour! My mother rented it for me for a whole week. We've had a long-term rental video player for a few months now. It's a luxury but one our mother justifies because we rarely go out. I'm thrilled. It means I can record music videos from TV and watch *Star Wars* movies and study dance moves from my favourite popstars. Especially Michael Jackson. As part of our rental agreement, the video recorder comes with two weekly movie rentals. My father is away for six weeks, working in the engine room on a container ship, so there's an air of ease in my life these days. I've been preparing for this weekend all week, helping clean the house, making it fit for visitors. I've never had anyone from school come over before. I'm looking at our house through a stranger's eyes and with just an hour before my friends arrive all I can see is everything that's wrong with it.

My mother is incredibly clean and houseproud so we've been dusting and polishing and doing yard work since yesterday. That's not the issue. As I look around I see bits of peeling wallpaper and most noticeably, the hole in the front door from the time my father hurled a coffee table at my mother. We filled the hole with newspaper and covered it with brown art paint and it looks like a papier mâché model. It reminds me of the skin on the skeletons of mummified remains in documentaries about ancient Egyptian tombs. If anyone asks what happened to the door we always say it was an accident. But that just leads to more questions. I wish we could just get a new door.

I'm standing in front of the TV and I'm dusting the area where we keep two very sacred photos. One of my nana, my mother's mum, Jean, and one of her first daughter, Vivienne, who passed away at the age of twenty-four. For as long as I can remember I've known of the family lore of the terrible tragedy of the death of my beautiful Aunt Vivienne, who I was told had married a man who was an alcoholic and very early into their marriage revealed himself to be gay. This revelation ended their marriage and left Vivienne in so much distress that it emotionally if not medically broke her heart, leading to her death. I don't recall ever meeting Vivienne, but her shadow stretches long and tragically over our family. I stare at her picture sometimes and she seems so innocent, so angelic.

It's almost time for my friends to arrive and I'm anxious. What will they think of my house? I'm ashamed to care but I do. My mother has been so great. She's just excited I've made friends. She's got snacks and drinks prepared and has made a big deal of the fact that she's going to 'keep out of the way' so we can have fun.

I stare at the picture of my mother's lost sister.

In our house, Aunt Vivienne is a saint. We talk about her in hushed tones but always in the highest regard. You could say she's been canonised, both in story and in image. I can't remember a time when her framed black-and-white portrait wasn't displayed prominently in our living room. She was, objectively, stunning. The silver-toned photograph emanates a sense of beauty and tragedy frozen in time, in the same way we think of a James Dean or a Marilyn Monroe; someone ethereal taken before their time but preserved at the peak of their potential. She is perfect to me because she remains forever young and beautiful, trapped in a two-dimensional image: porcelain skin, immaculately styled hair straight from the salon and a permanent twinkle in her eyes, like she has a secret to tell.

I stand back and realise that our TV looks a bit like a shrine – perfectly framed by the portraits of two beautiful women who passed away prematurely.

There's a knock on the door and my two school friends are here. Last time we hung out at their places they made me watch football and look at *Playboy* magazine. I hated that. This time we're going to learn the choreography for 'Dress You Up', the first song from the Madonna concert.

'Do you like Madonna?' I ask as they enter the room.

'I guess,' says one boy, unenthusiastically. Silence from the other.

Oh. This is gonna be a challenge.

They look around and I see them staring at the portraits. Do I tell them? I decide not to. Instead we sit down in front of the television, eat popcorn and I press play on the VCR. I'm glad the topic didn't come up because it still confuses me.

When Vivienne first separated from her husband, she moved back to live with her parents and was under the treatment of a 1960s doctor who prescribed 'nerve pills' to combat the incredible sadness she was experiencing. Unfortunately, I'm told she was allergic to the medication, and it thickened her blood, eventually stopping her heart beating. She had been complaining for weeks of cramps in her legs and so to soothe this pain had been taking the medication along with warm baths at night.

During one of her evening baths, she fell ill and was moved to her little brother's bed. Sometime in the middle of the rainy night, she silently passed away. She apparently lost consciousness and her poor family found her, too late. She died needlessly while being treated for depression related to her impending divorce. She was, by all accounts, considered an angel, and her passing caused a string of tragedies in my mother's family that still reverberates to this day.

The trauma sent my grandmother into a shock that she never truly recovered from. After the loss of her daughter, the poor soul descended into a cycle of suicide attempts. She passed away by her own hand, leaving behind my mother, who was nursing a six-week-old son, Peter, with the daunting task of soothing her little sister Jenny and baby brother Robbie and a broken-hearted Poppy, my grandfather, Clarry.

Jean's passing, like Vivienne's, was so mysterious to me as a child. She was someone I never met but always felt a connection to. That comforts me. Maybe it's just that I spent so long gazing into her kind eyes in the photograph of her and Poppy or maybe it's because our souls are connected in some way. I don't know. But she's magical.

Jean struggled with depression and suicidal thoughts much of her adult life. Back in the 'middle ages' of mental health care, the 1950s and 1960s, and after the death of her adult daughter, she was forced to endure some of the most horrific and brutal rudimentary treatments to help ease her pain. She had electric shock treatment – to no avail. It was heartbreaking that both Jean and Vivienne's lives were cut short. If she were a patient today, a simple antidepressant might have saved her life.

Back in my 1985 living room, I've spent the past forty-five minutes scrutinising the faces of my two male friends, watching their reactions to each and every song. When the music video finishes, there's an awkward silence. I realise that while I've been utterly enthralled and transfixed by the dynamism that is Madonna, my two friends have been bored. I feel a creeping sensation of redness come over my face.

Pointing to my Aunt Vivienne's photograph, one of my friends says, 'Who's that?'

I'm aware that my mother is in the kitchen and is going to hear anything I say. I may not be able to articulate it but I know that the tragedy of Aunt Vivienne caused a string of terrible events in my mother's life that, to my knowledge, began with the act of a gay man. When I first heard the story, Vivienne's husband was considered evil because he was a gay man who was responsible for the death of my aunt, a woman my mother adored. That death then resulted in the death of my nana. You can imagine how I feel. There are parts of me that I know are different; I've been called 'gay' at school and it hurts. What I've put together from my family history is that being gay is not only bad, but the potential cause of horror, grief and pain ad infinitum. Being gay is basically what killed my saintly aunt.

In a moment of pure panic and stupidity I say, 'That's my aunt who killed herself.'

I immediately regret it.

From the kitchen, my poor mother says softly, gently, 'She didn't kill herself, she died of natural causes.' I'm devastated.

CUT TO: Present day

I don't blame my mother for being grief-stricken or for how the circumstances of Vivienne's death were communicated to me. It was in the 1960s when this occurred – not the most progressive time for acceptance of homosexuality – and my mother's focus was not on her sister's ex-husband's sexuality. It was on the alleged act of betrayal that led to her sister's grief. Ultimately you could take sexuality out of the equation and it would have been a story of infidelity. But to my young, impressionable mind, Vivienne's death was the result of the fact that this man was gay. That was the cancerous element in the story my mind had developed and allowed to metastasise over time. Gay people equal misery, heartbreak and yes, death. Here's the harrowing, twisted and even more evil side of this story: through conversations with my mother and her family members and research for this book, it turns out that the 'gay' depiction of my aunt's ex-husband was a *false* rumour, one that had been started by my father. When held up to scrutiny, it turns out this was a piece of fiction invented by him and accepted as fact at the time. For what reason, we don't know. It makes me angry that I lived most of my childhood believing the stereotype of an 'evil gay man' and finding out this came from my father makes the tragedy sting even more. The suffering this 'fact' caused me was unquantifiable. Looking back, there was always a projection of homophobia around most things my father said and did.

My first experience of homophobic shame occurred when I was about six. It was the summer of 1978 and I remember that only because it's when my *Star Wars* obsession began. My Aunty Jenny had promised to get me a *Star Wars* show bag from the Brisbane Exhibition. For those not from Australia, the Exhibition or 'Ekka' as we call it, began as a sort of travelling carnival based around livestock and produce.

Farmers would display and compete with their various crops and animals against the backdrop of a fun fair. To make it commercial, there were fun rides, games and promotional novelty bags sold, usually themed, filled with various novelty goodies and candy, or 'lollies' as we call them in Australia, all in ways designed to appeal to kids.

They would run TV ads for weeks leading up to the Ekka and if you were going, you would have a list of the show bags you wanted to buy. Up until that point in my life, I'd never been, but since my Aunty Jenny was going and promised to bring me home the *Star Wars* bag, I'd become consumed with all things from a galaxy far, far away. The bag came with a Darth Vader mask, that's all I knew, and I was desperate for it. So desperate I sat on the roof of our house on Lake Road for hours waiting for her to stop by. I remember that afternoon took forever. I realised I could relieve some of the anticipatory tension I was feeling if I simply set up camp on the roof because of course I would have a better vantage point when my Aunty Jenny's car appeared on my street. The moment it did I scrambled down the drain pipe and into the front yard to greet her. There she was, as promised, my Aunty Jenny and Uncle Colin, frazzled from a day at the Ekka but holding my soon-to-be prized possession, the *Star Wars* show bag with the Darth Vader mask.

I'd wear that mask when I played with a boy who lived around the corner.

His name was Noah and sometimes we used to get naked when nobody was watching. None of it involved any sexual activity – we were around six and seven respectively – but I distinctly remember the exhilaration of taking off our clothes, knowing this was something we shouldn't be doing, and kissing on the lips the way cartoon characters kissed; a sort of 'peck' without really touching lips and the making of a smoochy, smacking-lip sound. That was the main attraction for me, the forbidden nature of *kissing*!

We were re-enacting what we thought of as adult scenarios that were, in retrospect, so incredibly innocent but felt *scandalous* at the time. We behaved the way a child might pretend two dolls were making love; with zero idea of how the act is performed but armed with a handful of images and romantic words gleaned from TV soap operas like *Days of Our Lives*. Sometimes I would wear Noah's mother's nightgown, at his request, and walk around his basement garage pretending to be his 'wife', calling each other 'darling' and 'love' as we play-acted this fantasy adult marriage. We acted as two people madly in love with each other but all we really did was lie about on cushions making kissy sounds, talking about what was for dinner. I made the dinner.

Noah, I could already tell, wished I were a girl. I knew he wasn't attracted to boys. As an ex-pre-school teacher I understand now this was what most psychologists would call 'playing doctors and nurses'. It's a natural, curious stage children go through, and it's normally dealt with by an adult explaining boundaries to children and educating them about body autonomy. If handled by a sensitive and caring adult it can be a positive moment to move on from. Scolding or shaming was definitely not the way to handle finding two children engaging in this behaviour. Sadly, it was not the case for me.

I enjoyed the thrill of getting to play out my own fantasy of being able to touch someone of the same sex without any of the gender policing that was occurring in my day-to-day life. Noah was very serious and secretive about our rendezvous, I suspect because he knew he wasn't gay and was always petrified someone would find us. I don't know what he was worried about, I was the one wearing his mother's diaphanous lavender size-eighteen nightgown, and it was not a good look!

One day, someone did find us. I don't know how it happened exactly, but I guess my father had been calling for me to come home, and when I didn't respond he came looking for me. Since there was nobody home at Noah's house, he went snooping around the garage and there I was, butt naked in some kind of renaissance painting repose, kissing a boy. The next thing I knew I was being spanked. Hard. My father dragged me out of there by my arms with such force I felt like my limbs were going to disconnect from their sockets. When we got back to Lake Road, I half expected a further beating but something very strange happened instead. Silence. Even though my entire family was home, my father said not one word about what he'd witnessed. Instead, he just told me to get back to my chores (picking up the grass clippings from the freshly mown lawn) and that, I thought, was that.

Spankings were something most people say 'just happened' back in the 1970s and 80s. However, I remember physical 'smacks' from my father being very painful. I recall once getting a spanking so hard it left a hand-shaped bruise on my butt cheek for more than a week. My siblings and some neighbourhood kids had been playing in our above-ground pool, making a whirlpool by walking in a circle as fast as we could. One child, a young girl, was having trouble keeping her head above water. When my father saw this he demanded everyone get out of the pool and my brother and I go to our bedroom, lie over the bed and wait for a spanking.

The feeling of fear and dread in that moment was excruciating because he took his time to come into the room. We were soaking wet, our swim trunks seeping into the red and yellow African style print of our bedspreads as we trembled, waiting for his fury to arrive.

About fifteen minutes dragged by before he came into the room. Each slap of his hand across our rear ends was punctuated with a word of condemnation about water safety.

Afterwards, my bottom was severely bruised, so badly that my mother was concerned. My father said it was because my pants were wet; that's why his hand had left such a mark. That mark turned red, then purple and then black over the course of a week. There is, of course, no logic to that theory. The truth was, this beating was a violent overreaction, yet it took me most of my life to realise that, wet hand or not, a parent shouldn't leave a mark on a child that takes a week to heal.

But this particular day – the day of being caught kissing Noah – there were no bruises. No further spanking.

Later that evening, a few neighbours gathered for a BBQ at our house. My father liked showing off our backyard because it was freshly landscaped; the result of having free labour from staff at the Sand and Gravel Supermarket – the business we owned briefly back then. We had a koi pond in the front yard, and all those fantastic shrubs for hiding behind. At the back was a grotto built from stolen bush rocks my father had simply taken from local rainforests and placed in an arrangement around a fire pit where he and his mates would drink beer until all hours, roasting meat and ordering up 'stubbies' – single-serve beers – from the fridge from us children, who would diligently serve them like unpaid waiters.

That night I was in the kitchen when my mother handed me a plate of rump steaks and asked me to deliver it to my father in the grotto. As I approached the group of men, dimly lit by the flickering fire, their robust conversation suddenly stopped. I instinctively knew they were talking about me and what my father had seen earlier that day.

'Steaks,' I announced meekly.

'Just put them down there,' my father said, motioning for me to set them next to the rest of the food to be cooked. I felt the judgemental eyes of the men. It was like each was wearing a pair of those X-ray glasses I so badly wanted that were advertised on the second to last page of the *Casper the Friendly Ghost* comics I collected. It felt like these men weren't just looking at me, but right through me, peering

41

at the images and thoughts in my mind. Who knows how powerful those X-ray glasses were. I'd never seen a pair in person, nobody in Australia I knew was able to buy anything from the novelty page of the comics because you needed to send a stamped, self-addressed envelope and pay for them in actual American dollars.

I'd stare at that page for hours, getting lost in the descriptions of the bizarre and mystical trinkets. I preferred reading that page more than the comic itself, not just because it was an exotic flea market for rare and exquisite wonders like 'sea monkeys' and coins that could hypnotise people (complete with twenty-five free lessons!), but because it hinted at the possibility of a land somewhere far away from where I lived. The possibility of a place I could escape to one day. A place where, with just one American dollar, you could be in possession of something truly magical.

Obtaining those unique treasures seemed a complex mission, however. Perhaps the barrier to the prizes was part of their appeal. How could an Australian child get an American dollar? And what was 'sales tax'? I didn't know the answers to these questions but I knew that children in another country were reading the same comics as me and they could take their pocket money and put it in a stamped, self-addressed envelope and send it to somewhere glamorous called *New York*. In less than a month they could be the ringmaster of their own underwater circus of sea creatures who did acrobatic tricks exactly as described in the ad. These children probably had their own bedrooms and teachers who cared about them and parents who didn't hit them and they probably weren't being gawked at by sweaty, drunk men like I was right now.

The silence was so uncomfortable. I set the steaks down as asked and quickly exited. Or so they thought.

Like the rest of the overly landscaped backyard, the grotto provided plenty of privacy. No sooner had I rounded the corner of their man cave, I crouched down to listen to what they were talking about prior to my interrupting them. I wasn't surprised they had indeed been talking about me.

'So you'll never guess what I caught Darren doing today,' my father gossiped. 'Playing doctors and nurses with the boy around the corner.'

The group burst out laughing.

'Kissing!'

The group let out a groan, as though they'd seen roadkill.

'I know,' my father went on, like this were some unspoken insult. But there didn't need to be any clarification of the insult. I felt it. It was more than implied. I was disgusting. I was repulsive. I was the kind of secret you whispered when the rest of the family weren't listening. Something ugly and embarrassing. The only way to deal with something like me was to laugh about it behind its back. This vomit-inducing, gross, ugly, unlovable creature. I ran inside and hid in my room.

The contrast between how my parents treated me was so extreme it's a miracle I survived the cognitive dissonance. My mother seemed to possess a preternatural understanding of me and the notion there was something fragile and special to protect. She did this by fostering my most instinctual parts, encouraging my artistic interests and musical preferences with love, compassion and genuine interest. I always felt completely adored by her and understood. I felt seen.

When I asked her for a Wonder Woman costume, she didn't try to change my mind, or suggest a male superhero. Rather, she took out her Artex fabric pens and painted fifty white stars on a pair of blue shorts, a gold American eagle on a red T-shirt, and bought glitter glue so I could apply it to the used toilet rolls that I repurposed as my arm bands. She even helped me make a golden lasso.

When I made up plays, she was often the only audience member. I remember rehearsing my one-act *Superman – The Play!* for weeks.

I put up crayon signs all over the Lake Road pine trees advertising the date of my performance. As the day and hour of my debut approached, I peeked out from behind the washing machine in the garage to ask my mother, 'Is everyone here yet?' She replied, so kindly, 'Just me, love.' I performed that show just for her. I was barely five.

As much as my mother tried to protect me from my father, she didn't have magical powers. His view of me was much like the greater world's. He was hard, cruel and had no tolerance for nuance. As I grew older, my innocence was harder to protect and I heard my father's voice, even when he wasn't speaking. It echoed in my mind, like the narrator of the film of my life.

The shame monster had its tentacles in me and came from so many different directions now. Like the ink from an octopus being released in a crystal-clear lake, finding its way between every river rock, crevice and tributary, the coverage was overwhelmingly effective. It needed only two things to survive: one, a contract with its host that I would always react like this, with an absolute terrorising fear of anyone finding out who I really was, and two, that I would keep the feeling a secret. As long as I abided by those two rules, shame would not tell anyone else I was its host. It was a wicked, evil contract I had signed without ever truly understanding the consequences. Like biting into a poison apple, the ferocious appetite to rid myself of shame had blinded me from the consequence of giving it what it wanted. This contract would suffocate me, torture me and rule me for a long, long time. I knew it. I felt it in my gut and my gut was never wrong. And yet I signed anyway.

That night I had a dream. A nightmare. The kind of lucid nightmare where you think you are awake, but hindsight reminds you it is impossible that what you witnessed was real.

INTERIOR – Bedroom, Lake Road, 1978

I'm lying in my bed, the bedroom door slightly ajar as it always is because I'm still afraid of the dark. Even though my brother has long since fallen asleep nearby there are many things that still terrify me. It's hard for me to drift off into a relaxed state most nights. I don't know what that feels like. Tonight, a few of my father's friends are lingering, making noise and playing records, so I'm on edge. Things could take a turn for the worse at any moment even though my mother has already gone to bed. My father is awake and he'll probably drink and party for a few more hours. I'm reminded of the times when he's been a friendly drunk. Those times, he lets me watch *Wonder Woman* while he drinks his six tallies of beer. During the ad breaks, I twirl in the hallway, wishing I could transform into the female superhero. He comments on Lynda Carter's breasts. Tonight there'll be no twirling. No TV. He's not friendly tonight. He's on edge, and that makes me so nervous I feel like I might throw up.

Mercifully, sleep comes to find me, sneaks up on me and creates a version of the room exactly like the one I'm in. Only in this dream version of the room, a horrible clown with hundreds of sharp, rotten teeth and yellow cat-like eyes slithers out from underneath my bed. I jump, terrified. It just smiles and says, 'I'll be back.'

I lay awake for hours, petrified the clown will return. It doesn't. Meanwhile the party is still going on.

Somehow, I drift off to sleep. I wake up in the pitch dark in silence. No clown. No music. No guests. Everyone has gone to bed. Maybe I can relax now. Maybe.

The Escape

Today is the day we're leaving him. I'm excited but nervous too. There's so much secrecy surrounding the details of this mission it's hard not to be apprehensive about what's at stake. If he finds out, we are literally dead. I know this. I've heard my father say a million times, 'If you hate it so much you can always leave,' but then, 'If you ever leave, I'll fucking kill you.'

My mother has recited versions of this cautionary tale so often I know it by heart. It's the reason we've never been able to escape. Not only could we not afford to live without his wages, but his revenge would be the end of all of us. My mother said he'd rather she was dead than happy. I fear she's right.

Today, she's risking death, and so is my Uncle Colin. My mother always said if anyone found out she had help leaving, they'd be dead too, so this operation must be kept top secret.

I love my Aunty Jenny and Uncle Colin. Aunty Jenny taught me how to draw feet and fingers. Before this, my pictures of Wonder Woman had circles for hands and feet. But with Aunty Jenny's help, my drawings of Lynda Carter now have sophisticated high-heel boots with pointy ends and even stars on the sides. I have learned how to create wrist cuffs, a magic lasso and draw red nails on delicate fingers. Aunty Jenny says I could be an artist one day. She is so patient with me. She also has her own two children, my cousins Matthew and Kim. Perhaps I'm envious of them because their family seems so happy. Sometimes I even wish that Aunty Jenny and Uncle Colin were my parents – especially my Uncle Col. He's very handsome, with his dark brown beard and piercing eyes. He's so gentle and kind. He gives cuddles and hugs and he doesn't smell like alcohol. I wish I had a father that didn't smell.

Sometimes my father will come home from the pub and be covered in sweat. His bald head a shiny, slippery, red, sunburned stinky ball of skin. He'll ask me to give him a kiss. I hate this. He reeks of cigarettes and beer and body odour and another smell I've never been able to pinpoint. Garbage, maybe. He smells a little bit like rotten garbage left over after the bins have been collected. Whenever he asks me to kiss him goodnight, I quickly use my pyjama sleeve to wipe the germs off my lips. Ugh. It's disgusting.

Uncle Colin, however, smells like Old Spice. It's my favourite smell in the entire world.

We're all in the kitchen, wrapping things up. Uncle Colin is helping us put knives, forks and plates in a box as well as essential groceries.

'One cup, one plate, one bowl and one set of cutlery is all he needs,' my Aunty Jenny says in a matter-of-fact tone and so that's all we leave behind.

I have mixed emotions being in this kitchen. It's the emotional centre of this house. It's where most of my parents' arguments take place and I can see it from my bedroom at night. However, it's also a place where I cuddle Fonzie, our dog, and where I eat ice cream with Milo sprinkled on top after school. It's where I help my mother put up Christmas decorations of brightly coloured foil bells draped across the bright yellow kitchen cabinets. It's where I sit up at the counter on winter mornings and eat my hot Weet-Bix my mother makes – with two big helpings of white sugar sprinkled over the malty, warm and comforting biscuits. It's a place of nurturing and happy memories.

Yet now it's more like a war bunker.

The beige and brown floral wallpaper and the bright yellow cabinets seem sad without their crockery and glasses. Instead of a vibrant flowery room I see it for what it really is; a dark, dingy space with black-and-white vinyl floor tiles lifting up from the cement, wallpaper peeling away at the seams and a layer of brown residue over everything, like a coating of sadness.

We slowly finish loading the trailer outside with boxes of our belongings and our suitcases. Soon we'll be on our way to our new home, Paradise Cove Trailer Park.

Yesterday my father left for six weeks, working as an engineer on a merchant ship called the *Ampol Sarel*. He hates it. For most of my life this is what he's done for a living. When he was younger he was a police officer in Sydney before he moved us all to Queensland, separating my mother from her friends and family. For a brief time we owned a plant nursery, the Sand and Gravel Supermarket, but he drank away all the profits and blamed the accountant for ripping him off. We all knew the problem was that my father spent more time at the pub than he did at the business. We almost lost our house to the bank because of it.

It was embarrassing because before this, we had a nice car, lots of friends and parties at our place. In the years that followed the closure of the business things became tough. Old car, old clothes. Fewer friends. No parties. My mother went back to work full-time doing night shifts as a nurse's assistant in a retirement home while my father worked long haul in sweaty, hot, noisy, greasy engine rooms floating on the ocean.

The time he's away is heaven. It's like a weight has lifted off the world, like someone has taken a can opener and ripped the ceiling off our house and there's nothing but blue skies above. The downside is that when he gets home, he's often what my mother calls 'dry drunk'. He's angry, always in a bad mood and they're always fighting. Not only that, while he's away, instead of saving money, he spends his free time at the bar on the ship. When it's time to come home, he must pay his bill, the bar tab. Sometimes it's more than he earned.

We have six whole weeks to establish our new lives as a family without him. I'm so proud of my mother for finally having the courage to do this. We've been begging her to leave him forever and today she's finally doing it.

The drive to the Paradise Cove Trailer Park feels long. It's in a part of town I've never been to before. Because I'm in primary school but my siblings are in high school, my mother tells us that instead of walking to school she'll have to drop me off. My brother and sister will take the bus.

We pull up to our new home: a concrete slab next to a white trailer with orange and yellow stripes on the side. The slab is for the annex and apparently that's where my mother will sleep and where our living room will be. I love it! Stepping inside the trailer feels like being on a camping trip. There's a table and wrap-around couch as soon as you enter, then a cute little kitchen and sink. The table folds down and the couches become a bed for Peter and me. At the other end of the trailer is another couch which will be Tracey's bed. The trailer smells musty and like sun-drenched plastic. Like that time we got an above-ground pool for the summer, back in the days when we felt rich. The framework of the pool lay on the sandy base of our backyard while the blue vinyl cooked in the Queensland sun for hours as the workmen desperately tried to figure out how to put the pieces of the framework together. Us kids were so keen to get in the pool we were standing in the middle of the oceans of aqua plastic before it was even upright. I remember being overwhelmed by the unnatural chemical smell of the pool lining, the opposite of the beach and everything it conjures up in your mind. I can still smell it now. It was like a big inflatable toy. That's what this trailer smells like. I think it's the plastic coverings on the seat cushions. Or maybe the curtains.

While we're unpacking clothing and putting food in the cupboard my Uncle Colin and his friend have put up a massive tent that makes the annex into an enormous room. I already feel safe here.

My brother says there's a park in the complex just for children and my mother says we can go play there so we go to check it out. It's not much – just a sandpit with a big spinning wheel in the middle and some monkey bars. But there are other kids and we quickly make friends. Before I know it, the sun is going down and we're being called inside. It's bath time and this is the only bit I don't love. There's no bathroom in our trailer. We have to use the one in the trailer park. It's a communal shower which means we must take everything we need with us into what feels like the sort of place where you change swimming costumes at the school pool. It's brightly lit and smells of bleach.

We wear 'flip flops' on our feet to the trailer shower and I feel a little silly walking around at dusk in my flannel pyjamas when all the other kids are still out skateboarding and riding bikes, but my mother is insistent we come inside for dinner. When I enter the trailer, I notice instantly the plastic smell has gone. Now the trailer is filled with home smells. My mother has made baked beans on toast and the aroma of warm bread and tomato sauce fills the air. Her perfume and hints of hairspray mixed with cigarette smoke have transformed the empty shell into a friendly space.

We have a lively conversation about the future and because it's a special occasion being the first night of our new lives, I'm even allowed to have a cup of my mother's Maxwell House coffee. We sit up for a while talking about what the next day is going to be like.

I am filled with a sense of peace, but I can tell my siblings are not thrilled. It's a school day tomorrow and Tracey has to get a bus from an unfamiliar location. My brother says he's embarrassed that people are going to find out where we're living. My mother says it's nobody's business. However, she reinforces that we cannot tell anyone in case it gets back to my father. That sentence sticks in my head.

Later I will wake in the middle of the night to a warm gush of liquid between my legs. I have pissed the bed like I will most nights for the next six months.

Something Wicked
This Way Comes

Summer 1980. I've had the best six months of my life. Sure, I've had nightmares every night that we've lived here but I honestly don't remember them. Living in the trailer is the happiest I've ever been. We've been in hiding from my father for so long that it feels like he'll never find us. The idea of a life without him is starting to feel permanent.

My mother works two jobs. At night she works at the nursing home, taking care of the elderly, and a couple of days per week she makes sandwiches at a café in a new strip of shops that has just opened within walking distance of our new home. She's exhausted most of the time and we don't have much money. Before we left our father, he committed us to an expensive car loan, and a huge chunk of my mother's wages is being spent on the repayments. Over the summer holidays my brother Peter and I often go with my mother to her café job because we're too young to be left alone at the trailer park. We are reminded to be on our best behaviour in case we draw attention from my mother's boss and get her into trouble. That's hard for us because we argue a lot.

The days are long at the café and my mother's boss is mean. I don't like the way he talks to her or the other lady who works there. My mother seems scared of him. He glares at us as we sit at a table on the footpath outside, as though we're a nuisance. I've got my colouring books and creative things to keep me entertained but it's harder for Peter because he's a much more physical kid. He likes to play football and other sports, so he's bored a lot of the time. The summer stretches out endlessly and I love it because there's no school and the movie *The Empire Strikes Back* is coming out soon. There are so many TV ads and toys to look at when we go to Kmart. I love looking at the catalogues that come in the mail and dreaming of owning some of the *Star Wars* figurines.

There's a boy at school named Arthur Lotts. It's an apt surname because he has more *Star Wars* toys than anyone I've ever seen. So many, in fact, that he carries them around in his arms like he's scooped them up from a pile on the floor. To me, they're so precious and expensive, I could never be so careless with them. At lunchtime Arthur is followed around by a horde of boys he lets play with the toys. I am never allowed. One day before Christmas break, he dropped his Darth Vader figurine and he didn't even notice it. Nobody did. As the boys all followed the pied piper of *Star Wars* off into the pine tree clearance where kids would play, I picked up the discarded toy and studied it. It was so beautiful. I traced my fingers over its shiny vinyl cape and extended the red lightsaber that hid neatly disguised in the arm. I made the *whooosh* sound. What if I kept it?

I looked over at the group of boys, deeply engrossed in their play. They were missing the main villain of the story and had no idea. I discreetly slipped the figurine into my pocket and took him home with me for the night.

I showed my mother and explained what had happened and begged her to let me keep him but she would hear nothing of it. 'No, it's not yours, sweetheart. You have to give it back.' So I got to play with one *Star Wars* toy for one night that year. The next day I went to school and prepared myself for the reaction I'd get when I gave

Arthur Lotts his prized possession back. I imagined the sense of relief on his face. Mum was right. It didn't belong to me and Arthur had probably been crying all night over the missing toy. I know I would have been.

INTERIOR: Classroom, 8.45 a.m., Mabel Park State School
A crowd of children huddle together, talking. One giant blond child holds court over an enthralled group of junior boys.

It's five minutes before the bell rings and everyone is getting ready to sit at their desks. I approach Arthur. He has his back turned to me.

'Hey!' I tap him on the shoulder.

He turns around and looks at me as though it's the first time he's ever seen me. I realise in this moment he is very tall. He looks like the oldest child in *The Sound of Music*. A tall, broad, blond Aryan statue of a man-child. I'm holding out his Darth Vader figurine, offering it up like a sacrifice. Gently, like I'm feeding a steak to a lion. He looks puzzled.

'You dropped this yesterday. I found it. I'm giving it back to you,' I say nervously.

There is no expression on Arthur's face.

'Oh,' he says casually. He swipes it from my outstretched hand and utters a barely audible, 'Thanks' as he turns his back and walks away.

All year I've been coveting (and I do mean the literal biblical use of the word) *Star Wars* toys in the toy section of the Big W department store on Kedron Road. I've spent a lot of the lead-up to Christmas in this massive retail complex where one half is filled with groceries and the other half is the epitome of 1980s globalism selling everything from beach chairs to televisions. Every time my mother goes grocery shopping I help her first and then she gives me fifteen minutes to go and look at the toys. I go immediately to the *Star Wars* displays and gaze at the eye-wateringly beautiful racks of merchandise. All of my favourite characters are there encased in tiny plastic windows, glued to cards decorated with stunning action stills from the films. I carefully take each item from the rack, delicately handling it as though it's precious cargo. I study every inch of the casing; my eyes darting up and down, left to right, reading the descriptions in great detail. I pore over the accessories, the fabrics and costumes noticing tiny details like the difference in paint colours chosen for the facial elements; often spending so long scrutinising the objects of my desire that I can detect subtle manufacturing differences in seemingly identical items. Each toy is unique. On the back of each box is a photograph of all forty-one figurines in the collection so far. You can collect them all if you can afford it. But they are very expensive. One dollar and ninety-nine cents. Each! Multiply that by forty-one and that's a lot of money, especially for a single mother.

I believe in Santa Claus, but he has never brought me a present as expensive as this, or as desired. I also know that even though there are certain presents my mother would buy for me, the *Star Wars* figurines are probably out of her price range. I don't care, really. I get so much joy from just looking at them. Owning them isn't as important as being around them. Each time we go to the store, my mother asks me, if I had to pick *one*, which would I choose. It's tough but it always comes down to my hero, Luke Skywalker.

Seeing Christmas ramp up, from a retail point of view – often from as early as October – is an exciting journey in and of itself. Before we left our father, the weeks leading up to the special day were such a source of excitement, particularly when it came to decorating the Christmas tree. My mother went out of her way to indulge my love of fantasy. We'd look up at the sky on Christmas Eve and she'd convince me that a red light on an airplane was actually Rudolph's nose. I believed her. On Christmas Day, we had lavish festive lunches with roast turkey and ham, spending half the day at our place and the remainder with other relatives. Food was in abundance. However, due to living in the trailer this year I am already lowering my expectations. I am completely fine with that because we are safe. Mum's going to get Red Rooster – a fried chicken take-out meal – and we'll eat it outside on the park bench at the trailer park. Later on we'll visit Aunty Jenny, Uncle Colin and my cousins Matthew and Kim who are aged five and three respectively.

It's Christmas Eve and I'm such a bundle of nerves and excitement I'm sure I won't be able to sleep. My mother encouraged Peter and me to exhaust ourselves – running and playing in the trailer park and re-enacting TV shows. I don't know if it worked but it's now time for bed. I'm freshly showered and in my PJs, looking at our charming but very small Christmas tree in the trailer annex and wondering how Santa Claus is going to find us this year. My mother assures me he will. I fall asleep as the colourful Christmas lights blur into a rainbow glow of hopes and dreams.

The next morning, Peter wakes up first, as he does every Christmas morning, and declares with an excited scream, 'Santa's been!' I open my eyes to a room literally overflowing with presents. What happens next is nothing short of a miracle. My sister and mother urge me to open one specific present first. It's a rectangular-shaped parcel about the size of a large lunchbox. I tear off the paper and immediately recognise what's underneath. *Star Wars*. It's a vinyl box and the cover is decorated with the most exquisite painting of various action scenes from the film. There's a black pop button and I unlatch it to open the lid. Underneath is a tray with twelve partitions and each one is filled with a *Star Wars* figurine! My eyes are as big as the moon. No, the Death Star! 'How did he know?' I ask, incredulously.

'There's more, underneath,' Tracey says.

I lift up the tray and sure enough there are *twelve more* figurines! This is the collector's carrying case containing twenty-four *Star Wars* characters. Every single one I wanted. Han Solo, Princess Leia, R2-D2, C-3PO, Yoda, my hero Luke and so many more. There are figurines I hadn't even seen before at the store! A medical droid! Bounty hunters! This is almost too much to fathom. I think I now have more *Star Wars* toys than Arthur Lotts! My mother looks at me with pure love. 'There's something else, just from me, open this one,' she says and hands me a larger box. I open it and to my delight, it's a large Luke Skywalker doll, a twelve-inch one, so big the lightsaber looks almost real. It's translucent blue, unlike the plain matt painted one that came with the tiny figurine. When I hold it up to the light, it sparkles magically. I'm obsessed with it. I think I like this more than any of the toys because my mother chose it herself.

I am the happiest boy on the face of the earth. I'm so safe here. I love this life in this trailer, sleeping so close to my mother, near my sister and brother. Surrounded by my toys. My world is tiny and manageable. It feels like I don't have to worry so much anymore.

It's a perfect Saturday morning and I'm playing with my *Star Wars* toys in the playground at the trailer park. There's a wooden platform that connects the monkey bars and I've set up camp here. I've rigged a makeshift pulley system with some string to connect the lightsaber of my Luke Skywalker doll so that when I pull it, it appears as though it's floating in air. Luke stands on his hands, with my invisible assistance. Yoda, his Jedi master, instructs patiently by his side.

'Luke, use the Force,' I say in my best Yoda voice.

I'm re-enacting the scene where Luke, on the swamp planet of Dagobah, has to use his special powers of telekinesis to lift objects without touching them. All while doing a handstand. In this particular scene, Luke is worried and distracted. He has visions of his friends in trouble.

I feel a tingling in my belly. I close my eyes and breathe, purposefully, confidently. I pull the string to raise the lightsaber from the ground.

'Yes!' I say, imitating Yoda.

But Luke can't concentrate. He's too busy worrying about his friends. Yoda is balancing on Luke's feet while Luke is mid-headstand, trying to make rocks float and draw his lightsaber towards him when a car appears. I look up. Luke falls. Yoda falls. My stomach falls. My world is destroyed.

I'm surprised nobody else is reacting to this. Shouldn't the earth be shaking? Shouldn't there be rivers of blood? It feels as though a thousand knives are stabbing me in the gut. I look around the playground and life carries on as usual. How could it possibly? There's a car, a bright-red F100 Ford pick-up, driving up and down the purpose-built 'streets' of the trailer park.

He is looking for us.

Found us he has.

Trailer Park Blues

I'm running as fast as I can. In bare feet, the red-hot bitumen stings even worse because of the grains of sand, which are in fact tiny razor blades as far as my skin is concerned. I pay no attention. My body is a disembodied torso that allows my legs to bound higher and higher and my arms to swing at gravity-defying angles such as to achieve a level of speed the mind finds impossible. On any other occasion my lungs might have reached peak capacity and I'd have been sabotaged by a stitch. But on this hot summer's day I am a perfectly honed specimen of a human designed to react immediately to fear. The fight or flight response is propelling me at supersonic speed towards the trailer where I know my father is headed.

My mother is in extreme danger.

You can imagine my shock when, instead of a physical altercation, I come upon what looks to be a calm negotiation. My father is with a friend of his, someone I don't know very well. My mother has a friend visiting for a cup of coffee. All four adults seem to be telling each other to take it easy, to relax.

I creep up to listen and the gist of the conversation seems to be that my father wants to apologise.

What?

He wants to *apologise*? Surely my mother can see through this. This is just a lie to get us back!

He says some bullshit about how he's going to stop drinking, about how he's cut down already and how he wants to take us out on a 'family night'.

What the hell is a *family night*?

I'm standing in the annex, watching my mother be persuaded and charmed by my father and I feel all the colour drain from my life. My stomach feels like there's a manhole inside it like the kind Wile E. Coyote would fall into chasing that pesky Road Runner. It feels like there's an endless, hollow well of emptiness at the centre of my soul. It's dread. It's fear. It's a future flash of certain tragedy to come. What was once a perfectly safe and peaceful bubble has now been pierced and is unsafe and vulnerable. Everything I've come to know and trust over the past six months is at risk. There's a snake in the garden, slithering among the magical world I've created in the absence of evil.

Eventually my mother and father agreed to start dating again. It seemed unfathomable at the time, but that's what happened. In the decades since I've had many conversations with my mother and learned so much about domestic abuse and the horrific toll it takes on the victim's self-esteem. In my mother's case, she was dead broke. She was working two jobs to try to feed and educate us, as well as pay off that car loan. Suddenly this man turns up and promises to stop drinking 'as much' and to 'stop hitting her' if she'll just 'give him a second chance'. She had no power and she was terrified. So she agreed to let him take us out on family nights. It wasn't like he took her to dinner or did anything remotely romantic. One of the first things that happened was he wanted access to his children. Not my sister, mind you. He sort of hated her because she was brave enough to openly hate him back. But he still felt some machismo-driven need to demonstrate some paternal qualities to his male offspring.

When I first had to spend time with him, I felt that familiar dread monster awaken in my stomach. It was a Saturday afternoon and he had come to collect us with the most unappealing plan: we were going to work with him the next day. For some reason at this point in his life he had a job as a garbage collector, driving a truck with one other guy and emptying domestic trash cans. He started early in the morning, so we were going to our old house with him to stay the night and get up at 4 a.m. for his 5 a.m. start.

When it came time to leave the trailer park, I pretended to be asleep. I was hoping that my mother would decide not to wake me and I wouldn't have to go. My heart was racing even though I was faking blissful, peaceful slumber. I listened carefully for any kind of indication they might let me off the hook, but none came. I was gently rocked 'awake' and told it was time to go.

The separation anxiety I felt was physically painful. I remember pulling away from the trailer park with my father and brother and there was a lump in my throat. I wanted to cry.

Upon arriving at our house at Lake Road I was shocked to discover it was now a disgusting, filthy mess. My father had clearly not cleaned it since we left. I'm not exaggerating. There were cigarette butts on the carpet. Beer cans everywhere. It stank. He must have been having parties or just partying by himself. Vinyl records were scattered around the living room, some out of their sleeves, scratched. It made me sad to the see the house in such disrepair, especially some of my favourite albums we listened to as a family, tossed aside like they meant nothing.

There were no sheets for our beds, so we had to sleep in the same bed as him and those sheets hadn't been washed since the beginning of time. Even though my brother and I had a shower before we left the trailer park, my father didn't bother having one before bed, and the stench of his body odour and cigarette breath as I lay down was overwhelming. I could barely sleep. It felt like I was in a haunted mansion. All the memories of the violence and the terror kept running through my mind. I wanted so badly to be close to my mother but I couldn't let my father see that. So I lay there, again pretending to sleep, trying to drown out his donkey-like snore and ignore the anxiety and loneliness I felt.

Suddenly it was 4 a.m. and a brutal analogue alarm clock was ringing, shocking me out of a shallow sleep. There was no time for breakfast or even anything to drink. We just got out of bed, got dressed and suddenly a massive garbage truck pulled up out front. The stench. That was the first thing I noticed. The truck smelled like trash cans that have had rotten rubbish in them because of course this was where all trash cans went to die. The rest of the experience felt like the longest day I've ever lived yet it was a standard eight-hour shift. Sometimes we hung off the back of the truck, sometimes people would give my father bottles of beer to say thank you (it was near New Year's) and sometimes we'd have to pick up bits of trash that fell out of the truck. The midday sun was glaringly hot by the time we took the fully loaded truck back to the depot to be emptied. That's when the only good thing about the entire morning happened: we went to a fish and chip shop and my father bought us breakfast.

When he took us home to my mother, I couldn't wait to wash the stench off me. Not just the scent of rancid strangers' trash, but the putrid smell of having spent the night with my father's still unwashed body and uncaring company. I knew he'd only had us to prove a point to my mother. There had been no bonding, no stirring up of good feelings. Just a further reminder of how utterly distant we were and how terrified I was to leave my mother's side.

Abduction

New Year's Eve, 1980. There's a storm coming and I don't mean just the one they've been warning us about on the radio. I feel it in my gut. I really do have the Force, just like Luke Skywalker. Something terrible is going to happen today. I can sense it.

We're spending the night at Aunty Jenny's to celebrate the New Year. It's going to be 1981 tomorrow and we're allowed to stay up until midnight. I should feel excited but I don't. I feel a sense of dread.

We spent the day at a riverbank with concrete pipes in it. Aunty Jenny says we probably shouldn't be swimming in them because it's dangerous, but the way the river water flows is kind of like a water slide made extra slippery from the green moss that lines the inside of the massive tubes. Besides, she's so safe in the water. One of my earliest memories is of being in her arms as she taught me not to be afraid of the Pacific Ocean. Clinging onto her warm, maternal body of love, safe in her arms as the waves swelled, ebbing and flowing. Each time I got scared she distracted me, making a happy 'Whooo!' sound and smiling to make sure I knew that it was fun and safe. When a big wave hit and splashed our faces, we laughed and she held me tight, her warmth and love all encompassing. That's what it is to be around her, total immersion in love.

Today she has her two babies, Matthew and Kim, whom she's watching, but she always makes me feel like she's my second mother. I love her so much. She's waving at me now as I swoosh through the slimy pipe. Uncle Colin is making hamburgers on a barbeque in the picnic area and we come out of the water and dry off from the freezing river to eat lunch. The sky is a pale green and my mother says that means hailstorms are coming.

See. I knew.

Now we're driving home in two cars. There's too many of us to fit in just one. My mother, Tracey, Peter and me in one car. Aunty Jenny, Uncle Colin and Matthew and Kim in the other.

Tonight on TV we can watch anything we want. I hope it's *The Muppet Show*! But first we have to take a bath. I'm freezing after my swim, still wet in my swimming costume. Matthew and Kim and Tracey and Peter have already had their bath and I'm next. I was supposed to share a bath with Peter but I didn't want to. I'm too old for that. So I get the bathtub all to myself.

It feels like being inside a cocoon, sitting in the warm ceramic bowl. The milky, soapy water comes up to my knees and I listen as the rain starts to hit the tin roof. Normally this is a calming experience; the sound of droplets on the metal has eased me into dreamland many times before. I should connect to that memory but tonight I've got that awful feeling again. What does it mean? Is it the Force? Is something bad about to happen? My psychic ability warning me? Should I do something?

I hear yelling.

Is that—? It can't be. It sounds like my father's voice.

Slow-motion urgency. Water clings to me, desperately, as I jump up. I look like a wave frozen in a glass sculpture. The contents of the bath are crying, its tears clinging to my legs like I clung to my mother's the first day she left me at pre-school. I resist the pull of gravity that urges me to stay in the safety of the bathroom. I know what is unfolding outside and there's no way I can pretend it's not happening. My mother is in grave danger.

With a towel wrapped around my waist I run out of the bathroom but find nobody in the house. The TV is quietly flickering static between stations and the rain is pelting hard against the windows. The commotion is coming from downstairs, outside. I quickly head to the front door, which is open, and bound down the chocolate-painted wooden stairs.

Headlights cut strict beams of light with the precision of a lightsaber through the black of night, peppered by flickers of raindrops. They extend out from my father's Ford F100 pick-up truck which is idling, driverless, in the front yard. My eyes dart around in the dark. It's chaos. Two men struggle in silhouette against the backlight of the headlights. My father is raising his fist, pounding it mercilessly and continuously into my Uncle Colin. To the right of the two men my cousins Matthew and Kim are screaming and clutching their mother as they witness this horrific act. My mother and sister are together, yelling for my father to stop. I can't make out much of what they're saying, but from what I gather, this is punishment for my Uncle Colin helping move us out of Lake Road and into the trailer park.

Now my Uncle Colin is on the ground and my Aunty Jenny is coming at my father, telling him to leave. Uncle Colin gets up to try to escape, but my father chases him, and the two of them run around and around the truck in the pouring rain until my father catches Colin again and beats him some more.

It's like something from a horror movie only this is my life.

When my father has finished with Uncle Colin he takes my mother by the hips and throws her over his shoulder like a sack of potatoes and forces her into the truck. Peter jumps in to try to intervene and suddenly the truck is pulling away. Within seconds my mother has been abducted with my brother on board.

I'm standing in the front yard, under the dull illumination of the moon, the rain pelting down, trying to make sense of what has just happened. My aunt and uncle console my baby cousins. My sister and I are in shock and yet unattended to. I feel utterly alone and abandoned.

Time is elastic in my memory but somehow we end up in my Aunty Jenny's living room, in our pyjamas, sat in front of the television on their brown velvet couch. I remember the texture so vividly I can almost feel it under my fingertips now. I think I hyper-focused on the details of that room to ground myself and calm my nervous system because what I had witnessed and what my mind was trying to process was just too overwhelming. Nothing is really explained to me. I've just seen my mother and brother abducted, watched my father beat up my beloved uncle and now there's this horrible silence as the abused family console each other and put their precious children to bed. My sister and I feel like this is all our fault. We feel a deep sense of shame, though no words are exchanged.

I'm shivering with cold and no matter what my Aunty Jenny and Uncle Colin think, feel or believe in that moment, what my eight-year-old mind takes from the situation is a series of beliefs about myself that will shape my life for decades.

I am all alone in this world and nobody can save me.

Nobody is coming back for me.

Even the people who love me only love me on a second-tier level; they love other children more.

I am the son of something monstrous, something evil and therefore I am monstrous and evil.

I am a burden.

I am unlovable.

I sit on the couch imagining all the things the adults are thinking about me, feeling the second-hand embarrassment and shame for my father's actions. It's excruciating pretending to watch television as though everything is fine, while inside my mind I'm full of un-answered questions.

Where is my mother?

When is she coming back?

Where am I going to sleep tonight?

I look at my cheap pyjamas, summer ones with shorts and a short-sleeve button-down shirt with boat patterns. I feel poor. Inferior. Genetically deficient. I'm comparing myself to my beautiful, young and innocent cousins, now fast asleep in their beds. So perfect and unblemished and so utterly blanketed by love. This experience for them is the first introduction to the life I have led every day since I was born. Now I've infected their world.

I look at my feet, still dirty from walking around the muddy yard. I feel the dampness in my uncombed hair. I feel like an orphan. I look over at my sister, eyes wide, still in a state of shock, sitting upright, back stiff, protective. She's staring at the television as though she's seen a ghost. We don't talk.

Sometime around midnight the phone rings. My Aunty Jenny answers and seems calm; she's nodding, she's 'uh-huh'ing. She puts the phone down and then she comes and explains what's going to happen next and what's going to happen next is my worst night-mare. My worst nightmare is delivered to me in the kindest, most dulcet tones because Aunty Jenny is one of the kindest most loving people in my life. She says my mother is safe at my old house at Lake Road. She explains that, after several hours of 'talking', my mother has decided it's the safest option for her to stay there the night. She'll come and collect my sister and me tomorrow.

I can't process this information.

Everything was perfect before he found us. I had my routine, my special safe place inside the trailer. I had my toys. I had a universe free of violence and a world without my father. It was the only time in recent years that I remember feeling safe. What had my father done on this night to earn her trust back? I didn't understand.

The next day is another smear through the lines of time.

The foreboding bubbling of the exhaust of the Ford F100 sounds the alarm in my stomach as my parents arrive. My father waits silently in the truck while my mother gets out with my brother. They have been returned and my father leaves without explanation or apology.

Adult conversations ensue. Apparently my mother was able to subdue my father by promising to hear him out. In his belligerent state, he was making promises about giving up drinking in a bid to win us back. She knew her life was in danger and so she did what she felt was the safest thing: she listened to his pleas until he fell unconscious and waited till the next morning when she knew he would be full of shame and regret.

That pesky elasticity of time swirls. I know we did not immediately return to live with him. We went back to the trailer park for many months still. During that time, he did indeed stop drinking and made attempts to take us out.

I remember visiting him, at the family home, early on in this process.

INTERIOR: Lake Road, January 1981

Entering the house I can still smell the stench of my father's six months of partying. Walking into my old bedroom and sitting on the bed I feel actual dust and debris. The mattress has no sheets, just the woollen bedspread. There is no pillow, no posters on the wall.

I can smell bacon and eggs, a staple for my father and something my mother cooked for him often. She'd gone out to buy some groceries because there was no food in the house. We sit and listen while our parents have a procedural conversation about how they are going to dismantle our life in the trailer park and move everything back to Lake Road – if my father can change. It's like watching a car crash in slow motion.

Part of the conversation involves the promise my father made that he is going to stop drinking. He made this declaration in front of us all but honestly, I don't believe it. But my mother says it is the only reason she might agree to letting him have access to us again.

Of course, I couldn't possibly have known the cost of this decision.

At the age of eight, my Aunty Jenny and Uncle Colin left my life and disappeared. I think they fled that night after the abduction.

While we eventually made our way back to the trailer park, the placenta of my innocent, safe and trauma-free world had been stabbed, violently, its contents oozing out like the insides of a Stretch Armstrong toy pulled beyond its limits. I remember seeing Arthur Lotts, the rich kid at school, destroying one of those toys when I was younger, ruining the 'unbreakable doll' illusion. It wasn't really an unbreakable miracle, able to withstand any amount of force. It too had limits. At the hands of a violent and curious mind, the world's strongest and stretchiest doll would weep, just like me. Once its insides were exposed there was no way to put them back in.

I can't imagine the impact that losing another sister must have had on my mother. Worse than death in some ways because although she knew Aunty Jenny was alive, she had no way of contacting her. Similarly, the heartbreak my Aunty Jenny must have gone through, leaving the comfort and security of her big sister and the life she'd built in Brisbane. The trauma of having to uproot her entire family and run for their lives. As an eight year old, I could only see it from my point of view. I didn't know that my father had threatened to kill my Uncle Colin if he ever contacted my mother again. Naturally, Uncle Colin took that threat seriously and took the steps to make sure his family was safe.

What unfolded was nothing less than a witness protection program–like disappearance from our lives. No forwarding address. No phone number. No contact. For a decade. I took it extremely personally. I felt abandoned by two of the people I loved most in the world. My child's mind unable to understand the decisions that were made, I internalised the scenario. Instead of realising that my mother went back to my father that night because she was afraid for her life, I thought she went back because she had given up. Instead of understanding that my beautiful Aunty Jenny had fled the city in fear of her life, I thought she had discarded me. I thought she didn't love me. Nothing could have been further from the truth.

Safe

The doctor asks me what has brought me to his office today. After some brief glossing over of my career and the stress of getting ready for the impending release of the second Savage Garden album, *Affirmation*, I explain that since coming out as gay and feeling unsuccessful at having relationships with men, I've found myself having very dark thoughts. How dark? Like, *driving across the Golden Gate Bridge and thinking about closing my eyes for enough time so the car might drive off the edge and plummet into the icy deathly waters below*, dark. Like, *how many sleeping tablets would I have to take to never wake up again* dark.

He asks about my childhood. I get defensive and tell him that I had it rough but that I'm just here to get some medication because my assistant who has been checking to see if I'm alive each morning thinks maybe I need an antidepressant. I'm angry at the prodding about my private life. I've spent so long getting over it, surviving it. I honestly believe I've put it to bed. There's a lyric in a song on the forthcoming album where I say that I believe my parents did the best they knew. I believe that! My mother was poor, she was not well educated but she was smart. Life had dealt her a series of blows until her only escape was to marry a man who physically abused her on their wedding night.

71

My father came from a family who did to him what he did to us. He was physically beaten as a child, and he watched his father beat his mother. While he drank heavily and beat us, he eventually stopped drinking and by 1999 I have 'forgiven' him. I remember watching an Oprah Winfrey special about taking control of your life where she specifically mentioned how, at some point, you have to stop blaming your parents for your problems and realise that you are the adult now and you are responsible for your happiness. That's me. That's where I'm at. I've forgiven him, I told myself.

Or at least, I thought I had. Whatever the case, my father seems to *really* like me now. Sure, he was the first person to call me a faggot and the first person to tell me I'd never make it, but now that I'm rich and famous, he loves me. Things are good. Aside from those pesky suicidal thoughts.

The psychiatrist then asks me a question that will change the course of my life forever. Just seven words. Seven words that crack open an iron fortress that has been keeping a part of me safe for decades.

'Did you feel safe, as a child?'

My lips begin to tremble.

'Safe?' I ask, as though I've never heard of this word before.

'Yes,' he says calmly. 'You do realise that as children we only have a few basic needs. To be fed, to be loved and to feel safe. Did you ever feel safe?'

I'm furious at the question. That fury turns to anger and then that anger gives way to a wave of deep, deep grief and sadness. It was as though someone had taken a pin to a balloon full of water. All of my bravado vanished. All of my alleged strength disappeared. I burst into tears. My body went limp and my defences were gone.

I realise that I never felt safe or secure as a child – or as an adult. From my earliest memory I was always anxious, worried, uncertain.

On guard. The swarm of wasps in my belly wasn't just a child's over-active imagination. It was the physical manifestation of anxiety and fear. An overload of feelings and emotions far too big for my still-developing emotional intelligence to process. Not only was I terrified of my father and what his unpredictable moods might unleash, I was also unable to rely upon my mother – who was herself a victim of his abuse – to protect me from him. Like my sister, Tracey, I was my mother's protector but nobody was protecting us.

I created an adult life where I would never have to rely upon anyone. I'd be not just a member of a band, but the lead singer. The star. Not just a working performer, but a millionaire. Not just a boss, but someone who employed all of his friends, paid for every meal and who never, ever had to face or fear rejection. I created a life where there is no possibility of feeling vulnerable because I am the person in control of every aspect.

It's exhausting.

After twenty minutes of crying, I am able to admit that maybe, just maybe, there is some unfinished business and some residual pain that I have never truly dealt with.

Did I ever feel safe? I cycle through the memories.

INTERIOR: Ford F100 pick-up truck, 1976
I'm four years old and I feel like the world is ending. That dread, that knot in my stomach I told you about, the twitching and gurgling discomfort is the larvae of the wasps, churning in my gut as my mother, Peter and I sit in the front seat of the F100 pick-up truck outside my pre-school. I'm sipping on an apple juice box. I'm distinctly aware that if I sip slowly, I can delay the departure.

'Come on, sweetheart, it's time to go inside,' my mother says gently.

A stab of pain as the insects in my belly begin to hatch. 'But I haven't finished my juice yet,' I say, sipping even slower now.

73

Peter seems calm, bemused even by my sudden anxious behaviour. Sip. Sip. Sip.

'Okay, Darren, this is getting a bit silly now,' my mother says. 'You can finish the juice inside. I'm sure the teacher won't mind.'

I am terrified to leave this car but I have no choice because suddenly I'm being lifted out of the seat and nudged towards the school gates. Every step closer the carcinogenic sensation in my belly intensifies. My mother opens the creaky metal gate, walks me up the wooden stairs to the reception; all the while I'm gripping her hand for dear life.

Once inside, I'm instantly panicked. I clock the room like a trapped animal. There's only one exit: where I came in! There are so many children and no parents. I'm going to be abandoned here. My mother is going to leave me with these strangers. Beads of sweat spring forth on my forehead. My pulse quickens. I feel like I'm going to die. There's talk of where to put my school bag and conversation about what happens to the sandwich that I've brought for lunch. I don't care. I only care that soon she will be leaving me. I latch onto my mother's legs. Two staff members swiftly grab me. They try to pull me away. I'm screaming. I'm holding my mother's thighs so tightly my fingernails dig into her skin. I scratch deep trenches of desperation into her quadriceps. I really do believe that if she leaves me here, she will never come back. I've never been apart from her before.

Somehow, I'm pried away from the safety of my mother's warm body and taken outside to a play area. A female teacher's assistant is trying to distract me by showing me a piece of playground equipment. My people-pleasing nature kicks in and I immediately pretend to be okay. I'm going to outsmart her by making her think I've calmed down and hopefully she'll leave me alone. I stop crying, even though internally I am holding back a sea of tears. Out of the corner of my eye I see my mother and brother with a teacher while she fills out

74

paperwork in the office. I manage to convince the teacher's assistant that I am not only just okay but actually very happy to be outside on the swing set. She foolishly leaves me unattended. Amateur.

The moment she turns her back, I leap over the fence, run for the F100 and jump into the tray, lying perfectly flat. My mother and brother have left the office and I overhear the teacher say that since I am so upset, it's probably best to leave without saying goodbye. My mother and brother agree and walk to the truck without looking back. They get in. I hear the doors slam shut. The ignition starts. And they drive away from this horrible place, with me safely hidden in the back.

We get halfway home before my brother notices the stowaway. Once discovered I am swiftly returned to the pre-school.

That day and every single nap time for the next year all I do is cry. 'I. Want. My. Mummy. I. Want. My. Mummy,' I sob, over and over and over. I cannot be consoled. I hate that entire year. And the teachers hate me. They complain about the 'cry-baby' who won't nap during their lunch breaks as if I can't hear them. I try to console myself under a random bedsheet that's assigned to me. It smells like unfamiliar detergent and somebody else's skin. Nothing can soothe the aching feeling of being alone.

INTERIOR: Living room, Lake Road, my sixth birthday

I'm in my pyjamas, clinging to the vegetable-shaped novelty pens and colouring pencils my mother has bought me, just so happy to have these incredible gifts. It's an ink pen in the shape of a bean! And another in the shape of a carrot! There are twenty-four immaculate Faber-Castell pencils and the most beautiful art paper to draw on. Oh, the things I'll be able to create!

I've got a belly full of my favourite meal, my mother's fried rice, just like I requested. Now a chocolate cake is coming out from the kitchen with six candles flickering on it. Life in this moment is about as perfect as it could get.

Just as we are about to sing 'Happy Birthday', the cake goes flying through the air, tossed in anger by my drunken father, and an evening of violence commences. Birthday cancelled. An all-night vigil takes the place of a celebration. This is no longer a happy moment. This is wiping cake off the walls and protecting my mother.

I never felt safe when I was a child. I could never relax. I could never count on happiness. I couldn't afford to. I had no evidence that any adult could protect me. Not my teachers. Not my neighbours. Not even my mother. Because nobody could protect her.

Music Saved Me

The year 1982 was pivotal. You could say it decided my destiny and made me the person I am today. Michael Jackson's *Thriller* album was released. *E.T.* was the biggest film in the world. Pop music was exploding and my escape into the visual landscape of music videos and the sonic universe of FM radio made my challenges at home much more bearable.

The year 1982 also marked the beginning of what would become years of pilgrimages to Woody's Music Store, the independent record shop inside Woodridge Plaza, the mecca of our retail dreams. It was the peak of 1980s consumerism and to me the shopping centre was everything television shows like *Stranger Things* and movies like *E.T.* captured about the period. The 1980s seemed innocent and 'mall culture' was, for a while at least, a cocoon of safety and wonder for my sister and me.

We'd walk there every Saturday after our chores were done. The journey was always the same. Left out of Lake Road, past Caribbean Drive, right on Paradise Road, then left onto Kingston Road and then right on Wembley, the massive street that connected all of Logan City suburbs. Sometimes we'd stop at the 7-Eleven along the way and I'd get a promotional Slurpee. This was especially exciting during the *Star Wars* years when *Return of the Jedi* was being promoted and there were so many branded cups and cut-out standees. I'd put my name down behind the counter for a poster once they'd finished using it but usually ten other kids had got there first. It didn't matter. Waiting and hoping was half the fun.

There were two places where you could buy records. The music department inside Kmart and the record store opposite it, Woody's. Now, there was no-one named Woody. At that time the owner was a very tall African American man we called 'Chuck' who was, honestly, intimidatingly cool. There were rumours that if you tried to bring a record back and claim it was scratched, Chuck would literally hurl it at you! Hence the nickname. We were petrified to ask him questions and the staff who worked there were chips off the Chuck block, so to speak. They had an air of aloofness about them and we were like boot-licking serfs, perfectly happy to placate their every whim because to us, they were the epitome of cool. They worked in a record store! What could be cooler?

We were, for some reason, massive Diana Ross fans.

How did this happen?

It goes back to my mother and Aunty Jenny. Both loved music. Before she was chased out of our lives, Aunty Jenny, being the youngest of my mother's siblings, introduced us to 'cool' 1970s records. Fleetwood Mac, especially. Carole King. An album called *Mandingo – The Primeval Rhythm of Life* and of course a lot of Motown. My mother was the person who got us into Diana Ross and the Supremes and in particular a song called 'Someday We'll Be Together'. My nana had bought the seven-inch single for my mother when she and my father had first spent time apart, and my mother would listen to it to soothe her loneliness. I remember this well because I used to play the song over and over and over. I learned to sing it note for note including all the high notes in what is now my signature falsetto.

One day I was playing the single and I accidentally scratched it. Oh no! What should I do? I was honest to a fault as a child (I guess I still am; I find it excruciating to lie) so I confessed. My mother reacted by breaking the record over my head! I'm laughing as I recall this moment, and she does too every time we remember it, because she was not a violent person. But my God did she love that record. She then blamed me for breaking it. Ha ha!

The point of all of this vinyl cracking on heads is to say we, as a unit of four – my mother, Aunty Jenny, Tracey and me – were passionate about music. Even though it was the midst of the 1980s electronic new wave – which I also loved – I was being raised on Motown and American West Coast harmonies. The soundtrack to the movie *The Big Chill* was more popular in my house than Michael's *Thriller*, simply because it got played more (and we couldn't afford to buy *Thriller*!). But Michael was all over the radio and television.

We knew all of Diana Ross's music, from her time with the Supremes through to her solo material. I was obsessed with songs like 'Swept Away' and 'Eaten Alive' – songs most people to this day don't know. I was aware of their production – Daryl Hall worked on the former; Barry Gibb from the Bee Gees and Michael Jackson on the latter. I paid attention to these things. Similarly, with the album *Thriller*, when I finally got my hands on a loaner copy, I pored over every detail of the liner notes, desperate to know what a 'Synclavier' was, as it seemed to appear on almost every track. Forty-one years later I'd have my own version of a Synclavier synthesiser, and I'd use it to produce sounds and record them on my own solo album, *Homosexual*.

Since we didn't have a lot of money, buying an album was an extremely sacred and special event. We often bought them using lay-by – that excruciating system whereby you select the item you want, take it to the cashier, put down a deposit, and essentially pay it off, interest free, over a period of time. Tracey would grab an album like *Silk Electric* by Diana Ross and put it behind the counter at Kmart and fill out a form, put down a dollar as a down payment and walk away, giddy, with the carbon copy receipt in her wallet. Each week, either from pocket money, or via her part-time job at a grocery store, she'd find the spare cash to pay a little bit more off until the record was finally hers. I got a vicarious thrill just being next to her when she did all of this because I knew the day we brought the record home we'd listen to it, with complete reverence, from beginning to end, often twice. The record was a piece of art and an object of great fragility that had to be handled with perfectly clean hands and always stored inside a plastic slip case (that was one dollar extra!).

On Sundays we did chores like cleaning the house. My sister came up with a plan where we were allowed to play one album each while we worked. Funny that her albums were often doubles, allowing her the most airtime.

It's 1983 and I'm in primary school and *Thriller* is the album the whole world is obsessed with and, let's face it, most homes have a copy. Not ours though. I had to go over to my friend Mark's house to listen to it. It was a play date but I had an ulterior motive: I had a blank cassette and was going to make a bootleg copy. While Mark recorded the album for me, I copied the lyrics from the record sleeve into my journal.

My cassette copy was soon worn down to a thread from playing it so much. I was obsessed with the songs and the hysteria surrounding Michael. I remember watching the historic twenty-sixth Grammy Awards when *Thriller* won eight awards and being fascinated by the seemingly terrified and shy man behind the glasses. I couldn't comprehend this was the same person who could excite me when he danced like an electric eel in 'Billie Jean' and frighten me when he turned into a zombie in 'Thriller'. But there was something about his private persona that I related to. An outwardly explosive and sparkling personality shielding an inwardly shy and gentle soul.

I received a dollar a week pocket money, but records were expensive back then – around $12 – whereas a dollar would get me a Coca-Cola, some lollies (or candy as we say in other parts of the world), a comic book and I'd still have five cents left over. At that stage, I couldn't seem to justify the expense of buying records.

When *Thriller* fever died down, everyone counted Michael out. Not me though. I patiently waited for his return. Soon enough, along came Prince, whom I was also obsessed with. In 1984 I got my first Sony Walkman and a cassette copy of *Purple Rain* for Christmas. I was also introduced to the concept of *stereo*.

Oh. My. God.

I would lie awake in bed at night, listening to the album on my Walkman in the widest possible stereo field and marvel at the production. I dissected every keyboard part, every harmony, every guitar lick, every drum-machine pattern. My introduction to production and sound design really began by listening to Prince through those orange foam headphones.

Then came albums like *Faith* by George Michael, of course Michael's *Bad* album, all the early great Madonna records including her debut and *True Blue*, and the genius of the Eurythmics. I absorbed their incredible melodies and fell in love with their huge pop sound. It was something that would one day influence my contribution to Savage Garden.

The development of my musical tastes coincided with the emergence of my sexuality. Madonna, Prince and Michael Jackson were my entire world by the time I reached high school even though I distinctly remember not feeling old enough to go. I still felt like a boy, not a teenager. I didn't want to part with my beloved *Star Wars* toys but I also felt ashamed to own them.

When our father was away at sea we'd rent movies from the local video store and have movie marathon weekends. It was a special time in my life because I felt like the four of us were really bonded. We each chose a film and sometimes suffered through some real duds, but I got a great emotional education watching John Hughes films like *Pretty in Pink* or having the spine stripped out of me in fear, hiding behind my hands, suffering through my brother's love of the *Friday the 13th* movies. Teen themes, love, betrayal and moral dilemmas were all played out on our tiny twelve-inch TV screen and we had lengthy discussions about what was right, wrong, fair and unjust. I also learned about the art of film during that period, watching so many B-movies, mostly horror and science fiction. I loved special effects and anything fantasy related. All of it fed my imagination and my tendency towards escapism.

My mother became friendly with the woman who worked at the video store and learned that her young son was also a huge *Star Wars* fan. The woman wanted to buy her son some *Star Wars* toys but couldn't afford to. I was essentially broke and desperate for money to buy my own family Christmas presents that year and my mother saw an opportunity. She told the woman I was growing out of my toys and was thinking of selling them. So a deal was struck. I willingly offered to sell my entire *Star Wars* toy collection to the woman from the video store for the enormous sum of $24. For a kid, that was a fortune in the 1980s.

Back then I had an illegal job helping the milkman deliver milk every Sunday. Sounds crazy but it's true. I started at age eleven and got paid $7 for seven hours' work a week. I'd hang off the back of the van, while true to cliché the milkman would flirt outrageously with the sexually frustrated housewives in the neighbourhood. He'd stand

and exude charm and testosterone while I'd work up a sweat darting between houses collecting empty glass bottles, replacing them with full ones, and bringing back the little envelopes of cash. I was terrible at maths and often struggled to work out the exact change to return to the housewives. I can't tell you how many times I either delivered the wrong milk to the wrong house, or the wrong change. People complained about my mistakes but my boss figured the cost of my wage was worth the occasionally disgruntled (and hot) housewife. I would describe him as the first morally ambiguous person I'd ever met; charming as hell but ethically so confusing. He would talk about being happily married but then tell me how much he fancied his customers! He was cheap too and never gave me anything for free regardless of how hard I worked. For example, at the end of my shift, he'd charge me full retail price for a small chocolate milk!

Between saving up $7 a week from the illegal milk delivery job and this offer of $24 for my *Star Wars* toy collection, in 1984 I had a decent amount to spend on Christmas gifts for my mother and siblings. It felt good to be able to buy them real presents with real money that I'd earned. But it came at an emotional cost.

Handing over my precious toys to the lady at the video store was like having a piece of my heart removed. I pretended it didn't bother me but in reality it was so much bigger than just parting ways with objects of affection. It was the sale of my innocence and a rite of passage to a stage in life I was not prepared for.

I Don't Belong Here

As soon as I enter the gates of Mabel Park State High School I'm like fresh meat in a lion's den. From my perspective, everything about me is underdeveloped. I don't understand the concept of rushing from class to class, I feel overdressed in the compulsory school uniform and I miss the affection and tenderness of my primary school teachers. Mabel Park feels very grown up and the kids seem cold and mean. I don't know anyone from my previous school except one girl, Nathalia Rayfield, but in my first few years we hang out in different crowds. I'm immediately cast as a nerd. In primary school, I was a dreamer, a sweet kid, a friend to most. Here in high school, I'm a piece of toilet paper stuck under the shoe of progress and that shoe did not stop running from torment.

The bullying started almost immediately.

I was labelled a faggot. Gosh, it hurt. It stung.

I had two friends. Ryan and Breck, outcasts like me, lumped together and designated as nerds via the mystical algorithm that decides the pecking order the second you pass through the school gates on day one. To survive, we had to spend our lunch break at the library. It was either that or be tormented and beaten by the bullies who ruled the school. They were relentless.

Ryan was a soft, naturally studious type, very responsible, serious and neat. Breck was a little more goofy, awkward but funny and overly sexual for his age. Both were obsessed with girls, something I distinctly remember was in contrast with me. I didn't think about girls at all. Yet all they could talk about was boobs. Both were from divorced families. We became close enough that we would sometimes spend time at each other's homes on weekends. When we were at Breck's, he'd want to show us his dad's *Playboy* magazines. I remember feeling really uncomfortable. When we were at my place, I'd want to watch taped music videos and replicate the choreography. I'm sure that felt weird for them.

My first heartbreak came from that friendship when I found out that Ryan and Breck were going to a water park, without me. Not only had they not invited me, they didn't want me to find out that they were going. A mutual friend leaked that they'd spent the weekend with them at Wild Waters – the massive water park in Brisbane's south – with my two supposed best friends. I phoned Ryan to ask why I hadn't been invited. He responded, 'Because you can be boring.'

I went to my mother in tears. She sat me down on the couch, laid my head in her lap and told me that this was my first experience of the world where people can be cruel. I can still feel her hands playing with my ears to soothe me. As I wept, she reminded me that I shouldn't take it personally. She warned that in life there would be more experiences like this.

I never really recovered from the betrayal. The way school was designed back then, by the second year, the subjects we selected pretty much put us on different paths in life. Theirs was manual. Mine was creative. I chose art, music, theatre and history. Ryan and Breck were mostly in the woodwork and metalwork department or doing maths classes. We gradually drifted apart.

Part of what separated me from the other kids was that I was secretly attracted to boys. I'd been stifling this urge since my first spanking at age five for kissing Noah, the boy who lived around the corner, but the real threat of violence had come during my final days of primary school.

It's 1984 in the last hot and sweaty months of the year before everyone in Mr Sordello's class goes their separate ways for the summer holidays. It's a bittersweet time. I've absolutely loved the last couple of years and I've really loved my teachers. Mr Sordello, especially. He's American and he talks all the time about the place I've been dreaming of my whole life: Los Angeles. Mr Sordello is a man, but he's not cruel like some of the men in my life. I think he'd make a great father and I while away my days thinking how lucky I would have been if he were mine.

I've seen some incredible things this year. First of all, my father doesn't hit my mother anymore. That's a relief. He doesn't drink, either. He's still mean, he still spanks us hard when he's 'punishing' us, and I still hate being around him, but for the most part, I no longer fear for my mother's life. Or my own. I do know my father frowns upon my 'artistic' qualities though. Peter is athletic and a natural at rugby league and my father fawns over him. I won a dance competition doing the bus stop to 'Upside Down' by Diana Ross but he didn't even acknowledge it.

Part of why I love being in the seventh grade so much is that I have the most intoxicating crush on a boy named Brad. He's the opposite of me in every way: floppy boyish haircut, dark eyes, olive skin, braces, and good at sport. Every time he walks past my heart leaps out of my chest then halts in mid-air – as if attached by a rubber band – trying to run as far away from me as possible, only to be returned to my rib cage with a definitively rejecting *thud*. Is this love?

86

I go home at night and sit in the bath, singing Lionel Richie's 'Hello'. I imagine singing it to Brad. Was it me he was looking for?

One day I receive my answer.

Brad had a best friend, Simon, who, looking back now, was very territorial. He was possessive and watched me like a hawk. Brad never seemed to care how much I talked to him, how my face blushed when he returned my gaze, or how often my eyelids fluttered when words fell out of his mouth. However, Simon sneered whenever I approached his sacred plus one.

One day, after school, the situation was made perfectly clear. Simon walked up to me when I was alone, made sure nobody could hear him and said, 'Stay away from Brad.'

'Huh?' I played dumb.

'I know you're gay. Stay away from Brad or I'll break your nose. Get it?'

I just nodded. He walked away.

How did he know I was gay? *I didn't even know I was gay. Was I gay?* Why was everyone calling me gay?

He wasn't the first person to call me gay. That trophy was awarded to my father.

That same year, I remember being in our front yard, having a silent stand-off with my father after he'd verbally abused my mother. He was perched low, squatting, feeding the goldfish he insisted we have in the disgustingly putrid koi pond he'd installed. I don't know what possessed me or what gave me the courage, but I mustered enough gumption to declare, 'You're mean!'

He took a second to study me. His eyes narrowed. Then he did something unexpected. He took off his metal wristwatch and hurled it at me, nicking my cheek and causing it to bleed ever so slightly.

'And you're a little faggot,' he said coldly.

*

Since the abduction, my father had been a 'dry drunk'. The expression was coined by the founder of Alcoholics Anonymous, an organisation my father never visited even though my mother did, to better understand the man she was married to. A 'dry drunk' describes someone who's sober but hasn't yet dealt with the underlying issues that led to their addiction. To me, it meant that although my father was no longer drinking, he was still incredibly angry, bad tempered and hard to be around.

There was always something us kids had to do that didn't seem urgent but that he made out to be an end-of-the-world priority. And it often involved his obsession with animals. It began with dogs. He always said he 'loved' dogs, but he was very cruel to them. He'd buy a bull terrier or a mixed breed of Staffordshire designed for pig hunting from a backyard breeder but the animal would spend most of its life in a kennel. That was, of course, unless it was being used to hunt pigs. In the meantime, my brother and I had to take care of it. Often my father would get a female and then breed her and keep some of her puppies. This meant building a massive concrete kennel in our backyard that looked more like something you'd house a lion in at a zoo. He'd go away to work for six weeks at sea and we'd be left in charge of feeding the dogs and cleaning the kennel daily.

We had so many illegal animals we were constantly in fear of being reported to animal welfare. Besides having more dogs than a residential house was allowed, at one time we also had a purpose-built exotic bird aviary that housed at least a hundred rare parrots. Not only that, over the course of our childhood our backyard was home to a carpet snake, two kangaroos, a black wild boar, a magpie, an owl, a cockatoo, a bald cockatoo, a kitten (that lived for about two weeks before our highly trained pig-hunting dogs ripped it to pieces before our very eyes) and the occasional seasonal puppy mill.

My brother and I were expected to take care of all of these animals and with particular attention while our father was away.

Having three dogs at a time and a father who made them sleep outside in a concrete dog run meant there was a lot of dog shit to clean up. Every morning before school we would take turns scooping up large quantities of very unhealthy looking stools and dumping them in containers in the backyard. They absolutely stank to high heaven. These containers were emptied so infrequently by our father that they became a breeding ground for maggots. Every morning the dog run had to be hosed down with disinfectant that washed right into the next-door neighbour's backyard. They would constantly complain about the smell and the run-off, which contained excrement, piss and Pine O Cleen. My father called them 'arseholes' for complaining.

Then there were the purpose-built bird cages whose bottoms were full of bird poop and seed husks. They would get wet and smell rotten and require shovelling out and rinsing and washing down regularly. The conditions the birds lived in were, in retrospect, terrible. Even though they belonged to my father, the responsibility to take care of them fell to us children.

In the summer of 1985 my mother and father went away for a week on the *Ampol Sarel*, the ship my father had been an engineer on. They left my sister in charge. I was thirteen, my brother fifteen and my sister eighteen. Tracey was technically old enough to look after us, but we were really too young to be left with so much responsibility. I stayed at our friend Lenore's house for much of the time but was still expected to do my chores before or after school. This meant looking after my father's birds and keeping the cages clean, which, when my father left, were full to the brim with filth. Peter was put in charge of feeding the dogs and cleaning up their shit while my sister, who was naturally maternal, was responsible for meals and our general wellbeing.

INTERIOR: Bedroom, any random night between 1997 and 2024

The screams. That's what I notice first. Neither human nor animal. A hybrid of despair and suffering. It's soft and coming from a place far away from me. I'm in a dusty wooden barn filled with bales of hay with high-vaulted ceilings and ropes hanging everywhere. Upon closer inspection I remember it's a sheep shearing shed, like the kind my father would have us set up camp in when he forced us to go pig hunting. It's a perpetual twilight inside. Dust particles flicker in the shafts of light originating from outside.

I know I need to get closer to the screams but every step I take, the walls of the shed become narrower and the bales of hay reach out like the innards of a scarecrow, gutted and left to die but strangely animated and malicious. It wants to crawl inside my mouth and slide up my nostrils, suffocating me. The dry, husky blades of grass scratch and push forward from all directions, until I'm caught in a spider's web of straw. I reach down to take out my pocket knife and am able to cut my way through some of it and make a hole big enough to fall through and land in a sloppy wet grain silo. Beneath me there's a squelching sound and a foul stench. Rancid. Rotten. Death and sewage. The black sludge comes up to my waist. I look up and all I see is corrugated iron and a tiny sliver of light, where a ladder on the inside of the silo leads to the top.

If I can just make it to the ladder.

That's when the screams begin again. They increase in volume, swirling upward and around the circular prison.

I look down and as my eyes adjust to the light I see the skulls and translucent faces of newborn birds, their eyes glued shut, their beaks crusty, their tongues white and dry. They're bubbling up from below like rice or pasta in a boiling pot on the stove. Then there are dismembered limbs. Wings. Rib cages. Wet feathers. With my eyes becoming more accustomed to the light I see I'm immersed in a dark, bloody sludge, so dark it's almost black. Within the sludge are thousands of dead or dying birds, each one drowning in its own shit. That's when the overwhelming feeling consumes me. This is all my fault. I did this.

I wake up in a sweat. It's just my nightmare again.

The 1985 summer holidays were hot. Temperatures peaked at 39° Celsius in January. On one of those January days, I forgot to do my chores.

As a teenager it didn't seem that big a deal. But when my parents came home, it suddenly became a *huge* deal. My father inspected the backyard to check on our 'work'. When he checked the bird cages, I realised that I had forgotten to fill their water bowls the day before.

My father called me over. 'What's this?' he said, pointing to the cage floor.

I looked down and to my horror, some of the birds were dead. Worse still, some were just babies. There was no water in some of the water bowls.

My father's reaction was volcanic.

He sat me down and told me I was a *murderer.*

At the time, I fully accepted the accusation. I felt sick to my stomach, like the worst person in the world. Worse than a child molester or a man who beats his wife. I had *killed* these innocent animals. I didn't know that the cages were overcrowded, that some of the birds might have been sick already, or that the extreme heat alone might have led to their deaths. I knew nothing of the guilt my father just felt for having left children in charge of animals and his need to project that guilt and blame onto me.

All I knew was how it felt to be called a *murderer.* It was an accusation that would imbed itself in my subconscious and torture me for much of my adulthood.

INTERIOR: Bedroom, any random night between 1997 and 2024

I'm a grown-up with a fantastic life. I can't explain how I know this, it's just a feeling that permeates my universe. This house is nothing like anywhere I've lived but it's also an amalgamation of every rom-com I've ever watched. A perfect family home. It's what you imagine the inside of a white-picket-fence house might look like. I can't quite make out the faces of the people who are gazing adoringly at me but they're my family and they love me. I feel that. I'm smiling, making something for dinner. Oh! It's a roast chicken. I'm taking it out of the oven. We're all sitting at the perfectly arranged dinner table and I'm about to make a toast when there's a knock on the door. Huh.

I excuse myself and get up and that's when it hits me.

I remember now.

It's the police.

The officer doesn't have to say a word. I remember what I've done.

I'm guilty. So guilty. My entire life is about to be destroyed. They've found the body. The one I killed and hid. It changes in various versions of this nightmare. Sometimes it's a DNA sample. Sometimes it's a bone fragment. Sometimes it's something grisly like a suitcase with a body contorted to fit inside. A suitcase that's been buried for twenty years; so long that I'd foolishly forgotten about it and dared to think I could move on and have a happy life.

But I can't. It's over. I have to walk back inside and tell all the people who love me that I'm a terrible, disgusting murderer. I'm lower than the lowest slithering slug. I'm repulsive.

I had just forgotten about it.

Vibrator

The bullying at school escalates in 1986 and 1987.

In Australia back then, the first four years of high school were compulsory, while the additional Years 11 and 12 were optional, but compulsory if you wanted to study at university. As a result, my ninth and tenth years of high school were full of kids who would eventually leave without completing the final two years.

But not without leaving a massive scar upon me.

It all started with one particular bully named Charlie. Looking back, I understand exactly who he was and why he behaved the way he did. He was a kid who must have hated himself for reasons that were never clear to me. He externalised that hatred into the most cruel behaviours as a way of protecting himself from ever being hurt or victimised. He weaponised his insecurities and it worked. Nobody ever targeted him. He was untouchable, like some sort of mob boss. He had a posse who all were equally afraid of or in awe of him – Marcus, Callum, Shaun and James – all of whom were willing to do his bidding.

Charlie came from a tough family. I remember seeing him being beaten by his dad in the school grounds. Instead of being softened by the abuse, he just regurgitated it upon the world. Look at him the wrong way? You'd get a slap. Answer one of his insults with a retort?

A punch. That's what happened to me. Following some variation of a gay slur, I answered Charlie back and it was on. He spat at me, I became outraged and ran after him. He found my humiliation so entertaining that he called me 'vibrator' – presumably because I got so angry that I physically shook.

So that became my name.

Vibrator.

For a whole two years, my name was a sex toy.

You can imagine how dehumanising and embarrassing it was and how I felt too ashamed to tell anyone who could help. The kids wouldn't say it in front of a teacher, because they knew they'd get in trouble. But they'd say it in the corridors, whisper it under their breath, or yell it at me as they walked by. They slapped me and spat at me and threw spit balls at me when a teacher had their back turned. It was constant physical and mental torture.

It's no understatement to say it made my life a living hell. But something fascinating started to happen as a result: I started the process of what I call 'the split'. Psychologists might call it 'dissociation'. For me, it was a way to disconnect from my surroundings in order to mentally survive what was happening. I'd done this to some extent when I witnessed the violence perpetrated upon my mother, and when I was immobilised with fear when I was younger, but this was different. This was a proper out-of-body experience.

Sitting in maths class, the target of rolled-up pieces of paper covered in saliva and vomited at me from behind, my reaction was to leave my body. Sometimes it became so severe that I'd put my head on the table, cross my arms and make a fortress for my face. The teachers did nothing. They saw what was happening and they allowed it. Some of the boys were so physically intimidating at that age, it may have been easier for the teachers to ignore it. Maybe they felt it'd toughen me up. I'll never know. Had they intervened, my life might have taken a different trajectory.

The moments between classes were worse. That's when the kids could physically hurt me. I became so used to having my shoes stepped on from behind, my ear flipped and my butt kicked. I took it every single time as though it wasn't happening to me. It was like I was a dead body, a corpse, my soul floating above, watching the abuse but not feeling it.

On the rare occasion that I defended myself, it would erupt in a physical fight, my face getting red, chants of 'Vibrator, vibrator, vibrator!' and so on. One time after biology class I fought Charlie back and his punch was so hard, so precise, my nose bled immediately. Still, no intervention from the school. Just threats of punishment for 'fighting'.

Another incident involved two huge twins – I swear they were mostly made of bone and testosterone. I was in history class and dared to disagree with one of their girlfriends. She casually told me her boyfriend was going to 'beat me up after school'. She meant it.

Soon, the news had spread that 'Vibrator' was going to get beaten up. I was worried. I had ridden my bike to school and was a sitting target. They knew exactly where to find me when the end of school bell rang. I went to my teacher and explained my dilemma. There was no urgency, no real concern for my safety. I was brushed off and assured that everything would be okay.

I remember sitting in English class in absolute terror, watching the seconds of the massive clock tick down to 3 p.m. The feeling of dread in my stomach was overwhelming. By this time, my best friend was a boy called Dean. Dean and I devised a plan to weave our way in and out of the swarm of kids leaving school, to try to blend in and hide our escape and eventually make our way to the bike racks.

We got to my bike without incident and for a moment I thought everything was truly going to be okay. Soon we were on our way, walking home, pushing our bikes, when suddenly I saw one of the twins.

'Hey.'

The blood drained from my face.

'You insulted my girlfriend,' he said.

I didn't even get a chance to respond. I turned away, intending to walk in the opposite direction and was faced with the other twin. He punched me square in the forehead. A king hit. I saw stars and fell to the ground.

Dean was a well-meaning but ineffectual C-3PO sort of friend. He was tiny and couldn't have physically stopped the altercation even if he'd tried. His way of supporting me was to use humour and distraction to defuse the situation. I don't fault him for that, but without the intervention of teachers or anyone else to stop what was happening I felt helpless most of the time.

In the aftermath of that assault, and it was assault, the school said I could press charges and have the twins face juvenile court. It was also implied that the best long-term solution was to let the school deal with it internally. You can guess how that went. The school *didn't* deal with it. The teasing and bullying from the twins stopped for a while but it didn't stop other kids.

One of the more humiliating experiences involved the ringleader's sidekick, Marcus. The week before his thirteenth birthday he made a big deal out of handing out invitations before first class. He had a pile of envelopes and derived a great deal of joy from reading out each student's name. One by one, the lucky recipient of the exclusive invitation walked up to Marcus and received their envelope, striding back to the group proudly. I knew I wasn't going to get an invitation so it was such a shock when he called my name out and held up a red envelope. I couldn't believe it. My face expressed as much.

'Seriously. Here. This is for you,' he said. He waved the invitation like a golden ticket to the chocolate factory.

I cautiously walked up to accept the invitation from his outstretched hand when he suddenly pulled it away and yelled 'As if!' and burst out laughing, cuing the entire ninth grade to join in. I understand in retrospect I was a fool to fall for such a prank but I was so desperate for the suffering to end, I really did believe that the tide had turned and something was about to change.

No such luck. I was a social pariah and it was suffocating.

There was no place I could go without the stigma following me. There were times on weekends when I'd see my bullies at the mall or hanging out at the local corner store and just their presence was intimidating. Even if I was with my mother and family it didn't stop them. At first I lied and made excuses for their behaviour.

'What did they just call you?' my mother would ask after someone had yelled out 'fag'.

'Oh, they're just joking,' I'd lie, for reasons I still don't understand. I guess I was just so embarrassed.

Around this time, my parents sold our house on Lake Road and bought a block of land an hour's drive south in a rural community called Jimboomba. The plot was five acres (about two hectares) with nothing on it besides a man-made dam to water livestock. The plan was that my brother, now an apprentice carpenter, would help my father build a brand-new home on the block. In the two years it would take to do this, we would all live in a tin garage on site. As I was the youngest child with the most at stake school-wise, I was lucky enough to have the privacy of my own trailer parked next to the garage.

Prior to moving to Jimboomba, my parents made a deal with the people who bought our house, giving them time to build the garage which was, on its own, a massive undertaking. I spent every weekend and most afternoons on site, helping my father dig trenches and pour concrete, while my eighteen-year-old brother and a handful of friends erected stud walls and installed illegal plumbing and electricity. They even put in a rainwater tank. We spent our time living between Lake Road and the job-site in Jimboomba until the garage was complete.

This was around the time Michael Jackson re-emerged from his three-year hiatus after the massive success of the *Thriller* album with his 'Bad' music video. While he'd been away his appearance had changed drastically. He seemed more feminine: he wore eyeliner, makeup with foundation and even lipstick and mascara. I noticed the difference in his image immediately and I was obsessed. The rest of my peers, not so much. It was considered 'gay' to like Michael Jackson in 1987. I remember when the album was first released, in the months we were still living at Lake Road but transitioning to Jimboomba, I rushed home from school, ran to Woody's and bought my copy on vinyl that I had pre-ordered. I listened to it, start to finish, for hours upon hours. I studied the liner notes, I scrutinised the photographs inside the sleeve and of course the heavily airbrushed and immaculate 'new' image of the late 1980s Michael Jackson. To me, he was perfect.

I saw myself in this androgynous, alien-like, luminous being who seemed simultaneously tortured and afraid of the world and yet full of rage and power. I watched the person being teased in the music video before transforming into a superhero and thought, 'That's me on the TV screen.'

While we were packing up things at Lake Road and getting ready for the move to Jimboomba, it was announced that Michael would tour Australia. I *had* to go. We had no money to spare but somehow between my mother and my sister we scraped together enough to buy two of the cheapest tickets on offer. Two seats way up in the back of what was then called ANZ Stadium in Brisbane.

In the music video for the single 'Bad', Michael played a version of someone just like me; a kid, bullied by his peers. Teased for being academic. And what did he do about it? He retaliated in the most creative way. Not with violence. He transformed, literally, through music. One push and shove too far and *BAM*! Musical stabs and suddenly he drops from a subway ceiling and he's someone completely different. Confident. Slick. Powerful. In control. A superstar.

So that's where I'd go in my mind when they bullied me. I'd assume I was a popstar. I was magical and capable of silencing my critics with my talent.

My Savage Garden stage persona was born in those moments. It wasn't all sadness and despair. The power of my imagination fortified my self-confidence. I guess I had the ability to see the long game, as though high school were a marathon. Sometimes when my head was in my hands on the desk, eyes closed, I wasn't crying; I was manifesting. I would think of the day when I'd be on stage, with thousands of people screaming my name, and I'd remember the moment I was currently suffering through as motivation. It all sounds very meta, I know, but that's how my mind worked. It could be called delusional, but it went so far as taking on a life of its own outside of school. I'd travel in the backseat of the car with my mother and sometimes I'd duck down, like I'd seen famous people do to avoid the paparazzi. I would fantasise about what it would feel like to be so recognisable that I couldn't go out in public. Sadly, most of the time, I ducked down because I'd seen one of my bullies in the car next to us and I didn't want them to see me, but instead of defaulting to victim mode, my imagination would turn the scenario into something cinematic, magical and positive. I wasn't hiding from Charlie. I was preventing pandemonium!

*

The move to Jimboomba was a brutal shock to say the least. You can imagine the lack of privacy. It was mid-1987 when my parents bought the block and by 1988 our entire family was living there. My then twenty-one-year-old sister was living in a tin shed with my parents and my eighteen-year-old brother. There were no walls. My parents' king-size bed was in one section, my brother had a single bed, and my sister slept on a couch. There was one cubicle wall with no door that housed the bathroom with a toilet and a shower – if you could call it that. It had a nozzle for rinsing off, but we had to fill a bucket with hot water and wash ourselves with a sponge first. That's how precious water was. In times of drought, of which there were many, we had to pay for water to be delivered.

Outside, my crusty, rusty 1970s trailer sat parked against the tin shed. If I needed to use the toilet in the middle of the night I'd put on shoes and open the garage's creaky tin door and wake everyone up. The alternative was to walk a hundred metres or so and pee in the grass. There was no paved or cement driveway, so in the rainy season it was just a muddy mess. Or a fun slide.

We were so far away from my school the bus ride took an hour. My art teacher, Mrs Sales, lived around the corner and for much of my senior school years she gave me a lift to Mabel Park. This was both a blessing and a curse. Imagine the pressure of having to talk to an adult, much less a teacher, for forty-five minutes twice a day. The part of me that felt like I had to keep up the appearance of being a 'good little boy' was working overtime. I did well at school, but the two subjects I adored most were music and art. Consequently, Mrs Sales expected a lot from me. That became a challenge for her when I was cast in school musicals and they would take up all my time and attention. She gave me a 'talking to' one day, telling me how worried she was that 'this musical business' was distracting me.

One day on the way to school, Mrs Sales noticed a picture of Michael I'd glued to the front of one of my notebooks. 'He's a very pretty man, isn't he?' she commented.

I didn't know how to respond. Yes, he was beautiful. I thought he was a work of art. But I found nothing sexual about him. I was neither attracted to him nor threatened by him. I simply identified with his fluidity, his gentle nature, and the pain behind his eyes. Still, I was afraid to agree with her statement in case it outed me as gay. At that point in time I was still floating on air from having recently attended his concert.

The date of Michael's concert was supposed to be November 27th, 1987. One night at a massive stadium. We had bought general admission tickets, which meant we would be standing in a grassy field along with tens of thousands of other people in a stadium that held over 45,000. Ever since Tracey bought our tickets, I had been plotting my way to get to the front of the stage. I knew the gates opened at 2 p.m. but the show didn't start until 8 p.m. and Michael probably wasn't going to be on stage until 9 p.m. My biggest concern? How I was going to hold my bladder. Seriously, that was what filled my anxious fifteen-year-old mind. I considered making a device to strap to my body, a sort of hidden catheter (believe me, I know this is gross), because I wasn't going to let anybody stop me from losing my place in the queue and I definitely wasn't going to pee my pants in front of the King of Pop! I worried about it way more than I should have and then a weird sort of miracle happened.

A rumour spread in the tabloid press that Michael would be performing inside 'a bubble'. I know that sounds crazy, but at the time, this was reported in the news. This bubble was apparently to protect him from 'germs'. Well, the result was, the already tarnished media image Michael had in Australia quickly deteriorated. He was already suffering from his image change, which seemed too feminine for Aussie audiences and did not go over well in our very machismo-driven culture. News of the fictitious 'hermetically sealed dome' meant that ticket sales virtually stopped in some parts of the country, not least in the deeply conservative state of Queensland. Instead of one night in a 45,000-capacity stadium, Michael's show was moved to two nights at the Brisbane Entertainment Centre – a venue that holds a maximum of 13,500. And there were still tickets available. The radio and TV networks were telling ticket holders to turn up to the venue and exchange their original tickets for new seats.

My sister and I assumed, since we had general admission tickets, we would be sitting at the very back of the Entertainment Centre. This was not the case. We showed up early and were surprised when we received incredible seats ten rows from the stage! We couldn't believe it. As soon as the lights went down, we bolted towards the stage and miraculously found ourselves in the front row.

That evening changed my life. That expression is used a lot and it rarely means what it is intended to. However, attending that concert changed my trajectory and made me into the man I am today. I remember every single detail. The yellow, blue and purple of the still half-empty arena seats when we arrived. The smell of stage fog, something I'm now beyond familiar with but at that point in my life was a sensory experience I associated entirely with the magic I was about to witness. I remember the feeling of anticipation in the auditorium and the first blast of the PA system being so loud I felt as though my chest would implode. The frequency of the bass reverberating in my bones. I recall being so excited as Michael ascended a backlit staircase that opened up from the depths of the stage and feeling like I was going to die with happiness. Each footstep was accompanied by a pre-recorded sonic *BOOM*. The adrenaline pumping through my veins built up in my throat until it just became an uncontrollable scream. *BOOM*. The top of his head was revealed. *BOOM*. One more step and Michael and his four dancers revealed more of themselves. *BOOM*. Now they had almost entirely emerged from the underbelly of the stage, cut by a cool white silhouette amid fog accompanied by absolute sonic hysteria from the audience. *BOOM!* Finally Michael had arrived and he . . . froze.

No music.

No movement.

He stood there, perfect like in my dreams, only even more beautiful. Skin like porcelain, hair blue-black as midnight, his eyes fixed on a point in the distance, seemingly undeterred by the wave of adoration coming at him at a hundred miles per second. All around me was hysteria. The kind we're used to seeing in archival footage of teens reacting to the Beatles or Elvis Presley. It was deafening.

Then he pointed – cuing the drums to start. The song 'Wanna Be Startin' Somethin'' began and all hell broke loose. The audience lost their minds. Anyone with a shred of inhibition left was compelled to move, to dance, to sing. I screamed out 'I love you, Michael!' and from behind me, I felt a sudden, painful *punch* in my back.

'Faggot,' a girl shouted.

I didn't have time to process what had happened. My idol was on stage. He was like a hurricane and a thunderstorm, moving like an electric eel; every whip of his leg, every snap of his finger sending the sold-out arena into outer space. His silver bodysuit clung to him like a second skin. The buckles on his skintight ski pants rattled and jangled so loudly I could hear them! That's how close I was. The screams. Oh my God. People acted as though he was a god. I witnessed uncontrollable cries. People fainting. There were waves of hands moving like a sea; a tide of bodies rising up any time he approached their section. It was like watching God create the universe. During the first few songs I was so close to the stage I could smell Michael's perfume and probably even the hair products he was using. That visceral experience of sight, sound and smell are forever etched in my memory.

I looked around the arena as he said, 'Look around. Look at yourselves. You're beautiful!' and I saw the ecstasy and joy of thousands of people mesmerised under the spell of one man. I thought, with complete clarity, 'I want to do this for a living.'

Still, the girls behind me – now there were two of them – kept on with their physical and verbal abuse. They began kicking the back of my legs every time I turned around to watch Michael on stage.

'You're gay!' one of them said.

There it was, even in the middle of one of the most incredible experiences of my life, that sickening feeling of dread. It was like a mathematical formula. Every time something good happens, something terrible follows. The wasps in my tummy. The awareness of conflict and the notion that ignoring it would not make it go away.

My sister picked up that something was wrong. She turned around and gave the girls a death stare. Nobody messed with her brother. But whenever she turned back to the stage, these girls would continue to kick my legs and insult me with homophobic slurs. It's such a strange and bittersweet memory. Being utterly transfixed by Michael Jackson and simultaneously having my behaviour policed by two strangers who seemed to hate me for no reason.

At the end of the concert, my sister and I made sure to wait around to ensure the girls left before we did. We didn't want a confrontation. We then went to the box office to see if there were any tickets left for the following night's concert. There were! So we bought two more tickets and those tickets were three rows from the front!

I spent the next day in heaven, knowing soon I'd be reunited with Michael; the smells, the sensations, the spectacle. I had a strange feeling of missing someone I'd never met but also missing the stage!

I couldn't wait to get back to the arena. The second show was even more spectacular because this time I was a student studying every move and every gag, observing the lighting and the sleight of hand. Working out how Michael manipulated the audience emotionally between songs, waiting just the right amount of time to get just enough applause before starting a new number. Waiting for the applause to die down and start back up again, like a tide, anticipating the incoming wave, making the audience beg for more. This was a masterclass in entertainment.

I made a pact with the universe that night. I decided to become famous. If I could go somewhere else in my mind when my father was beating me, or brutalising my mother, if I could leave my body when the bullies were attacking it, I had the ability to imagine anything. This would be my biggest trick ever. I would use the Force, magic, whatever you want to call it, to secretly, quietly, become untouchable.

I understood what was behind Michael's eyes. There was both a deep sadness but also a childlike desire to play, to spread joy, to control the flow of energy. I had no control in my life but I saw a pathway to having all the control I needed. Not in a malevolent way. Here in front of me was someone using their magnetic force for good.

There was something about me, since I was a little boy, that made me a target. Something that made me stand out and be noticed. What if I used that ability and instead of being embarrassed by it, decided that what people were noticing was that I was some kind of royalty? From now on, that would be my default definition of myself. In the same way that Luke Skywalker was a Jedi Knight but never realised it until the truth was told to him, in the same way all the characters in fairy tales are oblivious they had the power all along, I too would cast myself in that light.

Perhaps that had been my journey to this point. The veil had been lifted and I saw the world differently. I didn't want to be my father. I didn't want his love or his approval. I didn't want to fit in with the boys at school. Why would I? There was something magnificent about me. I decided that. And since I got to decide my worth, I didn't need to convince anyone. I would resist the urge to explain myself and my uniqueness to the world and instead patiently wait for them to find out.

Was there really something magical about me? I don't know. To this day, I don't know.

I just decided that there was, and so that's the way the rest of my life unfolded.

Break Me Shake Me

At high school things were going terribly. It didn't matter that in my secret life I was a 'royal magical popstar' – outwardly I was still a social outcast. It was still the wild west when it came to my battle with the bullies at school but I was slowly learning that 'victim' was not going to serve me forever.

One of the first times I ever fought back, properly, was with a runt of the litter. It was in reaction to something a kid called Elijah did. Every mob boss has one of these little rats. A powerless suckerfish that hangs around the shark and does menial tasks to stay alive. Elijah was Charlie's suckerfish.

The tuckshop (an Australian word for school canteen) was where local parents volunteered to sell food for lunch. It was a luxury in my home to have enough money for the tuckshop, but by the time I was fifteen I was earning a bit working various odd jobs and could afford to occasionally buy a treat like a can of soda or some candy. One day I was standing in line holding a jelly rat I'd just bought (very appropriate for what was about to happen next) when Elijah broke half of it off and ate it, right in front of me.

You can imagine, like Pavlov's dog, what rage this elicited. 'You owe me fifty cents,' I said through gritted teeth.

'What are you gonna do about it, Vibrator?' Elijah laughed.

A group of kids quickly formed around us. They wanted a fight. Elijah wanted a fight. He feigned a punch and I flinched in anticipation. Roars of laughter. He loved it. It humiliated me but also scared me. He saw the fear in my eyes so he did it again. Only this time, like a wound-up spring, I punched back and boy, did I have some spring in me.

INTERIOR: Fantasy
Three loud musical stabs. I'm wearing a leather jacket with buckles and ski pants with pointed black boots, just like Michael in the 'Bad' music video. I make deliberate shapes with my body, threatening Elijah within a few inches of his face. A pipe bursts and steam shoots out of it. Elijah flinches. Meanwhile all the kids behind me have transformed into my crew. We laugh at how scared the bully is now. The lights are blinding on stage. The drums begin and I start my performance.

CUT TO: Reality
In a split second Elijah was on the ground and I was punching the shit out of him.

The next thing I knew, we were being separated by a teacher and marched to the principal's office, where we were given a lecture about fighting. It didn't matter what Elijah had done. It didn't matter that he'd stolen half my jelly rat. We both received a caning across our hands because we'd 'fought'. It didn't hurt. I'd had worse from my father. I'm pretty sure Elijah cried. Little rat.

Part of me felt proud of my reaction. I felt 'cool' now. But a deeper part of me knew I had got there by dishonest means. I'd used dark magic to defend myself: violence.

Memory is a weird thing. It blurs and smears like watercolours on a canvas. I don't recall if it was that afternoon or perhaps weeks later, but Elijah tried it on again. Walking home from school I found myself alone. Someone behind started kicking rocks at me. I turned around and sure enough, it was my little rat, seeking a rematch. Fool.

I instantly summoned the rock star, the untouchable superhero. I was like Michael Jackson in the 'Beat It' video, undeterred by the gang members with their knives and steel pipes. What I had was different. There was a golden aura around me. I was untouchable.

I didn't give Elijah a second chance. He tried to do the fake punch thing again and I'm not proud to say I exploded. The force I managed to conjure up scared me. I was all fists and anger and torrents of rage. I had him pinned on the ground and was pummelling him when he spat in my face. In those next moments Elijah was every kid who had ever picked on me. Every homophobic slur uttered towards me. Every slap I'd received, every moment of shame I'd felt. Maybe he was even my father in that moment. I was a fury of violence directed at him, as he lay underneath me and I punched his face with my fists. It was as though that scary needle-toothed clown from my nightmare years before, the one who promised, no, threatened, 'I'll be back!' had returned, but not as I expected. Not as something to be afraid of. No, he'd returned *inside* of me. As me.

I punched and punched and punched and when I thought he'd had enough, I summoned up the most grotesque amount of phlegm I could and spat it at his face, returning the insult and degradation I'd experienced when he did the same to me. I watched him squirm and beg for mercy. He didn't get up until I let him. When I did, he scampered away like a cockroach, terrified.

He never bothered me again.

I left the scene, horrified at what I was capable of.

I felt like my father.

I had become a monster to defeat a monster.

I was reminded of the trials of Luke Skywalker. The final moment facing his father, slamming his lightsaber down upon his enemy, time and time again in fury until the villain he once feared was now just a frail old man, having fallen back, defenceless, one hand sliced off and struggling for breath. Luke could have ended him with one more blow but caught himself, realising he had become the very thing he vowed never to be.

Is that who I now was?

The villain?

INTERIOR: Car, 1998. A man, mid-twenties, blue-black hair, drives on a freeway

I'm driving to the Brisbane Entertainment Centre in my brand-new car, a midnight-blue Mazda Astina. God I love this car. I've never owned a new car in my *life*. This is the first new thing Colby, my wife, and I have bought besides a house since the explosion of Savage Garden. It's not a luxury car by any means, but to us it feels like a Rolls-Royce. Just two seats and black-tinted windows. The new car smell almost overwhelms my cologne. I love new car smell!

Tonight I'm playing the first of two sold-out shows at the very venue I saw Michael Jackson perform at a little over a decade ago. It's a completely surreal experience. I'm going to be walking in his very footsteps. This is where my life changed forever.

I'm listening to 'Wanna Be Startin' Somethin'' to get me in the mood. I remember what it feels like to be a fan, the excitement of seeing my idol emerge from the depths of the stage. I'm thinking about how I'll create that same feeling at the Entertainment Centre tonight, when all of a sudden I see flashing lights in my rear-view mirror.

Police, I assume.

I must be speeding. I check the speedometer. Nope, I'm under the limit. Huh.

The lights flash again from behind. The person in the car puts their head out the window and signals for me to 'pull over'. I assume there's something wrong with my car so I slow down, indicate and pull over, just like the car behind me does. I'm sitting there, doors locked with the engine idling. The driver in the car behind me has switched its engine off. They get out and walk towards me but they've left their headlights on so all I see is a silhouette. I keep my windows up, to be safe.

There's a knock on my window. I look up and see a man in his late twenties, maybe early thirties. He looks like he's had a rough life. But he's smiling from ear to ear. Giddy. Happy.

'Darren!' he says, with joy in his voice. 'It's me!'

I roll the window down.

'Sorry, I don't . . .' I begin.

'It's me! Elijah! From Mabel Park State High! I'm going to your concert tonight! I recognised you a few miles back and have been trying to get your attention. Can I get your autograph?'

I am frozen in disbelief.

Elijah hands me my album, on compact disc. And a pen.

I can't find any words. Has he forgotten our last confrontation? Is he oblivious to our past? I sign the CD and hand it back. Elijah is like one of the teenage girls I've seen at shopping malls all around the world. He has that fanatical look in his eyes, like he's starstruck.

'I'll see you tonight! I'm in the front row!' he says as he walks back to his car, shaking his head in a kind of 'golly gee I can't believe it' way.

Sure enough, later on that night I look down into the crowd at the sold-out arena and spot him among the 8500 other bodies. Front row centre, my high-school bully is screaming out my name, arms outstretched, in adoration.

The Coolest Job in the World

In 1987 the coolest thing in the world happened to the shyest kid in the universe thanks to what's usually a bland, obligatory high-school moment: work experience. While other kids spent time in a mechanic's garage, the art department of a newspaper, or a hospital, I somehow found the balls to walk into the hallowed halls of Woody's Music Store and ask those obnoxious arseholes if I could serve my work experience time there.

Chuck, the American owner, didn't really give a shit. He was just thrilled to have the free help. Sharon and Andrea, the famously frosty assistants, were wildly unfriendly at first. Of course they were. That was their schtick and what made Woody's so attractive. But I loved them. It was like a line to the hottest nightclub you desperately wanted to get into. It was almost a badge of honour to be ignored by them. I remember being so intimidated as a customer, trying to ask a question or, God forbid, give them money. Imagine doing work experience as a shy fifteen year old!

But the second I got behind that counter I felt elevated. The 'record bar', and that's what it was called, was like a stage and had an effect like wearing a costume. There was something about going behind that hot-pink enamel partition that made me one of *them*.

112

Before my first day, I thought a lot about how I would present myself; what I would wear and how I would do my hair. When I turned up, although still shy, I was instantly a different person to the boy who was bullied at Mabel Park State High. Behind the record bar, I was cool. Standing there in my sky-blue Penguin polo shirt, my acid wash jeans and my knock-off Ralph Lauren deck shoes sans socks, I was the perfect 1980s teenager from a John Hughes film. Within the confines of the temple of cool and free of the artificial rules that held me down at high school, I was judged purely by customers and other teenagers.

I even became something of a heartthrob.

At first I didn't see it. I was too busy blushing and freezing, trying to take in all the information being thrust upon me by Sharon and Andrea. Their new staff orientation had all the brevity and obligatory nature of a safety warning recited by a bored teenager working at a theme park. It went something like this: 'Here's how you operate a cash register. You'll get one lesson. It'll be five minutes in duration and if you ask follow-up questions we will humiliate you.' At least, that was the tone. Then there was the complex system of filing stock. To prevent theft, only empty cassette cases and album covers were displayed on the shop floor. When a customer brought the empty case or cover to the counter, it was my job to find the physical product from a library so complicated it made a university Dewey Decimal System seem like first-grade maths.

Each record company had a code and each cassette or album had a serial number, often seven or eight digits long. The records and cassettes were arranged alphabetically by record company and then numerically by product code. That's if the store clerks had put the products in the correct place when the stock originally arrived. A simple mistake would result in an excruciating wait for a customer and a harrowing experience for me. If I wasn't dealing with staff mistakes, I was learning the harsh lessons of my own rookie errors, dealing with furious customers who would come back an hour later, outraged that their Cyndi Lauper album cover had a Def Leppard record inside it. It was trial by fire.

At the end of the week, Chuck kept my number and told me he'd call if he had any more work. I honestly thought I'd never hear from him again. But then something magical happened. Chuck sold the store to a man who would become a mentor and father figure to me for most of my adult life. Gary Beitzel was the least rock and roll person you'd expect to take over Woody's. I met him at the end of 1987, just as the bullying at high school was coming to an end and the summer holidays were about to start. I got a phone call to come into the store; Gary was looking for a casual staff member to work Saturdays and Thursday nights. Back in the 1980s, this was known as 'late-night shopping'.

Before this innovation, shopping centres operated on a strict Monday to Friday 10 a.m. to 5 p.m. and 9 a.m. to 12 p.m. on Saturdays basis. Midway through the 1970s new trading hours were introduced and Thursday nights at the mall became a sort of teen pilgrimage. Before I got the job at Woody's, my brother would drag me to Kmart on a Thursday night to 'cruise for chicks'. He'd get dressed in his tightest denim, bought at the hottest store, Just Jeans, and carefully gel his naturally curly blond mullet. His fashion was on point – depending on the season, he'd team his jeans with either a tropical-themed tank top or a pastel cable-knit sweater. Below, usually Ugg boots or flip flops. He was exceptionally good looking and the girls loved him. Compared to my brother I felt like a blimp. I was always naturally a few kilos heavy and not particularly athletic. Peter, on the other hand, was a football player, effortlessly thin and lean. A blue-eyed Adonis.

Looking back at photos from that time, it saddens me to realise I was actually adorable! I got a lot of attention from girls but I didn't understand what it meant. I was so used to being bullied I thought they were mocking me. One night Peter and I were wandering around the mall in circles, trying to get any girl's phone number. A few would come up and say hello. I just assumed they were interested in my brother. But then a girl came up to me and nervously said, 'Hi.' She waved her hands excitedly.

'*Do I know you?*' I responded sarcastically and kept walking.

Peter was gobsmacked. 'Why did you do that?'

'She was teasing me!'

'She was *into* you, dude!' he replied, incredulous.

I had no idea.

My time doing the rounds on Thursday nights with my brother abruptly ended when he got a girlfriend and I started working at Woody's. My social status skyrocketed. I was about to skip years of social climbing and head straight to the most coveted position of popularity a teen could hope for. I was about to become 'the guy who worked at the record store'.

When I came in for the interview with Gary I was struck by two things: his loud fashion sense and his gentle, calm nature. Gary was very hip for a dad. He had blond highlights in his hair and a perm. He wore wild, patterned shirts, wide-legged, pleated pants and cool shoes. He was fashionable and not gay. This struck me immediately. There was something feminine about his style, but he was 100 per cent comfortable in his masculinity. He appreciated beautiful women and adored his wife, Carli, who worked part-time at the store. They had two young children, Dion and Monica. I was taken by the sense of stability and normality that Gary fostered within the family. There was so much love there. Gary had a sense of duality like the comedian Robin Williams. He could pretend to be an adult but first and foremost he was a child inside. An enthusiastic, joyful, happy child in a man's body. He loved music as much as I did and we really clicked. More than that, the part of me that desperately needed a father was soothed by his natural ability to care about my wellbeing. We adored each other.

That summer, I worked almost full-time at the store during the school holidays and as a result, my self-esteem soared. It coincided with the end of my junior high school years and the start of what I think of as the beginning of a magical time in my life. I was turning sixteen, I had just seen Michael Jackson in concert and when I went back to school, most of the kids who bullied me had dropped out. Their futures took some unfortunate turns. Some didn't achieve grades that would allow them to continue onto higher education, while others got themselves into difficult situations. One kid was now a father, and another would serve time in prison for drug dealing. My peer group was suddenly free of the core group of kids who had made the first few years of high school a misery. One kid who used to be a part of the pack that bullied me quickly turned into a neutral threat without the influence of the grunts pressuring him. He was actually smart, good at art and funny. Things I would never have known about him years before.

It was in art class and in drama class that I got to really bond with two kids who shared my vision for performance, music and fashion. The first was Nathalia Rayfield. I first met her in 1984, in primary school, and she was just about the most glorious thing I'd ever seen. A Madonna look-alike, Nathalia had transferred from a different school and was an instant target for bullies. To me, she looked like a reincarnation of Marilyn Monroe, with her unapologetic bleached blonde hair and natural beauty mark. She wore Michael Jackson T-shirts and danced to 'Billie Jean' and 'Holiday' at lunch with her ghetto blaster. She was cool personified. But I was terrified to talk to her at first.

Then there was her boyfriend, this pretentious but very pretty boy named Patrick. Patrick exemplified every single fashionable thing about the 1980s. Round, tortoiseshell glasses? Check. Bouffant, curly hair shaped into a Flock of Seagulls quiff? Check. Long, nay, *extremely long* white socks, bunched around his ankles and those black canvas slip-ons we called 'kung fu' shoes? Check! Patrick wore a real leather belt and a tie and sometimes even leather brogues. He was androgynous and not particularly talented at any one thing but so stylish and with a charisma that made him stand out. The three of us had a camaraderie and competitive energy that bound us together – especially during school musicals.

I have to thank my music teacher, Susan Lansdown, for first spotting my ability to sing. In Year 8, when I was a completely terri-fied newbie, she noticed my fledgling voice and recruited me for the school choir. This might sound like something very normal but back then, I was one of only two boys in the choir. It was considered *very* gay to sing in the choir so of course at first I refused. But then I heard them. They weren't singing religious songs or classical music but pop music. I instinctively knew what to do. I joined.

For the next three years, I stood next to a piano with fourteen girls and one other boy, Dean, and belted out melodies and harmo-nies. I was enthralled by the smell of the spruce wood of the piano soundboard, and the distinctive and ecstatic feeling in my chest as the frequencies of the keys reverberated.

In Year 11, the choir was invited to audition for Mabel Park's first musical, *Man Of Steele*, an homage to *Superman*. It was written in the 1970s and had vague references to the main characters from the famous comic without ever infringing on copyright. So there was a 'Superman' type, a 'Lois Lane' type and a 'Jimmy Olsen' type. I was encouraged to audition for a lead role, so I did, even though I was petrified.

I'd only sung in public for the first time a year before. I'd written a song on guitar about Marilyn Monroe, and somehow ended up being invited onto a local radio station to perform it. I didn't have a guitar pick, so I used the plastic tie from a loaf of bread! I remember being very proud of myself.

Then, the year of the first school musical, there was a 'musical soirée' night, and I sang a version of the Tracy Chapman song, 'Fast Car'. The choice of song was very deliberate. I was trying to confess what my childhood had been like, without being too literal. The lyrics felt somewhat autobiographical, and I think a part of me thought that if I sang the song with emotion and with conviction, someone might come up to me and say, 'Hey, did that really happen to you?'

That didn't occur. What did occur is the musical department and most of the school realised I had a distinctive singing voice – one I'd been hiding for years. When I sang the song, I closed my eyes and I felt every single word, to the point I had to stop myself from crying. When I opened my eyes I could see my vulnerability and authenticity had connected with the people in the room. When I sang at the audition for the school musical I could feel something similarly magical happen. The room sort of stopped in silence. It was as if the atmosphere changed. I was incredibly nervous but thrilled at the same time and I liked the feeling.

I had been singing like a canary all my life at home and with my friends but had never had that kind of reaction before. In fact, it became a joke in the Hayes family that I often sang louder than the radio, to everyone's annoyance! My sister and I now laugh about how little my family encouraged my singing as a child because it was simply a fact that I could sing. I remember once listening to the radio and the Stevie Nicks song 'Stand Back' came on. I must have been about twelve at the time. I was belting out the chorus when my exasperated sister begged, 'Can we just listen to Stevie sing for once?'

I'm often asked if my mother or siblings knew I was a good singer, and the truth is, I don't ever recall anyone telling me I was anything special. I think that was a gift, in a way, because it allowed me to sing uninhibited up until around age sixteen. When people did notice my voice, it was a surprise.

All of my friends auditioned for *Man of Steele* and there was much anticipation on the day the cast was announced. Not many people got leads but I was cast in the Jimmy Olsen role. I felt vindicated. All those years of singing in my bedroom, singing to the radio, thinking I had something, I was never really sure. Through this one casting, I had been validated. I *could* sing. Nathalia got a role as a cheerleader and Patrick was cast as Perry White, the editor of the newspaper.

What followed was my version of heaven. For the next six weeks, we would rehearse most afternoons after school. I instantly felt at home. Dance rehearsals, vocal rehearsals, dialogue rehearsals. The bonding was unlike anything I'd ever experienced. I felt sad every time a rehearsal came to an end, and I had to go home to my trailer in Jimboomba. The songs weren't all that good, but I loved the ensemble aspect of the show. It reminded me of seeing Michael Jackson and all his musicians and backing singers come together to create one big sound.

Because of the limitations of our teenage cast and the large age range of the roles some of the staging was objectively hilarious. One song, 'We've Got the News', featured a bank of typewriters staffed by teenagers in high heels and smart-casual office outfits that made them look like kids playing dress-up. I and several 'reporters' wore unintentionally oversized men's suits sourced from the local thrift store, rushing about the stage in a melodramatic frenzy while our 'boss', Patrick, with white hairspray applied to his temples and Santa Claus frosted eyebrows, barked orders at the newsroom. Later in the show I sang a sweet and funny solo ballad, 'I'm Just A Loser', which got laughs in all the right places.

Opening night at the Kingston Butterbox Theatre was electric. I really did feel like a star. My mother and sister were there and it felt as though I was revealing a secret to them. Neither was surprised at how joyously and easily I took to the stage.

The next day was even better. Because we were still buzzing from the night before, the atmosphere backstage was electric. I can't help but laugh when I think back now to the amount of white pancake and eyeliner we wore in that tiny theatre. We really did think of ourselves as serious thespians. Why we all needed Shirley Temple pink blush the size of a flying saucer on each cheek is still a mystery to me but I'm sure it stemmed from some advice about how stage lights are 'very bright'.

The musical for the next year, my final year of school, was a much bigger deal. First of all, our music teachers knew who the talented kids were, and cast them in strong roles. We were to perform a version of the 1960s musical *Bye Bye Birdie* – a sort of homage to Elvis Presley but at its core a story about a soft-hearted manager named Albert and his love, Rose. I was cast as Albert, and my icon, my muse, Nathalia, was cast as Rose. We were so excited. The stakes were higher too. This musical was to run for more nights and rehearsals were to culminate in a week-long camp.

This was 1989, a wonderful year for pop music. I was obsessed with Madonna's *Like A Prayer* album and was still in my love hangover period for Michael Jackson's *Bad* album, and dancing was something I took really seriously. Nathalia, Patrick and I performed our own version of 'Smooth Criminal' at another musical soirée that year and incorporated pieces from Prince's *Batman* soundtrack. I wore my pants very high to show off my white socks and black penny loafers, just like Michael and Madonna, and had begun experimenting with hair dye. We were obsessed with fashion on and off stage. On 'free dress days' at school we were permitted to wear our own clothes instead of our bland school uniform and I was often in an oversized paisley shirt, Levi's 501s with the cuffs rolled up, and Doc Martens loafers. I'd sneak tiny bits of makeup on and there'd be obligatory vintage rosary beads under my shirt. Of course I reeked of patchouli oil too because that was the scent of Madonna's *Like A Prayer* album.

The musical was a huge success and I sang the schmaltzy ballad 'Put On A Happy Face' each night to sighs of delight and rapturous applause. Afterwards we had a massive wrap party. I wished the high would never end.

Are You There, God, It's Me, the Masturbator

I don't know when I developed an obsession for telling the truth, or perhaps for confession, but one of my earliest memories of ruminating on guilt involves an incident with the son of a good friend of the family when I was about ten. His name was David and back in the 1980s, he was known as something of a 'bad influence'. It's hard to say how a twelve-year-old kid gets a 'reputation' but stick with me. The incident occurred when my mother gave us money to go to the local shops to buy 'essentials'. In the 1980s this meant milk, bread and cigarettes. Back then, adults would let kids buy anything as long as you had a note from your parents. My mother gave us $10 for her items and an additional 50 cents each as a reward/incentive. Essentially she was doing us a favour. We were two bored kids and a walk to the Argonaut corner shops was always an adventure. She trusted us to get there and back and she obviously trusted us to bring home the change.

At the store, once we'd found my mother's 'essentials', we used our 50 cents to buy a can of soda each and some candy. We received various coins in change from the $10 and that's when the devil in David whispered in my ear, 'Let's buy something else!' He pointed to a novelty machine near the entrance. You'd put a 20-cent coin in the machine, twist the metal handle and out would pop a toy ferret on a string or a fake gold ring that would turn your finger green in a day or two.

'We can't! That's *stealing*!' I said in my most Victorian voice.

'Yeah, but who's gonna know?' David persuaded.

'Well, I will!'

'It's just 20 cents. What's the big deal?'

So I gave him the money and we both got a plastic egg with a useless toy inside it. I regretted it the second the stolen object was in my hand.

The moment we got home, I couldn't live with myself. I handed over the milk, bread and cancer sticks. Then I showed my mother the toys we'd bought and confessed. She was so disappointed in me. I'll never forget the feeling of disappointing someone I loved so much. Telling her the truth didn't soften the blow or rid me of the feeling of guilt. She didn't understand why I had stolen from her, especially as she would have given me the extra money if I'd asked for it.

What followed was a year of obsessively telling my mother every single thought that came into my head. Every intrusive idea, every devil on my shoulder, every ugly image. It got so bad that one day she had to sit me down and tell me it was okay to have thoughts that I kept to myself. Message received. In order to maintain our pristine relationship, I had to get control of this compulsion to vomit up every idea that pulsed between my synapses. It didn't, however, quiet the slowly forming self-critical voice growing stronger as each year passed; a feeling of guilt that seemed to exist independently, regardless of my actions or behaviour. It seemed to be developing in parallel to my puberty. Perhaps it was the dawning realisation of my sexuality, or a deferred or inherited shame I felt from the secrets I had to keep about my father's behaviour, I don't know, but when it came to feelings about sex, I was absolutely riddled with horror.

Soon enough, though, I went from being repulsed, overhearing stories of the boys at school who would talk about girls, to being fascinated about sex.

My introduction to 'the birds and the bees' was like something from a 1950s sitcom. When I was around five years old I was at a rodeo, something our father had dragged us to, and saw calves next to cows. I innocently asked my mother, 'Where do the babies come from?'

My mother was excited that it was time for 'the talk'. 'Ask your father that question tonight.'

That evening after dinner, I was about to clean my plate and leave the table when my mother said, 'Darren, remember that question you asked me today? Did you want to ask your father?'

Things then got very serious.

My father stood up from the table, took a volume of the *Encyclopedia Britannica* from our bookshelf and we went into my bedroom. He'd never ever read a book to me, but this felt like story time. It was all very formal. He sat next to me on the bed and read from the book. I remember looking at the cover which showed a picture of deer. Inside there was a picture of a deer and a doe, essentially humping. He explained that in the animal kingdom, when a deer wants to make a baby, it puts its penis inside the vagina of the doe, a 'seed' comes out and it goes into the doe's 'belly' and grows into a baby. He said the same thing happened with men and women.

I sat there, repulsed, looking at the picture of the two wild animals, the male astride the female in such a violent position and asked, 'Did you do that to Mum?'

'Yes,' he said.

And that was how I learned about sex.

I left the bedroom and returned to the living room and couldn't look at my mother the same way. The poor thing. She must have wondered why I was so judgemental. I imagined my father doing what the deer had been doing and felt both sorry and angry at her for letting that happen. I was also full of questions. A penis was soft and floppy. How was it supposed to stick itself inside something? That wasn't explained. There were, however, moral specifics that were very explicit. Being raised Catholic, my mother often reiterated in our house that although there was nothing wrong with sex, one should never do it with a person unless one intended to marry them.

Got it. Stick the floppy penis inside the vagina to release the seed to make a baby but only if you're getting married. Gross. Why would anyone want to do that?

Years passed and I entered the first year of high school. The boys talked incessantly about masturbation and again, I didn't understand what all the fuss was about. I'd touched my penis before and it didn't feel particularly good. Then one day, around the age of thirteen, I was in the shower and I discovered what all the fuss was about.

Oh. My. God.

Are you kidding me?

What just happened?

And when can I do this again?

Against the backdrop of the bullying, suddenly I had an urgency to get home every afternoon and use the bathroom. The feeling of having an orgasm was so beyond any earthly experience I'd ever imagined. It was the height of pleasure, a rocket ship to ecstatic bliss so intense I didn't understand why humans did anything else. And yet it came with guilt. And not just regular guilt. Oh no. Mine was extremely macabre. Mine involved an irrational fear that I had somehow impregnated someone.

Let me explain.

Since my understanding of the science of sex was that sperm was just a 'seed' that came from me, and I was spending time in the shower and in the toilet, essentially spreading that seed, I had decided that those seeds must have made their way into the bellies of the women in my house! I knew it took nine months for a baby to be born, and so for many, many months I was convinced someone in my family or a cousin or visitor who had been in our bathroom was going to come by one day and announce they were pregnant with my baby!

I would go to sleep at night with the most dreadful feeling in my stomach wondering when I'd have to explain to everyone once this mystery baby was born why it looked so much like me. Everyone would know immediately that I had been masturbating! I dreaded the outcome so much I practically scripted the day this poor woman gave birth to mini-me. The little I knew about periods didn't help. I had no idea what they meant. I just knew that my sister and mother got them and in my mind that meant all women were a fertile breeding ground for my filthy horror babies.

Would I go to jail?

After nine months passed and none of the women in my life were pregnant, I concluded I was either infertile, or that God had forgiven me for my acts of self-pleasure. One of the two. And I could relax about masturbating. The reprieve from anxiety was brief. Once I stopped praying to be forgiven for masturbating, I would pray to God to help me stop fantasising about boys. I simply switched out the guilty feeling of being a sexual sinner to feeling guilty about being attracted to boys.

Everywhere I turned were signs I was going to hell. The constant creeping threat of AIDS and the fear of a virus that we were all told came from gay people was relentless. Rock Hudson's cause of death was now fact. He had died from having sex with men. The 'gay plague' was taking over the news. The only way you could catch AIDS was by having sex or injecting drugs but I didn't believe that. I truly believed it was a 'thought disease'. And so I did everything

I could to hide my desire, coaxing it into the deepest recesses of my mind.

If I could keep the biggest secret of all – that my father had beaten my mother – for all these years surely I could hide something that only existed in my mind from ever materialising as a behaviour. The shame of my childhood and the abuse we endured was a secret full of hard evidence that was hard to hide. We became experts at it. My father put his fist through the wall? We fixed it with paper and glue. Bruise on my mother's cheek? Makeup would cover it. But this? This was a thought crime. It haunted me and I had no outlet for it. I couldn't speak to anyone for fear of being labelled gay. I just sat with that awful feeling, that feeling of rot, of deeply embedded guilt and isolation, certain that I was not only a terrible person, but that my life was going to be cut short if I ever acted upon my feelings.

It played into this larger view and belief I had about myself. I was terrified that if anyone truly knew who I was, they would hate me. I guess you could say it was the beginning of my imposter syndrome. From a young age I had been keeping parts of myself hidden from the outside world. First, the secrets about the violence in my family. I was acutely aware of the embarrassment and shame associated with having a father who beat his wife. I was so repulsed by the social stigma of being one of those families the police regularly visited, or where friends and neighbours had witnessed the most humiliating, degrading and shocking parts of our private lives, that I had become an expert at doing what many victims do: covering up the evidence. In doing this, we all unwittingly carried the shame of my father's actions. At the same time we became his perfect public relations machine. The whole world knew him as Bob. Good time Bob. Happy go lucky and charismatic.

And from the outside we did seem like a great family. But on the inside, we were deeply unhappy. At my lowest ebb, I feared I was incapable of being loved. I believe that's why I decided to become a popstar. I thought that if I could become somebody else, I could start over. I could erase the past version of me, tainted and scarred by everything that had happened, and become someone entirely new, with all the qualities I didn't have. Confidence. Good looks. Success. Money. Safety. I'd receive all the love, attention and validation I was lacking. And I'd fill the God-shaped hole at the centre of my being that lay open and exposed for all the world to see.

Sometimes my heart felt like the hull of the *Titanic*, fatally wounded by a 300-foot gash. I lacked the perspective to see that no amount of fame, like the constant stream of icy-cold ocean water I was willingly allowing to flow into the underbelly of my own fallen ship of a heart, could keep me afloat. Little did I know that the soon to come endless stream of attention and applause would fail to rescue me and would, in fact, cause me to plummet to deeper depths of despair. Nothing could ever compensate for the damage that had been done to me until I accepted and understood I was standing on a sinking ship and asking for more of the thing that had hurt me in the first place. Asking to be loved for something I wasn't was a recipe for disaster.

Much of my misery was coming from my own internalised guilt for suspecting I might be gay like the man who had 'killed' Vivienne and sent my nana into a depressed state. None of this was rational, or as it turned out, true. But I didn't know that at the time. My young, shame-filled heart took it all in as fact; being gay was not only forbidden, but a terrible thing.

My thoughts about my own sexuality were formed during the peak of the AIDS crisis. Every single piece of messaging I watched on television about being gay was linked to this apparently deadly virus for which the only cure was to not have sex and not be gay. Many Australians who grew up in 1980s will remember the infamous 'Grim Reaper' TV ad which was screened at 7.30 p.m. each night. Like a horror movie, the aim was to instil fear into Australians, scaring them about the risk of AIDS in order to slow the spread of the virus. You'd be watching the movie of the week or a family sit-com and all of a sudden be confronted with a group of people lined up on a bowling lane being mowed down by death itself. The voice-over began, 'At first only gays and IV drug users were being killed by AIDS', before cutting to a close-up of a little girl, crying. 'But now we know every one of us could be devastated by it,' the voice-over continued while corpses were cleared from the floor and replaced with a new set of terrified children and families.

I would watch the commercial in fear, assuming my family all thought it was directed at me. I was scared that I had AIDS, simply because I had sexual thoughts about boys. The ad alone, I believe, stunted my sexuality and split my personality. When you think you can die from being physically attracted to someone of the same gender, you learn very quickly to kill that part of yourself.

We were told the most common symptom of AIDS was swollen throat glands. I massaged my glands, checking them feverishly every day, sometimes every thirty minutes, until, you guessed it, they became inflamed. 'That's it!' I figured. 'I have the virus!' I'd had sexual thoughts about Dirk Benedict, the actor who played Starbuck in the 1970s science fiction TV show *Battlestar Galactica* since it first aired. I remember telling my sister as we watched an episode one Friday night that I thought he was 'cute'. I felt all the oxygen leave the room. My sister's reaction was innocently puzzled. 'But he's a boy,' she said. She didn't mean any harm. But my shame monster was triggered.

Oh. My. God. She knows. She knows and she disapproves. I feel so guilty. I'm going to pray to God tonight.

129

I prayed that night and most nights for years for God not to make me gay. I had this feeling in my stomach I can only describe as grief-stricken dread. There was something inside me so rotten, so disgusting, so putrid that only God could eradicate it.

Please dear Lord, please take it away from me. I don't want to die. I don't want to leave my family. I don't want to get knocked down like a human-sized bowling pin in the Grim Reaper ad and come back as a corpse. I don't want to give my family AIDS. Most of all, I don't want anyone finding out.

I begged God to make me 'normal'.

I don't consider myself religious. I'm not a subscriber to any doctrine. But I do believe in a higher power and if pressed, I'd say that we are, collectively, all that higher power. But the day I had a glimpse of the potential that a higher power was listening to me was on one of those nights of prayer, when my suffering was so great I felt I couldn't withstand it any longer. I was crying in my bed, begging God to make me 'normal' when I suddenly felt this overwhelming sense of compassion and love wash over me. There was this presence, a parental or maternal feeling, that took me in its arms and held me and assured me that I was loved exactly as I was. I can't explain how I know this, but the message I received was to put down the burden I was carrying. I was too young and too innocent to be so hard on myself. That night, my tears stopped and I slept calmly for one of the few nights I remember from my childhood.

This one night of respite from shame didn't make the fear of having AIDS subside, however. I still feared that simply by thinking about boys I had somehow contracted this 'plague'. I begged my mother to take me to the doctor. 'Feel my glands,' I pleaded. My mother's job at the aged care facility meant she understood the basics of health care so she was empathetic.

'Hmm, they do feel a little swollen. Maybe you have a virus,' she said.

A *virus*! She just said it. She said it and she doesn't even realise what virus it was.

Consequently, we went to see the doctor.

INTERIOR: Woodridge Plaza Medical Centre, 1986

I'm sitting in the chair, my mother next to me as the very handsome young doctor feels my throat, looks at my non-existent tonsils and takes my temperature. I realise in this moment, it's not that I'm afraid I've got AIDS, it's that I'm so exhausted from carrying the fear and the guilt and the shame of my feelings for boys, that I just want the doctor to tell my mother the truth about me. If he tells her, this weight will lift from my shoulders and I'll finally be free of this crushing and all-consuming guilt.

In my mind the scene will play out like this:

Dramatic lighting. Melodramatic music plays.

It's Barber's *Adagio for Strings*.

Close-up on Darren.

Darren's eyes widen as the camera zooms in, Spielberg style.

We see beads of sweat on the boy's forehead. Extreme close-up on Darren's face and we see tears well up in the corners of his eyes.

The doctor places both hands on Darren's shoulders, giving him a knowing look.

The camera pans along the doctor's masculine hairy arms and to Darren's face.

Darren nods to the doctor, giving him permission to reveal the toxic secret.

'Mrs Hayes, I have some terrible news about your son. You might want to sit down.'

Suddenly a mirror falls from the wall and smashes.

All three heads turn to the source of the noise.

Mrs Hayes jumps up from her seat in fright. Bursts into tears.

She sits down, unable to stop crying.

'What is it?' she demands, fear in her voice. 'Is it cancer?'

'It's worse,' the doctor says, taking a deep breath. 'He's *gay!*'

CUT TO: Reality

In the end, the doctor found absolutely nothing wrong with me, my mother was slightly confused about her hypochondriac son and I still had the feeling of dread safely embedded in my stomach. The doctor must have missed something. How could he not know? It was so obvious. *Everyone* thought I was gay.

That night my mother took me to a Pizza Hut, just the two of us, and we ordered a fancy meal off the menu. The cheapest thing to do back then was to have the 'all you can eat' buffet. For a modest amount, you could have all the pizza and salad you wanted. But not tonight. Tonight we ate like kings. We ordered personal pan pizzas. One each! It was so extravagant and I knew we didn't have money to spare. I felt so lucky to share this time with her. It was as though she knew something was on my mind and although she couldn't solve it, she knew how to soothe my aching heart.

Girls, Girlfriends, and the Three-Letter Word

It was in 1988 and via the school musical I discovered I was the object of desire of the opposite sex. By age sixteen our second school musical *Bye Bye Birdie* had been a huge success and allowed me to showcase my natural singing voice. I was feeling more confident and inspired by pop music, dance and fashion. I was working Thursday nights and Saturdays at Woody's and had my own money to buy clothes and music and satisfy my new obsession with collecting remixes on 12-inch vinyl, studying every nuance between the differences from the album cuts to the club mixes. My personal style was developing. Madonna and Prince were at their artistic and commercial peak and I was still enthralled by Michael Jackson. I would choreograph dances and practise until the sun went down in the building site of the home my father and brother were building.

One evening after practising my moves, I came down for dinner to the garage, where the rest of the family were living. My father said he'd been having a lot of fun watching me on 'the big TV'.

The rest of the family looked smugly at each other, stifling laughter.

'What do you mean?' I asked.

'Oh, we've all been enjoying watching you dance on the big TV!' He pointed up to the building site.

I immediately understood what he meant. Against the silhouette of the sunset, the frame of the house was like a picture screen and he and the rest of the family had seen me doing my moonwalk and crotch grabs. I still laugh when I think of that.

I'd also saved up to buy a keyboard and had written a couple of songs: one called 'Goodbye', and a very sad one called 'Wilting'. That one was about my father. One night I decided to play him the songs. I called him to the 'big TV', plugged in my keyboard and sang him 'Goodbye'.

He sat there, motionless and silent while I poured my heart out for him. When I finished there was an uncomfortable silence. 'Huh,' he eventually said. And then left.

It was such a strange reaction. I don't know what I was expecting. Praise, I guess. But in the absence of that, even some constructive criticism would have been nice. He responded as though he were embarrassed or somehow ashamed of me. It was like he had to leave as quickly as possible. I stayed in the moment, utterly confused. Then I played the second song, 'Wilting'.

I'm wilting in your fading light, there's sadness in my eyes tonight, I'm drowning in your sad neglect, it's hard to do but I'll live without your respect . . .'

At school I had become increasingly close to a girl named Chloe. She was nothing like Nathalia, whom I'd always had a harmless crush on but never seen as a romantic connection. While Nathalia was blonde, fashionable, incredibly feminine, and a sensitive artistic and theatrical personality, Chloe was a brunette comedic music fan and much more of a tomboy.

In the past, on lunch breaks, it had always been me and Dean, but now it was me, Dean and Chloe. The root of our connection was music. She sang a little and whether it was singing along to the top forty or the soundtrack to *Little Shop of Horrors* – a movie musical that had come out a few summers before – we soon discovered our voices harmonised well. It was exciting to meet someone who listened to harmonies and understood background parts the way I did.

She was a year younger than me but because of the school musical we spent a lot of time hanging out and getting to know one another. Rather helpfully, she lived a bare fifteen-minute drive from my parents' place and it was nice to have a friend who was from my 'new' neighbourhood. Her parents were also renovating a house and lived on a large farm, so we spent a lot of time outside of school helping our parents.

I never thought of her in a romantic way – I never really thought of any girl in a romantic way – but we had a special bond and a deep connection. One day at her parents' house, while we were pulling up nails from old wooden floorboards, Chloe started singing the Queen song 'You're My Best Friend'.

I realised she was singing it about me.

My heart fluttered and it dawned on me that there was something romantic, not just platonic, brewing between us.

We spent increasing amounts of time together during the school musical rehearsals. It felt like I became more attractive, just being on stage. I found the attention confusing but flattering, of course. I was just so innocent back then and didn't share the same interest in sex that the other boys did. My motivations were romantic, poetic and kind and when I look back I see I was just a gay best friend to many girls. Unfortunately, some girls didn't realise this and it caused some confusion.

One day, a mysterious transplant and rebellious Seventh Day Adventist named Valerie arrived at our school. She pursued me aggressively and *told me* that she was my girlfriend. And so she was.

There was no discussion. I remember she took me out on a 'date' – essentially taking the train to a movie in the city – and at the station on the way home, she kissed me.

She kissed *me*.

I was incredibly flustered. After the kiss, she *unbuttoned* my 1980s new-wave embroidered shirt and my entire face went red. As her fingers trailed down my neckline, she touched the hair on my chest. She seemed to like how nervous I was. Thankfully things stopped there and we went home. I remember the feeling of being in way too deep and knowing that there was something either very regressed about my interest in girls, or very advanced about Valerie's interest in boys. It felt dangerous and exciting but also like I was growing up too fast. I didn't want to have sex. I didn't even really want to make out. I just liked the romance and the chemistry of flirtation. I liked writing love letters and the sentimental rituals of having a girlfriend.

Valerie was a chorus member in the school musical. We started writing each other little love notes and soon the entire school knew we were 'an item'. I found her mystical and fascinating and I got butterflies around her. In retrospect I think I just liked that she looked like Madonna from the cover of the *Like A Prayer* album. Plus, she wore patchouli oil.

At the end of *Bye Bye Birdie*, our school music teachers gave what was supposed to be just one award to three of us – Nathalia, Patrick and me. It was a week's tuition at a private theatre camp in the city. It meant I wouldn't see Valerie for seven whole days.

The camp was held during the school holidays and was free. It even came with spending money! It happened at a time in my life where I really needed privacy and time away from my father and the building site. I know my schoolteachers selected us because they saw our potential and to this day I'm so grateful for what was a passport to freedom.

When I got to the university where the week of intensive work-shops was to be held, I checked into my dorm room and was delighted to find I would be sharing with the first openly gay person I'd ever met, a young kid who introduced himself as Shahgopal Lee. I had never met anyone like him before. We had an instant connection. Shah, as he was referred to, would grow up to become a famous drag queen in Melbourne. Sadly he passed away at just thirty-eight. However, back in 1988, he was a magical unicorn and spoke openly about having sex with men. I felt so comfortable with him. I wasn't attracted to him and this is probably where the difficultly I had defining my own sexuality began. He was one of the rare gay men or openly gay people I knew who were so unlike me that I assumed I just wasn't gay.

At the theatre camp, we were encouraged to sing, dance, write songs and learn choreography. I joke with my now friend, 1980s legendary popstar Debbie Gibson, that I learned every step of her classic 1988 hit 'Electric Youth'. I felt like a rockstar performing it. During the final day, a rumour got back to me that somebody at school saw my girlfriend Valerie at a local mall kissing someone else. Even though it was a silly and innocent school romance, it stung. The feeling of betrayal was new to me and it felt very adult. As we were on school holidays, I didn't see Valerie for a week or so, but when school resumed, we spoke and she admitted she had a new boyfriend and that was that.

The drama queen in me feigned heartbreak for a few weeks. Our respective circle of friends avoided each other and everyone took sides. Despite the heartbreak, deep down I was relieved to be free from something that felt way beyond my emotional and physical capabilities. I felt like I could be a kid again.

My friendship with Chloe blossomed as the year progressed and I asked her to be my date at the Year 12 school formal. In Australia, this is the equivalent of what Americans call a 'prom'. The months leading up to it were so exciting and the reason I failed chemistry. Instead of studying, I would sketch designs of my outfit. I knew exactly what I was going to wear: a costume entirely inspired by Michael Jackson. It was a tuxedo with a custom-made shirt with long collars to allow for silver wing tips. I worked with a local seamstress to design a jacket that would have western belt buckles sewn onto the shoulders, just like Michael Jackson wore. I also bought a stainless steel Triumph motorcycle emblem and had a leather maker turn it into a cummerbund. My hair was long enough to put into a ponytail and I'd decided to dye it blue-black.

My plans were dealt a blow when my father noticed my hair was getting long.

'When are you going to get your hair cut?' he demanded.

I was hoping he hadn't noticed.

'I'm not. I'm growing it.'

'No you're not.'

'What do you mean? I'm wearing it in a ponytail for the school formal.'

And that's when he responded with the first of what would become a regular ultimatum; a demand to obey him or be thrown out of home.

'No son of mine is going to walk around with long hair like a girl. Get it cut or you can find somewhere else to live.'

He was deadly serious.

It took me twelve months to grow my hair and five minutes to cut it off.

In a tiny act of defiance, on the night of the school formal, I wore eyeliner.

My sister drove Chloe and me to Nathalia's house, where we met Dean and his date, a German exchange student. Nathalia wore her hair peroxide-blonde and long, set in a loose wave. Draped in a beautiful strapless black velvet gown, matching velvet gloves and faux diamonds around her neck, she was the spitting image of Marilyn Monroe. She looked like a movie star.

We felt magical that night. It was as though the rest of the room were teenagers, but we were rockstars. Even our teachers seemed to treat us this way. I remember how I felt when I first arrived at that hellhole Mabel Park High – bullied, spat on and tormented – and comparing it to the way I felt now. I walked on air and didn't give a fuck what anyone thought. I was my own person, my own true style icon, my own true inspiration. I'd fought hard to become the kid who felt confident enough to vogue right there on the dance floor.

Icarus Falls to Earth

After school ended, Chloe and I kept in touch. She spent New Year's Eve with me and my family and stayed over. In the middle of the night two confessions were made. The first, that we had feelings for one another. The second, I told her about my childhood.

She was the first person in the world outside of my family that I'd ever shared the secret with. Maybe it was the intimacy of being alone with a girl for the first time and feeling comfortable in my skin, or maybe it was that we both came from somewhat broken homes. Whatever it was, it all poured out of me as the sun rose. It was so cathartic to finally share the secret of Lake Road. I cried, she cried. Telling another person seemed illegal but at the same time emancipating. I had betrayed my family – mostly my mother. But isn't that how abuse endures? The victims are so ashamed of what has happened to them, they hide it, therefore carrying around the weight of the events on their shoulders, all the while letting the perpetrator maintain their pristine public persona. My father was 'good old Bob'. Everyone loved him. They had no idea of his temper until he unleashed it upon them. The minute they did, they were literally run out of our lives. I told Chloe everything. From my earliest memories of watching my father beat my mother, to my most recent experiences of being 'disciplined' physically, having my hair cut off, how he spoke to me.

The next day, we were boyfriend and girlfriend. We shared a sacred bond. She was my first girlfriend, only my second relationship with a woman, but one that would last for two and a half years. She was my first everything and I genuinely thought we were going to get married. She was a year behind me at school, so I'd graduated by the time we were officially girlfriend and boyfriend.

Anyone could see that I was supposed to go on to study music, theatre and drama. My friends Nathalia and Patrick auditioned for a university known at the time as Kelvin Grove, a technical college that offered courses in acting, directing and production. Neither Nathalia nor Patrick got into the acting program but they were accepted into the teaching course. I wanted to audition but my father told me I would never make it in the music business and that I had to study something 'sensible' or, you guessed it, be thrown out of home. That meant I applied for, and got into, the University of Queensland to study a Bachelor of Arts majoring in journalism. I thought I could get a job writing for a music magazine and get into the business via the back door.

I was utterly miserable at university. I hated every single subject, especially literary theory. My most dreaded class was 'style' which consisted of learning all the rules and adhering to a restrictive list of writing regulations journalists had to abide by. I found it suffocating and joyless. It seemed as though journalism was just writing in the least interesting way possible. Adjectives were a sin. Don't even think about using a metaphor. The shorter the piece, the better. After about six months, I built up the courage to tell my father that I was going to quit and work full-time at Woody's until the following year, when I'd audition for the same acting school I'd wanted to audition for the first time.

My father told me I was a dropout. A nobody. A deadbeat. He told me that in six months' time I'd be 'living in the gutter' and that I'd 'never make it as a musician'.

I stuck to my guns. I left the University of Queensland and started working full-time at Woody's. I was still allowed to live at home, but I had to pay 'board'; a sort of rent, if you will. It was an hour's drive to work. I tried to save as much money as I could but driving my first car – a hand-me-down from my sister – cost a fortune. The infamous bright-yellow 1972 Kingswood had originally belonged to my father. He sold it to my sister. You read that right. Sold. He didn't give us anything. My sister had been saving up for years to buy her first car, and when it was time, my father somehow convinced her a piece of junk that needed a new motor was her best bet. Years later, she simply gave it to me. She was always so kind. I called it the Batmobile because it reminded me of the Tim Burton Batman symbol. It was a generous gift but the car was a gas guzzler and the commute to Woody's was an hour's drive each way. The cost of running the 8-cylinder rust bucket tore through my wages. That's if it was running. Often it would break down and I was paying for new parts as the car slowly disintegrated over time.

Tracey was working as a waitress, pulling crazy hours at the Sheraton Hotel in the heart of Brisbane. When she left high school she studied hospitality and was destined for a career either in the culinary arts or hotel management. It felt so glamorous to meet her after her late shifts in the city before driving home to Jimboomba. The hour-long drive was our chance to listen to music and sing at the top of our lungs. We loved 'the city', which never lost its charm. Having grown up in the suburbs on the south side, which was looked down upon, going to the city felt luxurious. Now we were both spending time there, it felt like something great could happen at any moment. Magic felt like it was lingering just around the corner.

My relationship with Chloe was intense. It moved at a pace I wasn't prepared for. We made mix tapes for each other and pined for one another when we were apart. We were in love.

I remember her coming home from school one day and declaring proudly, 'I'm on the pill!' and me answering, 'Why?' Again, I was such a babe in the woods. Soon we were sexually active and it felt natural and wonderful to me. In spite of other gay men's experiences, my take on sex with women is that, because I didn't really know who I was and had nothing to compare it to, I just assumed that was what the experience was supposed to be like.

Human touch felt amazing, regardless of gender. I shelved my sexual attraction to men because I thought every guy secretly thought other men were attractive, they just never admitted it. I passed off my queerness as merely a quirk or a shameful guilty pleasure I was too afraid or too wise to mention in public. I didn't realise back then that it was an essential part of who I was.

Before I met Chloe, I'd never fantasised about seeing a girl naked. I'd never wondered what it would feel like to have sex with a woman. But once I crossed that threshold, human nature took over and any lingering feelings I had about boys were put on hold while puberty and the thrill and ecstasy of sex took a front-row seat. The emotional connection of being physical created a bond I'd never experienced with another human being. It felt sacred. I leaned into the romance and the intimacy of sex and it helped quiet the voice inside that questioned my sexuality.

Things at home, however, were not so great.

Although my father had stopped drinking, his temper was still out of control and he made life miserable for my mother, brother and me. Much to my sadness, Tracey moved out. She'd been my safety valve. When things got bad, she was always up for a drive down the South Side Freeway to the Gold Coast, or a trip to the Queen Street Mall to see a movie, or just to walk about the Myer Centre, which back in the 1980s was a glamorous multi-floor and high-tech mall. But now she was living with her boyfriend and she was gone. Worse, she'd started working on a ferry called the *Abel Tasman* that crossed between Melbourne and Tasmania, and was away for six weeks at a time. Just like my father when we were kids. Except I missed her tremendously. I'd write her letters and send her mix tapes of songs I was discovering. She'd write me letters too and the day I received them I'd devour every word. She'd come home with exotic gifts like *Dungeons & Dragons* handbooks she'd bought in this glamorous city called Melbourne.

I was eighteen by this stage but still found my father incredibly intimidating. He'd lose his temper and slap me around the head or the ears. He'd call it 'cheek' if I dared question him. He ruled the house with an iron fist and was puritanical about my relationship with Chloe. I'd seen him do this with Tracey. He called her a 'slut' for seeing a man without marrying him first. The fact that she moved in with her boyfriend, at the age of twenty-three, meant she was 'immoral'. My father chased my brother out of home at the age of eighteen, too, just for having a girlfriend. It was ironic because we're certain my father cheated on my mother several times. I think I even caught him once. The fact that I would drive over to my girlfriend's house, at the age of eighteen, and come home late, meant that she was also a 'whore'.

My friend Dean had moved into an apartment with his girl-friend Alice. He was able to do this with financial assistance from the government. There was a program for kids who lived in abusive homes and they encouraged me to investigate this. The assistance allowed you to apply for a monthly grant to help with food and rent.

I went and explained my living situation and the counsellor said that I qualified. The only thing was, they'd need to talk to my mother to verify my claims.

I was so worried about how she might respond, but I figured I'd try.

It's so absurd to me, looking back, that I wasn't sure I'd qualify for a grant specifically designed for kids living in abusive situations, when my entire life had been a series of abusive situations, but that was the cumulative effect of years of living in the conditions I was raised in. 'Normal' was subjective.

One Sunday afternoon in 1990, Chloe and I were at my parents' finally completed home in Jimboomba when my father asked me to do something for him in the yard. We already had plans to go to the movies. I asked him if I could do it the following day and he exploded with profanities. Chloe made the rookie mistake of answering him back and he launched at her, threatening her physically for being 'cheeky'. She had never seen that side of him before. It was as though my father was talking to my mother, years prior. It frightened me, terrified Chloe and we both instinctively ran from the house, sprinting down the very long country road.

When we were far enough away, we hid in the tall grass of a paddock. But my father came looking for us and we watched as his truck drove up and down the street. It was terrifying. I had flashbacks of being a kid, holding my mother's hand, hiding from my drunk father. Chloe was crying, I was stoic, frozen, numb. We waited, crouched down in the long grass for about an hour until the sun went down before going to a neighbour's house. We asked to use the phone and called Chloe's father to come pick us up. The humiliation was the same as being a child when I called the police. Now the secret was out and on full display. The shame monster was hovering above me.

I don't know how Chloe and I moved past that incident. The plan had been that I would apply for the loan from the government and just put up with the situation at home for as long as I could. Once I had committed myself to Chloe physically, I was sure we were completely in love and assumed we were going to get married. There's nothing quite like that feeling of thinking you are the only two people on earth who have ever been in love. Parents couldn't possibly understand. The world didn't get it. Only we did. It was going to be the two of us together forever.

Until it wasn't.

A year went by and when Chloe graduated high school, we decided we'd both audition for the acting program at Kelvin Grove. We were going to be stars! Together! Forever! Dean's girlfriend, Alice, did the same thing.

The day of the audition we were ready for our lives to be changed forever. The casting panel put us into different groups so I didn't see how Chloe or Alice performed but I found the exercises to be exciting and challenging. I had a gut feeling I'd done well but I really couldn't tell what they were looking for. I felt intimidated by some people and cringed when watching others. Afterwards I asked Chloe how she felt she went and she said she was confident she'd get in. We wouldn't find out for some weeks.

The day of the results rolled around and in those pre-internet times we had to attend the campus and see if our names had been posted on a bulletin board. There were lists for every course and we had preferences for which program we wanted to be in, whether it was production, education, directing or the highly competitive and coveted acting program, which only took fifteen students from the entire country. I was offered a place in every course, including the acting program.

Chloe's name didn't appear anywhere.

I was devastated. We were in love. We were going to go to university together to become stars together. What would happen now?

On the sombre bus ride home I made a stupid, self-sacrificing offer. 'I can't imagine going on this adventure without you. We were supposed to do this together. If you aren't doing the course, then I'm not going to do it either.'

'Okay,' she replied.

Okay? That's it? She wants me to give up my place?

So I did.

I gave up my offer to attend my dream school and instead re-enrolled to study early childhood education, as a way of keeping my father happy and not getting kicked out of home.

At the time, I thought it was a way for Chloe and me to stay together. She didn't have a back-up plan. She didn't qualify to get into any other universities and so she got a full-time job at a chain record store/hi-fi outlet. Within weeks she'd moved out of her family's home and into a place with her older sister. Suddenly she was hanging out with her new work friends, reconnecting with her old high-school friends and abandoned any dreams the two of us had together. It was as if she'd grown up, given up and moved on in the blink of an eye. She broke up with me and was soon with someone else.

My entire world fell out from underneath me. Chloe had provided a sense of stability in an uncertain world. I'd shared my deepest secrets with her. We'd planned a future together that was now disintegrating before my eyes. I was left without my performing dream, because I'd given up my chance to study acting, and here I was sitting in an orientation class of a Bachelor of Education in

Early Childhood with a bunch of hopeful pre-school teachers wondering what the hell I'd done to divert so far off my path.

I was in shock.

I phoned her and begged her to take me back, which in hindsight was a ridiculous and degrading thing to do. I cried every time. Eventually she told me to stop calling, so I did.

While I had lived with anxiety my entire life, this was the first time I'd ever experienced what I now realise was depression. I didn't want to do anything. I couldn't imagine the future. It was like I had nothing to live for. I lost all the joy and I lost a lot of weight. Pictures of me back then still bother me. I looked pale, emaciated and exhausted. I spent days finding places to cry, privately. All I wanted to do was sleep, to switch my mind off. To remove myself from reality.

I stopped socialising. I stopped eating. I spent all my free time in bed sleeping as late as I possibly could. My mother was really worried. I just couldn't shake the disinterest in life, the hollow feeling in my chest. I couldn't imagine ever being happy again. On top of it all, I was now doing a university course I had no interest in. My days blended into one another. I also lost my best friend, Dean, because his girlfriend Alice was friends with my now ex, and they all hung out together. I felt completely discarded.

Before we broke up, Dean, Alice, Nathalia, Chloe and I had all bought tickets to see Prince in concert. We'd slept in sleeping bags in the Queen Street Mall overnight to get the best possible seats. We took a boom box, played Prince music, ate pizza, laughed and joked. When the box office opened the next morning, however, we were shocked to learn the first thirty rows had sold before anyone had a chance to buy them! Like the true rebels we thought we were, we started a protest in the street, chanting, 'Fans first!' We attracted so much attention we got on the local news station. But it was to no avail and we eventually accepted that we were going to be sitting thirty rows from the stage.

When Chloe broke up with me, the matter of the concert was addressed almost immediately. It was decided, without my input, that she, Alice and Dean would drive to the show together and I would make my own way there. Alone. There was so much emotion attached to that Prince concert that I didn't know how I'd cope seeing Chloe there, in person, after months of being apart. Aside from that, the group's rejection and having my best friend, Dean, side with the girls, felt like another betrayal.

Thank God for Nathalia who insisted I come to her place before-hand where she was having a pre-party, and then go to the concert together. I'd be like Molly Ringwald in *Pretty in Pink*, walking into the prom with Ducky, devastated but defiant. My sister bought me the most beautiful, white, long-sleeved dress shirt with colourful embroidery down the centre line where a tie would normally sit. I wore it with a grey and blue plaid blazer with Levi's 501s and Doc Martens. I was rake thin thanks to the depression. When I left home my mother said, 'Hold your head high!'

At Nathalia's apartment in Petrie Terrace, Brisbane's coolest suburb, I pretended to be strong, but I was dying on the inside. I would leave the party and duck into the toilet and cry, then re-enter as though nothing was wrong. That feeling from childhood, like there was a monster inside my stomach, about to eat me from the inside out was back. The feeling of dread and the inability to see a future was overwhelming. It didn't matter what anyone was saying to me, I felt like I was underwater. I just nodded and smiled but wasn't listening. I was the walking dead. Even on the car ride to the Brisbane Entertainment Centre, where Prince and the New Power Generation were playing, I feigned interest singing along to '1999' and 'Raspberry Beret'. I felt nothing but black sludge inside my heart.

Once inside the arena we found our assigned seats. My 'friends' had already arrived. I had to walk past Chloe and I said 'hello' but she ignored me, like I was a stranger. It's one of the most painful memories from youth that I have. I sat at the end of the row, next to Dean and Nathalia. As the show started, I looked over at the person I used to trust and who I thought loved me. She had her hands in the air, full of reckless abandon. Thrilled. In party mode. Screaming with joy.

I was numb.

By the time Prince sang 'Nothing Compares 2 U' my heart couldn't take it anymore. I burst into tears. Nathalia rubbed my back.

At the end of the show, Alice, Dean and Chloe filed past me as I sat in my seat, devastated.

'Aren't you even going to acknowledge me?' I degraded myself by asking. Chloe ignored me and kept walking.

Dean stepped in and told me to 'get a hold of' myself.

Our friendship ended that night.

He left with the two girls and I sat there crying in Nathalia's arms.

Much later on in my life, when I'd become famous, Dean called our hometown radio station while I was on air. Because there's a delay on live radio, I was lucky enough to hear his voice and the producers saw my expression. I'd turned white. They asked me if I wanted to drop the call. Yes, I mouthed. Thankfully they did.

A few years after that he got in touch via Facebook and apologised for what had happened all those years before. He said he'd felt like he had to side with his girlfriend and that he wished he'd made a different choice. I forgave him, we were kids. I was in Brisbane years later and we spent some time together and it was nice to reminisce. He asked if he could visit me in the US some years after that but when we spent real time together we both realised things were not the same. Sometimes a friendship is not meant to last forever, and I made my peace with that. I loved the time I spent with him as a kid and I loved the time I spent with Chloe as a young kid finding first love. They're the parts of the memories I cherish and keep with me to this day.

Back in Jimboomba, I was so overwhelmed with sadness and the intolerable feeling of being stuck in a situation at university that I didn't want, my living situation was the last thing on my mind. I abandoned the idea of applying to move out under the government assistance scheme. My secret stash of saucepans, cutlery and appliances would have to wait. Life went on. I was in the middle of a practice teaching placement at a primary school and had just enough energy every day to hold it together, put on a fake smile and do the work assigned to me. Any chance I got, I'd hide in a supply cupboard or a toilet cubicle and cry. The depression blinded me. I had no ability to see a future. It drained my energy and sapped me of all joy. In the end, time helped cure my first episode of depression. But it wouldn't always be like that.

INTERIOR: Bedroom, Sausalito, 1999

It's noon and there's a knock on my bedroom door. I groan. 'Just leave me be,' I think. I've been staying up until I'm exhausted and I can't keep my eyes open anymore. Until the dread in my stomach has given up and I find a piece of silence in the world. Most nights I soothe myself by putting on a video cassette of *Return of the Jedi*. I usually fall asleep somewhere in the middle of the film.

There's another knock on the door. It's my assistant, Leonie, who lives with me. She's checking to see if I'm alive. I'm not stupid.

She comes down the little stairs that lead from the door to my private quarters to my bed and begins her daily ritual.

'It's gorgeous outside. Do you want to go for a walk?'

I don't want to do anything. Last night the pain was so bad I just wanted to die.

She manages to find me in the forest of pillows, puts a tooth-brush into my hand and gets me on my way.

An hour later, we're sitting at the bottom of Bridgeway Avenue, Starbucks muffins and lattes in our hands. I still feel a crushing sense of doom but the sparkling effervescent bay, its brilliant blue hue, shimmers with a glint of positivity.

'I'm worried about you,' she says.

Everybody Knows You're Gay Before You Do

EXTERIOR: Morning, school playground, 1983

Children of all ages are gathered in play. Some play handball with a green tennis ball, some play hopscotch on the pavement with chalk. One boy stands in front of a group of children, instructing them like a movie director . . .

I'm obsessed with Michael Jackson's *Thriller*. I can't get enough of it. Last week, I won a dancing competition where the prize was a ticket to watch *Making Michael Jackson's Thriller* on video cassette during lunch break. The school had been selling tickets, for one dollar, but we couldn't afford that. However, they announced a contest where you could win a free ticket just by doing the 'bus stop' to the Diana Ross song, 'Upside Down'. It seemed like a no-brainer. 'I'm gonna win this,' I told my mother. She cautioned me not to be so confident just in case I got my feelings hurt, but I knew in my gut I was going to win.

And I did.

Needless to say, after I saw the film I became transfixed with the production stages of filmmaking. I *had* to recreate this music video, live, in front of my entire school. I would play the part of Michael Jackson, obviously, but I needed my Ola Ray, the beautiful girl who played the frightened date, opposite. I had someone in mind: Tammy. She was so beautiful and looked just like the actress in the music video. The only problem was, she was shy. That's okay. I could coach her. And her hair. Ola wore her hair in an 'up' style so I needed to fix Tammy's hair too.

One morning before school, I'm standing in front of Tammy, playing with her hair. I take her scrunchie and rearrange it in different ways until I get it precisely how I like it. Just as I'm about finished I receive a swift slap on the bottom. Ouch! It really hurts.

I turn around and see the teacher on duty, standing behind me.

'Leave her hair alone,' she says in a stern voice, 'and come and see me in my office, immediately.'

Tears well in my eyes and I follow her, my head hung low, in shame.

Once inside her office, she closes the door and takes a seat, while I stand to attention. She takes me in with a glacial stare. 'You're a little fairy, aren't you, Darren Hayes?' She uses the word with such disdain.

I don't know what this means, but I know it's bad.

'I'm not sure what you mean,' I respond timidly.

'You know *exactly* what I mean,' she sneers. 'If I catch you playing with the girls again you'll be in detention all week. Now get out of my office, *fairy*.'

I leave the office and never play with Tammy's hair again.

INTERIOR: University classroom, 1991

I'm late, again. I'm always late. Maybe it's because the traffic from Jimboomba to Brisbane City is horrendous or maybe it's because I absolutely hate this course and do not want to be here with every fibre in my body. Why the hell am I doing a teaching degree? I don't belong here. I dress in paisley print shirts and jeans rolled up with white socks showing and my burgundy brogues polished to the nines. My hair is dyed a gentle shade of red and sometimes I wear rosary beads. Everyone else here looks like a clone, conservatively dressed and designed to fit in. Well, everyone except this one girl, Colby. She's what you'd describe as 'alternative'. She wears similar clothes to me but is more gothic. She's fused beauty makeup with industrial boots, Doc Martens of course, paired with cool denim and over-sized floral shirts or sometimes dark, billowing peasant dresses. She's a huge fan of The Smiths and Morrissey. However, what struck me most when we first met was her amazing hair. That was the topic of the first conversation we ever had. She has it cut in a perfectly sharp concave bob and it's dyed the most luscious, dark purple, almost black colour.

'I love your hair colour. What is it?'

Aubergine, apparently.

I didn't know what an aubergine was. But I loved the colour.

And that's how we bonded.

Colby had the most beautiful face. Thick, voluptuous lips, ice-green eyes and perfect skin. She really knew how to use makeup; eyeliner and brows were her strength. She reminded me of those 1980s Patrick Nagel portraits. Pale skin, dark hair, androgynous features and striking eyes. The cover of Duran Duran's *Rio* is a perfect example of the style.

Today, like most days, I am not only late to class, but my eyes are puffy from crying. Crying on the drive to university, crying during the breaks between classes, crying on the way home. But during class, I hide my sad inner world and am somewhat of an extro-vert. I sit with Colby a lot. She seems cool and nonchalant. And she smells divine. Always. She's anti-love, anti-marriage, anti-mush. That is *exactly* what I need. My heart is broken and my misery needs company.

It's especially difficult because I'm on the same university campus as my friends Nathalia and Patrick, only they are now second-year students studying theatre. Occasionally I see them with their theatre friends and feel so out of place. They smoke cigarettes and dress in all black. They've got tattoos. Nathalia is as warm and magical and generous as always but some of her new friends have these fake, pretentious theatre accents and look like lost members of The Cure. I find them insufferable. Maybe it's because I wish I were doing what they were doing, but still there's a level of self-indulgence. I see it as insecurity masquerading as confidence. Nathalia never has that. She wears her heart on her sleeve.

I'm lucky that occasionally she gets me cast in their productions. I don't know how she gets away with it, but she manages to convince her crew that this kid studying early childhood education should be in their end-of-semester productions. I'm so grateful. During my time in kindergarten headquarters I occasionally get to feel what it's like to be in a proper theatre production. I find their rehearsal process laborious and tedious at times but the thrill of being a part of the process is a joy. Ultimately it's the performing that is the true payoff. I love it. One of the first productions I'm in is a musical where Nathalia and I are part of the 'house band'. I get to sing backing vocals to pop songs by the Pet Shop Boys and other popular artists of the time. Nathalia is a muse, even here at university, with hair newly fashioned into a curly platinum-blonde bob, like Madonna's from the 'Express Yourself' music video.

Today, after class, a group of kids are going to the pub.

I don't drink. I made a vow I would never drink because of my father. I'm certain that if I let that poison into my body, I'll turn into the monster version of me, just like Dr Jekyll and Mr Hyde. I tell everyone I really don't want to go, but Colby and a few of our mutual friends remind me of how miserable I've been, and tell me it will be good for me. So I make my way to my car after class and drive to a beautiful beer garden in a pub called the Normanby in an area called Red Hill. When I get there it's like a flashback to my childhood. Adults sitting outside at wooden picnic tables drinking tall pints of beer. Some are smoking. I hate it. Even the smell of beer makes me want to vomit . . .

INTERIOR: The Waterford Hotel, 1979
I'm barefoot again, by choice. There's a riverbank near the pub and my siblings and I have been unsuccessfully trying to catch yabbies (or 'crayfish' as they might be known elsewhere in the world) for most of the afternoon and now the sun has set and it's nearing home time.

Mum has promised me we'll stop at the gas station on the way so I can buy a Smurf. I've been collecting the blue gnome-like toys ever since I saw them advertised on TV. There's a particular one I really want. He's a wind-up, regular Smurf, not the 'tennis player' or the 'nerd' or 'Papa Smurf' or any of the other specific ones. Just a regular blue little man with a white hat and pants, except he *walks*! I plan to put him in the back garden where I'm convinced actual fairies and friendly goblins live. There's only one problem. The gas station closes at 8 p.m. and we are running out of time. We were supposed to leave over an hour ago so my mother could stop on the way home and get milk, bread and some fuel for the car, but my father won't stop drinking.

I go inside the pub and I can see my parents having a tense conversation. I can't hear their words but it's clear they're arguing, yelling at each other, trying to be heard over the band playing a horrible cover version of the ballad 'Don't It Make My Brown Eyes Blue'. I'm anxious I won't get my Smurf. I want to say something but I don't want to make things worse. Then my father's demeanour changes. My mother seems to have convinced him to leave the pub early with the promise of getting more beer to take home. We all pile into the car and as he sits in the front seat I'm struck by how happy he seems, like a child getting McDonald's for the first time. He's beaming with joy as he orders 'six tall ones' – six 750-millilitre bottles of Castlemaine beer, or 'Fourexx' as it's more commonly called. The guy serving hands my father a cardboard box containing the bottles. As he takes the box, my father's arm grazes my face and I'm hit with the smell of beer on his skin, mixed with his sweat and nicotine. I want to rub my face to remove the stench but he'll notice. So I sit with the feeling of revulsion.

I ask if we're stopping at the BP gas station, but unfortunately, it's already closed.

CUT TO: Reality

Even though I want to leave, something makes me stay. It's Colby. She's changed outfits and she's wearing a cool blazer with a patterned shirt underneath, Levi's and her signature Doc Martens. She smells incredible and her makeup is impeccable. She really is stunning. We sit next to each other and just talk. Something about being around her feels soothing to the soul. I'm able to tolerate all of the outside irritants because I want to spend this time to get to know her.

Later, in classes, we become closer. During lectures I'm a complete clown, my disdain for the course and some of the condescending lecturers can't be hidden, but my grades are good. My daily ritual of crying has ceased and I'm fully immersed in the university social scene. I barely study but I still do well because most of the assignments involve writing and I seem to be good at that.

As time passes, my friendship with Colby becomes something everyone notices. We become those two people that everyone is saying are 'an item' when we really aren't. One night a group is going to a nightclub called Mary Street. I ask Colby if she's going.

She remembers it as me asking her out on a date. I just remember when we got to the nightclub we didn't stop talking all night and as the bar was about to close I said, 'I'm gonna marry you one day' and she said, 'I know'. And that was that. As the sun came up we were driving our separate cars home from the city and we stopped in the middle of a deserted street. I got out and kissed her. We were together from that moment on.

Our love was pure and real and magical. It was nothing like my high-school relationship. We were two people with family scars and a deep yearning for a life of security and safety. Colby was my best friend and my first real love. We were inseparable. So inseparable in fact that one day I came home from seeing her one night and my mother had packed my bags. 'You spend so much time over there you might as well move in with her.' So I did. Looking back, my mother was probably sad that her baby had grown up. She couldn't bear the gradual and slow loss of her now only child, and so she made the decision for me. I'm glad she did; it was beyond time. I was twenty-two yet such a baby in many respects. It forced me to grow up.

Until recently, Colby had been sharing a house with her older brother and sister in the beautiful northern suburb of Wilston. I spent a lot of time there during the first six months or so of our relationship, but her brother was about to get married and needed privacy so Colby was soon scrambling to find a place of her own. Her family was welcoming but her sister immediately distrusted me because she thought I was gay. It was the strangest feeling to be accused of something I didn't think of myself as. We would eventually become quite close, but in the beginning, her walls were up and she was not shy about expressing her reservations to my face.

Colby and I moved into a tiny apartment near where I was born, close to the Brisbane Mater Hospital in the suburb of Herston. The place was so small it barely qualified as a studio. It was essentially one room, with a kitchenette and a shower and a toilet. We joked that if you sat on the bed you could touch every wall. We pretended to be adults but the truth is, we were kids playing dress-up. The times we spent there were so innocent. We would pool our money and if it came to a choice between paying a bill or going to a restaurant we would go to a restaurant. That's how we lived.

Part of my degree included a practice teaching placement assisting a fully qualified teacher. I remember many occasions when parents would turn up to the pre-school, see that I was a male student teacher, and immediately remove their child. The presumption was that I was a paedophile simply because I was male. I think the further presumption was that I was gay. Both presumptions were horribly ignorant and misinformed. I don't think this would happen today, but in the early 1990s it was common for mothers look at me with disgust while they cradled their children defensively. Their reactions triggered all of the internal hatred I had about being gay.

It was disappointing those parents couldn't see the benefit of a male role model in what was then a traditionally female teaching position. But when I spent time in kindergarten, I could see the children of non-traditional families respond positively to having a male as a caregiver and over time so did their parents. I left most of my teaching placements with genuinely glowing evaluations.

Colby worked for her parents at her family's video store, Rainbow Video, and I worked as many hours as I could at Woody's, as well as part-time at Rainbow Video. Somehow we managed to scrape together enough money to pay our rent, university course fees, and for food. But as happy as I was with my new life away from my father, I was unfulfilled at university. I'd walk into lectures and sing into the lecture microphone some days to get the need for attention out of my system. I'd openly criticise the course, the teachers, the lifestyle choices. This got on the nerves of one fellow student who one day in the library turned to me and said, 'If you hate it so much why are you here?' I told her I was here because my father was forcing me. She asked what I wanted to do instead and I said I wanted to be a 'rock star'. 'Why don't you just do music then?' I remember being so offended at the accusation that one could simply do what one desired! 'It's not that easy!' I quipped.

But that evening I told Colby. She gave me a copy of *Time Off*, a local guide for live events and pubs and clubs. Towards the back of the magazine were 'want ads' where bands posted various listings like 'bass player needed for grunge band' or 'singer looking to join band'. Colby urged me to read that section and audition for a band looking for a singer.

The first attempt was a disaster. It was a death metal band and I was not a good fit. They loved me but I hated them. The second attempt was curious. I almost didn't call. The ad in 1991 read:

SERIOUS LEAD VOCALIST WANTED FOR
COMMERCIAL MUSICAL OUTFIT PRESENTLY
FINANCED BY MAJOR PUBLISHING COMPANY

Intriguing. Intimidating! Tempting!

I called the number and spoke to a guy named Daniel Jones.

Daniel was very charming on the phone. He told me that his band was called Red Edge and they were just about to be signed to Warner/Chappell Music. Apparently the publisher loved them and their songs but felt they needed a more commercial-sounding singer or 'front man'. Daniel's brother, Oliver, was the singer and lead guitarist. Daniel played keyboards and they both wrote the songs. If successful, I would be hired to sing their songs.

We talked about what music we had in common. We had none. I mentioned I liked Michael Jackson, George Michael, Prince. Daniel talked about Australian rock bands. We were worlds apart, sonically.

I decided on the call they weren't the right fit for me and since I had no experience, I was probably just going to waste their time. But Daniel insisted I audition anyway. We agreed to meet at his house the following week, on the south side of Brisbane, further south than where I grew up, in a newer development called Loganholme. It was near a massive shopping mall with the most 1990s name one could imagine – the Logan Hyperdome.

I didn't give much thought to what I would sing, what I would wear, or what my strategy would be. Yet I had this sick feeling in my stomach. Not a negative feeling. More a feeling of inevitability. It was like my whole life was about to change but not necessarily in a way I wanted it to. Just like when I was a kid and could predict what would happen at home, I knew this audition was going to be successful. I could feel it. But I could also feel the universe had just shifted on its axis. I had set in motion a chain of events that was going to forever alter the course of my life.

Bait and Switch

The day of the audition, Colby drove me to Daniel's house, a modest brick home in a cul-de-sac in Loganholme. From the very second I arrived it was daunting. In a brick addition to the front of the house, the two Jones brothers had set up a home recording studio. The door was open and inside were four people: Daniel, his brother, Oliver, Jamie, the bass player, and Jamie's brother, Scott, who was on drums. The first thing that struck me was that there was no room for me in this room. A warning? A metaphor? I don't know. The feeling was unmistakable though.

The second thing I noticed was they'd affixed grey acoustic foam panels to the walls and had set up a workstation with monitors, a basic computer and a rack of equipment that looked completely unfamiliar to me. There was an overwhelming smell of cigarette smoke. My parents had long since quit smoking but it was a weird sensory trigger. It seemed to be embedded in the building in the same way I remember Lake Road. Daniel's parents peeked out from inside the main house. They seemed lovely, smiling and positive and so welcoming. I clocked their London accents immediately.

The third thing I noticed was the atmosphere. It was emanating from one person, Daniel's brother, Oliver. He seemed to convey, with just a look, that I wasn't someone to be taken seriously. This feeling split the energy in the room. He lit a cigarette, which struck me as odd. Even back then, when smoking was still socially acceptable, you didn't smoke indoors.

Daniel was polite and seemed eager to hear me sing and get to know me. The others asked me about my experience. The questions came from everyone in all directions. Rapid fire. Of course I had no experience. Some musical theatre. Some roles in the now third-year drama student productions at Kelvin Grove thanks to my friend Nathalia, but no, I wasn't a professional musician. They seemed disappointed.

'What do you want to sing?' Daniel asked.

It was at that moment I made probably the most bizarre, left-of-field choice I'd ever made.

'I'm going to sing something from the musical *Little Shop of Horrors*, a capella.'

They exchanged glances.

'Okay, go for it,' Daniel said.

And so I did.

Now, if you've ever seen or heard *Little Shop of Horrors*, you'll know it begins with a song called 'Skid Row' that features a solo intended for a powerful soprano Black female voice. That's what I chose to sing. It was loud, it was soulful and although in TV interviews I've said that my voice 'cracked', it in fact did not. It was pitch perfect; it was just in a higher key than I had anticipated. But I nailed it.

As soon as I finished, there were two distinct reactions. I saw Daniel's eyes widen. There was a recognition. Like he'd found a diamond in the rough. And then there was a stifling of laughter from the others. Jamie left the room, covering his mouth, presumably to release an uncontrollable chuckle. Oliver stayed but his face was sceptical, stoic.

Meanwhile I'd gone bright red. The knowledge that I was being mocked and judged was very obvious to me. This was not a friendly audience.

'Do you know any other songs?' someone asked.

'Sure, do you know any U2?' I responded.

They seemed to know only the rock songs, 'Sunday Bloody Sunday' and 'Pride'. But no ballads. I wanted to show them my soulful voice. Eventually we decided on 'With or Without You' and when I sang it, the entire room was silenced.

I knew I was good. They knew I was good. Nobody was laughing now.

Daniel lit up a cigarette, his parents stopped by again with a cheerful hello and offered me a cup of tea. They were so sweet! We exchanged some pleasantries, but Oliver and the others were quiet. I was so grateful for the kindness of Daniel's parents. In a room full of coldness, they were like a warm hug.

I said my goodbyes and joined Colby in the car. She looked at me expectantly and I gave her the thumbs up. She didn't seem surprised. We drove to the Logan Hyperdome, walked around the food court and got some dinner. She asked me how it went and I said, 'I have a feeling one day I'm not going to be able to come here without being recognised.' I was in a daze. Like time had slowed down and sped up simultaneously. I now recognise this feeling as your soul lining up exactly at the point it is destined to be.

It was a glimpse of the future. I could see it so clearly. It wasn't necessarily a feeling of relief or celebration, but more of a prophecy unfolding. I could feel it all, the success, yes, but also the sacrifice and underneath it all a sense of danger, a feeling of impending loss and an understanding that I had just crossed a threshold. I had taken my first steps into a life that I had created out of necessity a decade earlier. All those years of feeling terrified, unsafe and powerless as a child, dreaming of a life where I had the confidence and the control of a popstar. As time had been slowly ticking away, this dream had been slowly growing, like a seed planted and then forgotten, but now bearing fruit.

I was about to get exactly what I asked for. But what had I sacrificed?

A few days after the audition, Daniel called to tell me I'd got the gig. The ad in *Time Off* said they were looking for a lead singer for a band financed by a major publishing company. Turns out that wasn't entirely true. Red Edge was a covers band, playing Australian rock classics in regional pubs and clubs on weekends. They had been writing original songs and submitting them to Warner/Chappell. Maybe they had received a small amount of money previously to record demos but the truth is, the publishing company hadn't offered them a deal. Yet. I don't know if it's because they didn't like the songs, or they didn't like Oliver's voice, but either way, the decision to hire a 'singer' – which is how they referred to me – was a strategic ploy to try to get the publishing company to actually sign them to a contract.

I listened to some of their original songs and honestly didn't love them. I wanted to. But I just didn't connect to them. I was expected to step into Oliver's shoes and sing their songs but also to tour and be in their covers band. It was a lot to take on. I liked their ambition more than their music and figured being in Red Edge was something worth investing in. Still, I could sense an inevitable confrontation between the two brothers was on the horizon. Oliver was the lead singer and I was replacing him, which perhaps explained why my reception at the audition was so icy.

Before the role was officially mine, I was told there was one more hurdle: a live test. The band had a show at a local pub that weekend and they wanted me to come and sing one song: an original written by Daniel and Oliver called 'Angel'. They'd given me a copy of the song on cassette tape the previous week, and I went to a rehearsal where I'd sung it, over and over. I felt pretty confident about my ability to deliver although I felt no emotional connection to the song. I didn't relate to it stylistically and I had no stake in it because I had no part in its creation.

I showed up at the venue with my mother and father on the evening of the gig. My father insisted on coming, suddenly invested in my singing career after never previously showing one iota of interest. He dressed up for the occasion and presented to the world his new persona: Bobby. Bobby Hayes wore a long-sleeve silk black shirt, a vest over the top, jeans, cowboy boots and, yes, a cowboy hat. My poor mother had to sit with this Village People impersonator of a husband. Colby came too and the four of us sat at a table until the band took a break. Daniel and Oliver came over to say hello and Oliver took no time explaining to my father why I'd been hired. 'We have the songs, we have the talent, we just need a monkey out the front,' he said.

So I was the monkey.

When the band finished their break, they started their next set by introducing me, and I got up to sing 'Angel'. At the end of the song, the crowd politely applauded, the band seemed happy enough and we went home. The earth didn't move and it wasn't my career-defining 'Motown 25' Moonwalk moment, but it was a start. Still, I felt oddly flat.

I didn't enjoy the experience. I was angry about what Oliver had said and was still processing what Daniel had told me about what the future held. I was to replace Oliver, touring the pubs and clubs on weekends. I'd get a cut of the live fee, just like the rest of the band, and I'd continue to work on the original music that Daniel and Oliver were writing. This was in the hope that if my voice suddenly transformed the songs into something the publishing company wanted, we'd move forward as an originals band and get a publishing contract and, I presumed, a recording contract next.

Rehearsals were gruelling and challenging for my voice. I rarely saw Oliver. He would come in for the original songs but then leave and I'd spend the rest of the time working on covers that weren't at all suitable for my vocal range. Their repertoire consisted of mostly Australian rock: The Angels, Australian Crawl, Cold Chisel and the Hoodoo Gurus; as well as songs by international artists like Dire Straits, Journey, Poison and Bon Jovi. I'd grown up with this sort of music but it was never played on the top forty pop stations I listened to. I was buying Kylie Minogue remixes at that stage, obsessing over Madonna's 'Vogue' and Michael Jackson's *Dangerous* album and yet here I was trying to remember the words to 'Khe Sanh' – Cold Chisel's rock anthem about a Vietnam war veteran. None of it made sense to me emotionally or musically and none of it resonated artistically. It was only occasionally when they'd drop a song by Lenny Kravitz or Billy Joel that I felt any joy.

Worse still, singing this stuff was hurting my voice.

My first proper gig with the band was in a town called Toowoomba, about two hours' drive from Brisbane. The band was driving up in a van, with the PA and all of the equipment in the back. They were staying overnight at the pub, and I was expected to do the same. I had work and university commitments that meant I couldn't leave when they did, so Colby and I drove up separately. I spent the entire trip listening to Red Edge's 45-song playlist on her car stereo and going through my 45-page lyric book trying to remember the words to the songs, most of which, although classics, were new to my pop ears.

The venue was an old Victorian pub. As soon as we arrived it was time for soundcheck. But first we had to unload all of the equipment and set up the stage. The room seemed enormous. But I imagined when full, it'd feel less intimidating. I had no idea how to set up for a gig and the band delighted in mocking me. You could call it initiation or hazing, but it felt mean spirited.

On stage, I had my lyrics at my feet, naively thinking I could refer to them during the show.

After the soundcheck was done there were hours before the gig so Colby and I 'checked in' to our 'room'. Essentially it was pub accommodation, mostly for staff. The room stank of beer and cigarette smoke and God knows what was on the bedspread. It felt like it was made of concrete. Time stood still and my anxiety spiralled. I was so nervous I vomited. Somehow I made it on stage and at 7 p.m. we started the first of our four 50-minute sets.

There were just three people in the room.

I looked down at my lyric sheets, took a deep breath and we began.

We started with something fast, probably a Robert Palmer song like 'Addicted to Love' and powered through the set. Disaster struck when I used my foot to move a lyric sheet and accidentally kicked over my water bottle, saturating my lyrics. They were now useless. It's no exaggeration to say this first show was an absolute disaster. When we finally finished we had to wait for the bar to close before we could clear the stage and pack the equipment away. The band took great pleasure in making fun of the fact I had no experience in rolling up a microphone lead. Still, I lifted and packed and did everything they did. When the job was done they all stayed up drinking but I went to bed. I could barely talk my voice hurt so much.

I was depressed and disappointed in myself. Worse, I hated the experience. It wasn't anything like I had imagined as a kid and it certainly wasn't anything like the job that had been advertised in *Time Off*. Colby and I rose early the next morning and drove home to the safety of our apartment. I seriously questioned what I'd signed up for. I looked at my diary – I had two more shows the following weekend and had to work the next day at Woody's. I didn't know how I was going to do this. I still had university commitments and my job at the video store, but Thursday nights and Saturdays and Sundays were now booked up with Red Edge gigs for the foreseeable future.

So I made a difficult decision: I was going to have to leave my beloved Woody's.

Farewell Woody's

I really didn't want to leave Woody's, but something within told me to move towards the fear, the uncomfortable. I'd worked there for five years and on my final day my boss Gary bought me a very expensive pen as a farewell gift. I still laugh about this because a pen seemed such a formal and corporate gift, yet there was nothing remotely corporate about Gary. He was a goofball and a child inside an adult's body but he was also the only father figure in my life. We shared a bond over music that I didn't even share with the members of the band. Even though he was an emotional man, who would cry at a song lyric or be physically expressive with his hugs, he found it difficult to express love in words or gifts. The pen seemed an oddly unmusical and weirdly conservative choice but I think the gesture was intended to express something about my worth, possibly to encourage my songwriting. Plus, back then, an expensive pen was, well, expensive. I'd always known that I was going to be a musician, but whenever I met the local record company sales reps, I kept my secret well hidden. I think both the reps and Gary were shocked that I was joining Red Edge full-time.

What followed felt like a film about a young soldier who's drafted for military training. I was literally thrown in the deep end. We'd perform four hours a night, driving two or three hours each way.

I'd get up the next day exhausted and dehydrated with an untrained voice that felt husky and damaged, and do it all over again. Even though I was becoming more confident on stage, and no longer needed the lyric sheets, I felt so out of place in the venues we played. They were usually smoky pubs full of drunk, straight rock fans who just wanted to hear other people's songs. I could feel the indifference and the flow of energy being blocked by me. It reminded me of those times hanging out with my brother at the mall, when girls would come up and I'd mistake their attention for mockery. Because I had a girlfriend, I had no interest in the audience in a sexual sense, whereas the other guys loved hanging out with the girls after a show. I often felt alone and sad, and would comfort-eat in my room, trying to get some sleep before the inevitable early morning call. I felt older than my counterparts even though I wasn't. This just wasn't my world, wasn't my music and wasn't really within my vocal ability. My voice felt like it was about to disappear from overuse.

I went to see an ear, nose and throat doctor who took one look at my throat and was so alarmed by what he saw he recommended I rest it immediately or risk permanently damaging my vocal cords. Basically, I'd never had any singing lessons, I wasn't using my instrument correctly, and the amount of singing every night was unsustainable. My first reaction was to leave the band, go back to Woody's and just forget the whole sorry episode. I called Gary and explained the situation. I told him I thought I'd made a terrible mistake leaving the store, that the band wasn't what I imagined it would be and on top of it all, I was losing my voice. I begged him for my old job back. I did not receive the reaction I was expecting.

Gary gave me a lecture about how I should have thought about all of this before I quit. A sort of 'I told you so' speech. He explained he'd already given my job to someone else, a girl called Claire who worked at his other store, Skinny's, and that he'd 'have to think about it'.

Well, I told him to stick the job up his arse. It was one of the only arguments we ever had. I felt hurt and degraded, begging for my job then being humiliated by someone I adored. His tone seemed so pious and unnecessarily preachy and I didn't have the ability back then to keep my temper in check. I overreacted and temporarily burned down a relationship with someone I admired simply because of my pride.

At the time, I just couldn't see an upside to staying in the band and continuing with a singing career. Of course, I see now, had Gary given my job back and had I quit Red Edge, I wouldn't have had the career I've had and I certainly wouldn't be writing this book. Alas, hindsight is a gift that gives clarity only with the benefit of time. I slammed the door shut on Woody's and limped back to Red Edge – who had no idea what I'd been planning – and just got on with it. It didn't stop me dropping by the store, though, and that's how I met one of my best friends in the world, the girl who replaced me. The girl I hated at first sight.

Her name was Claire Marshall and she was apparently the world's biggest Michael Jackson fan. Oh really, Claire. We'll see about that. I would go into the store once a week to visit my friends – and to show Gary he hadn't won – and Claire would be there, bending over backwards to befriend me. I was such an arse. All I could see was 'the girl who stole my job'. Poor Claire. She'd been told by everyone how lovely I was. 'You *have* to meet Darren, he's amazing,' the staff said. The pressure to fill my shoes, she later said, was enormous. Still, I put her through hell.

Back in Red Edge world, I found a singing teacher who gave me some basic advice including some vocal warm-ups, tips on 'steaming' my voice (a method of warming up the vocal cords where you inhale hot steam) and drinking plenty of water to keep hydrated. I saw a speech pathologist who taught me how to use my voice, everything from the way I spoke to refraining from cheering at concerts or laughing too loud. I actually learned to laugh silently! A practice I still use when I'm touring. Nothing is more bizarre than watching my reaction to a joke, mouth wide open, head thrown back in silent 'laughter'. I did all this because I needed to keep my vocal folds as healthy as possible.

Red Edge meanwhile were still trying to get a publishing deal. The Jones brothers asked me to do a photoshoot and I showed up in a white tank top and Levi's jeans, partly inspired by the look Herb Ritts had crafted for Michael Jackson's 'In the Closet' video. When the proofs came back Oliver pointed out my man boobs. I felt humiliated.

Separately, I asked my friend Nathalia to do another photoshoot and she took the first ever pictures of Daniel and me together, along with Oliver, Jamie and Scott. Daniel at that point was obsessed with the look of the band INXS and he told me to try to get some 'striped jeans'. I didn't have the money or the knowhow to find such a specific item, so I got some white denim jeans and painted black stripes on them. They were barely dry in time for the shoot, which was on the grounds of an old farm in front of a wooden shed.

We then went into a professional recording studio to write and record a song. Daniel and Oliver wrote a backing track and I wrote a melody and a lyric. The first line was, 'You've got that look, I'm always scared to see.' When it came time to record the lyric, Oliver pulled an ugly face and said, 'What, this one?' The entire studio roared with laughter.

I can imagine it must have been hard for him getting phased out of his own band. I think he made jabs at me because his position was slowly becoming redundant, and his reaction was to diminish me. Even though I could see that his behaviour was as much about his relationship with his brother as it was about trying to take me down, it still hurt. I didn't ask to be in the middle of a family dynamic and it was very tense most of the time. Thankfully Oliver wasn't touring or playing live, so I only saw him in the studio.

When the song was finished, recorded and mixed, it sounded beautiful. It was the first time I'd heard my voice professionally recorded. The song was called 'Trust In Me'. I remember sitting in the car with Colby, playing it to her for the first time. Both of us were amazed at what a leap forward the sound had taken. Even though the genre wasn't my style, or hers for that matter, there was no denying it was the most commercial sounding thing the band had done. It was the harbinger of death, though, because after the recording, Oliver was officially out of the band. One day I realised I hadn't seen him in a long time and it was quietly revealed to me that he was no longer a member. He was now a solo artist. The 'band' just consisted of Daniel, Jamie, Scott and me.

Over time, my stage persona started to change. I sat in my skin more confidently. And the more shows I played, the more confident I became. I made the songs my own and found a way to bring some George Michael and Michael Jackson into the way I sang them. My look changed dramatically. I dyed my hair black and I got an earring. Suddenly I was playing with the attention and the energy from the crowd and I was aware that I could control it, much in the same way Michael Jackson or Michael Hutchence did. I can't say that I was consciously aware of it, but it was as though this was the mani-festation of the person I imagined I was when I was being bullied at high school. I was slowly wearing a costume, putting on protective layers, adopting ways of moving and patterns of behaviour that were like a performance artist. A superhero costume, maybe, to boost my confidence on stage and protect me from criticism. Whatever it was, it worked. After six months of singing covers with Red Edge, I had real swagger, earned through sweat, hard work and yes, tears. After almost a year of playing everywhere from a room of three people to a packed venue in Lismore, there wasn't a single space that intimidated me. I knew how to harness the stage and I knew my worth. I felt like a star.

Oh, and the band? They weren't laughing at me anymore. I was now an asset. I had fans. My own fans. And I knew how to roll a mic lead.

One day Daniel came to us after a show with an offer. Red Edge had been approached by a promoter with a contract to perform for six weeks at a casino in Alice Springs.

This was a crossroads and the axis of power had shifted dramatically. I did not want nor did I need to go to Central Australia to continue being the world's most average covers band. Daniel had advertised for a singer for a band with a pending publishing deal and yet here we were, a year later, about to do six weeks on the inland equivalent of a cruise ship. My journey with this cast was complete. I was out of there. Besides, U2 were coming to town to perform their career-defining and genre breaking Zoo TV tour, designed by the legendary set and lighting designer, Willie Williams. I was not going to miss that. I knew everything about the tour already: the set list, the stage design, the costumes. I was obsessed.

I was far more interested in seeing U2 and learning from them than playing 'My Sharona' to a bunch of drunk tourists. A year ago I would have sold my soul to be in a band. Now, I felt like I *was* the band, all on my own. I told Daniel that I was no longer interested in being in a covers band but that I *was* interested in being in a duo with him, writing original songs. It was a bold move. He responded by handing me an instruction book for the keyboard he played on stage – an Ensoniq ESQ-1 – and told me if I learned how to play it, he'd consider my offer. Touché.

I never did learn how to play that thing, by the way.

Red Edge and I played our last gig in late August 1993 in the tiny NSW town of Ballina. That same day, the media exploded with reports that Michael Jackson had been accused of molesting a child. At the time I couldn't conceive of Michael ever hurting a child. He had meant so much to me my entire life. He was the reason I survived the bullying; he was the reason I started singing. Seeing his face plastered all over the news was heartbreaking. It was as if my own childhood had been destroyed, the innocence that I had fought so hard to keep intact shattered into a million pieces. After our final gig, I danced alone on the club floor to his sister Janet's new single, 'That's the Way Love Goes'. Afterwards I slept in yet another smelly, beer stench of a room. When I woke up, the band was already packed and ready to leave for their trek to Central Australia.

As the van drove away I felt oddly emotional. I was glad I wasn't on board facing the prospect of the terrible six-week job they'd signed up for. At the same time it was the end of an era. I knew I'd never play in a covers band again. I had six hours until the bus left and it was the loneliest six hours of my life. I walked around for a while, found somewhere for breakfast and then the rain started. I had no umbrella. It was a Sunday and practically everything was closed. I remember thinking, 'I wish there was a movie theatre' and when I turned the corner, sure enough, one magically appeared. Disney's *Aladdin* was screening in an hour. It meant that I could get out of the rain, get warm and, most importantly, disappear into a comforting childhood world of wonder and innocence.

I bought a ticket, some hot popcorn and sat in the back row and cried. I was the only person in the theatre. Those hours of safety and comfort, watching a 35-millimetre film, snug in my warmest jacket, eating comfort food and dissociating from my circumstances were all very familiar to me. It was a practice I'd return to at every traumatic moment in my life. There was always a movie, food and a blanket. Thank God for that little cinema.

When *Aladdin* ended I went to the bus station. I could feel the future in front of me like a bolt of electricity, dangerous and exciting at the same time. I could see a path where I was going to become famous; it felt inevitable, almost as if I had no choice in the matter. But underneath all of this was a gentle warning sign, a fear of getting what I wanted. I knew the dangers of fame. My idol Michael Jackson was being stripped of his honour in real time, just as the gates to infamy were being revealed to me. Recognition, success, celebrity, fame – a gilded cage – was within touching distance. There was no question I was going to achieve all of those things. Why was I afraid? What was my body trying to warn me about?

I curled up in the back seat of the bus and settled in for the three-hour trip home. The anxiety monster in my stomach let me know it was awake, kicking and doing somersaults like a demon pregnancy. Outside, the Australian bush flew by in a rush of green, blurred by the rain on the window like some kind of surrealist painting. Inside, my headphones gently delivered the spoken words of Michael's song, 'Will You Be There'. I couldn't have possibly known it, but I was receiving a warning, a cautionary tale in song. I was about to face some of the most challenging moments in my life and I'd find out very quickly that I was to face them alone.

We Just Work Together

It's 1993. The U2 concert was spectacular. Willie Williams, the show designer, is a genius and I have a whole new set of stage moves thanks to the reinvented Bono. He's no longer the earnest tree-hugging activist from 'Where the Streets Have No Name'. Oh no. Now he's dressed in head-to-toe patent leather, a gleaming parody of a rock star with wraparound shades and Elvis blue-black hair. The same colour as mine. Who wore it best? I think I said as such in the video confessional at the venue when I lined up to deliver a message, hopeful it would end up in the fan montage played on the gigantic video screens at the end of the show. Alas, no luck.

I'm sitting with Daniel at a park bench outside his new place around the corner from his parents' house. He's back from the Alice Springs residency with Red Edge. Apparently it was a lot of fun, if lounging by the pool, drinking beer and enjoying the sun is your thing. As a vegetarian vampire, I find the whole description terrifying.

We're discussing how we might be a band and what music we have in common. I'm obsessed with U2's last two records, *Achtung Baby* and *Zooropa* – especially the industrial sounds – and am very aware of the drum sounds that the American producer Teddy Riley is using on Michael's *Dangerous* record. I'm also obsessed with the vocal production of Babyface and his new, softer work with Madonna on her album *Bedtime Stories*. I love Björk. I love and own a lot of physical music, on CDs and vinyl, mostly pop and alternative music. But to my surprise, although Daniel is a massive music fan, he doesn't seem to own that many albums. The few that he does are strikingly different in genre from the ones I do. He loves Sheryl Crow and has a handful other mainstream pop albums. I'm into Depeche Mode's *Songs of Faith and Devotion* and want to introduce him to Kate Bush and Peter Gabriel. But it's not really working. We eventually agree on one song, an artist we both love, Sade and her single at the time 'No Ordinary Love'. Hallelujah.

Out of the blue, he says to me, 'When are you going to get your teeth fixed?'

My *what*?

Oh, there's a gap by my right incisor and my left one is kind of twisted but I'd never thought there was anything wrong up until this point.

'You're probably going to have to get your teeth fixed if you want to be a popstar,' he goes on.

I go home that night and examine my teeth in the mirror and all I see are the irregularities. I end up spending money I don't have on a dentist who uses a composite resin to create a smile that 'fixes' my teeth. Even so, I still don't open my mouth in photos. I'm self-conscious about how I look. It's like I don't trust what I see in the mirror.

Daniel has set up a studio at his new place and we work on a single drumbeat that emulates the industrial drum sounds of U2's 'The Fly'. It's for a song called 'A Thousand Words'. He comes up with a chord progression in front of me on his keyboard. I suggest changes if I don't like where things are going or give the thumbs up when I love it and after a few hours we have a structure: intro / verse / chorus / verse two / chorus / middle eight / solo / choruses to fade. I take an instrumental of this arrangement home on cassette tape with the intention of writing a melody and some lyrics away from the studio. At the apartment I share with Colby in Chermside in Brisbane's north, I get out my thesaurus and write some lyrics. I come back the next week and sing it to Daniel, verbatim, just as I've written it in my journal. This becomes the way we write songs.

Sometimes Daniel will have instrumentals ready for me; sketches of ideas that I'll listen to until I find one that sparks my interest. Sometimes I'll come into the studio humming a melody. It's in my head and we have to frantically get it down before it disappears. On occasion I'll arrive with an entire song in my head, and he has the challenging task of deciphering it. He's extraordinarily patient with me, cleverly extracting the chords I hear in my head, relentlessly going through different inversions as I sing my melodies, as I nod 'yes' or 'no' until he hits upon the sound I envision. Sometimes he'd have a complete piece of instrumental music, which was the case with 'To the Moon and Back'. That song was cinematic and complete from the second he gave it to me. I took his beautiful backing track and knew exactly what to do with it – I came back the following week and sang the lyrics and melody just as you hear it on the record today. I only had one thing to add, musically, which is the orchestral coda you hear at the end of the song. Again, testament to Daniel's ability to transform my then untrained musical ideas into reality, he painstakingly listened to my humming of what I thought the section should sound like and then came up with the most beautiful arrange-ment you hear on the finished record.

Our songwriting chemistry was effortless. I knew that a match like ours was rare and we were lucky to have found each other, creatively. As we progressed, we became even more prolific. For example, I could be walking to the train and the rhythm of my feet would give me a tempo and I'd come running into the studio with a finished tune in my head, as was the case with a song like 'Santa Monica'. It seemed like every time I turned up to the studio, Daniel had a new instrumental he was excited to present to me. We were on fire.

After about six months we had amassed a decent catalogue. Our plan was simple: write and record as many songs as possible, make some demos, and send the cassettes out to every single person in the music industry. Daniel worked at a printing factory and was able to get artwork done for free. I was working at the video store almost full-time at this point.

The drive from the north of Brisbane to his place in Loganholme took about forty-five minutes each way. I was obsessed with working out and losing weight, trying to live up to the image that I thought was going to be necessary to be a popstar, so in between shifts at the video store, I was always at the gym. If I wasn't at the gym, I was at Daniel's recording songs. I carried around a washing basket with a change of clothes, rice cakes, peanut butter and bananas (because that was just about the only thing I could afford to eat).

On Daniel's birthday the following year, 1994, I bought him a present. It was nothing huge, just some skin products from the Body Shop. He looked at the present and then at me with a puzzled expression on his face. 'What's this for?'

'It's a birthday gift.'

'Yeah, but what for?'

'Uh, because you're my friend. And it's your birthday.'

'I didn't think we got each other birthday presents.'

To him, maybe it seemed I wasn't a friend. A colleague. But not a friend. When I thought about it I guess it made sense. He never asked me to hang out after our recording sessions. We rarely spent time together outside of the studio, and he was right, he'd never bought me a birthday present. What was I thinking?

I sat there awkwardly while he opened his gift, awkwardly thanked me for it and I awkwardly left.

I drove home and thought over all of the things we'd talked about as a 'band'. It was right there in front of me the whole time. We weren't really friends. We just worked together. We were a team, with specific roles. They were very clearly broken down from the songwriting all the way through to how we would present ourselves to the public. He wanted me to do all the photos while he wanted to stay 'in the background'. His emotional investment was so different to mine. I thought about the great duos of the past I admired. Hall & Oates, the Eurythmics, Wham! Hell, even Bono and the Edge. All of these people had emotional intimacy first and foremost. They started off as friends. But my relationship with Daniel was purely business. I can't say I wasn't warned.

It's 1995 and I've just woken up from a dream and I'm heartbroken. It's like I've experienced a death. I can still smell his skin, the patch of stubble around his jaw where his ear and cheek connect. There's a distinct scent of his invisible pheromones lingering in the air and my chest is aching with the electricity of . . . love? Yes, the love I felt. No, I should say 'feel'. Because it's alive and enduring.

But he's not real.

These are just the remnants of a fantasy conjured up by my brain from sleep.

It feels like a past life experience. Or a future one?

I get out of bed and this sadness, this grief, fills my heart. I remember everything. It's like I lived an entire lifetime with this man in my dreams. How is this possible? I look over at Colby, still sleeping peacefully. She notices, obviously, that something is wrong and I pass it off as nothing. How can I explain it to her?

As days pass, the memory of this dream and this man will not be shaken. I feel depressed. It's as if I'm in mourning for the loss of something or someone I've never met but I swear I feel the absence of like a missing limb. Perhaps I'm mourning the death of the fantasy that my interest in men is just a 'fad', just a passing phase.

I'm reminded of something I did in high school, in secret. In 1989 I went to see *Pet Sematary*, the movie version of the Stephen King horror novel. In the film, I became transfixed with the male lead, Dale Midkiff. I must have gone to see that movie, in secret, five times. I'd go into the city at night and come home with my sister after she'd finished her shift at the Sheraton Hotel. I had the same feeling of sadness like I did in my dream when the movie ended. I thought I was in love with the character onscreen. So I kept having to go back to see him, night after night, to see him 'alive' in the beginning, before he was corrupted and tragically damaged by his actions. But it wasn't just that his character 'died'. It was that I knew there was a potentially alternative timeline, an alternate universe where I too could fall in love with a man, but it only existed in fantasy.

Earlier, in 1982, I had a home video fantasy love affair. It was with an actor in another horror film, *An American Werewolf in London*, and my object of affection was the lead, David Naughton. Again, a character who had a similar tragic end. But if I watched the movie from the start, I could see my perfect Adonis, young and full of life, and I could feel these *feelings*. I remember being depressed about having forbidden romantic thoughts about a fictional character and knowing I could confess them to no soul. I used to think about him dying and cry. It wasn't that I was sad about the character passing away. Rather I was aware that the possibility of a life where I could love someone who looked like the actor was impossible. Even at the age of ten I was grieving a life I thought was forbidden.

Waking up from my dream in the present is worse. This person is nameless. Faceless. But so real. After a week of going to bed every night hoping I'll dream about him and waking up every day disappointed he hasn't shown up, I decide to immortalise him in song. I take out my notepad and write the lyrics to what will become the Savage Garden hit 'I Want You'. On a cursory listen it sounds like I'm describing a psychedelic trip, but I'm actually explaining how I remember to access the memory of this secret love. Whenever I want to see him I just close my eyes.

The next time I'm in the studio with Daniel I tell him I have an idea for a song based around this lyric. I don't tell him what it's about, it'll be my secret. The melody will be like a bass, it will pulse and throb between one or two notes but basically stay the same, but the chords will move. I don't have a chorus yet but the verses will be this trippy dream lyric I can't seem to get out of my head. A song about wanting. A song about being in love with a man.

By now we have more than enough material for two demo cassette tapes. The first features black-and-white images mostly of me taken by Nathalia along the Brisbane River. I'm wearing black jeans and a vintage houndstooth-patterned, long-sleeved shirt. We call ourselves Bliss and this is printed in silver foil on the cover, thanks to Daniel's connections at the printing company.

Daniel shows me a music industry guide which contains hundreds of names and addresses. He is a genius at this marketing stuff. We make 150 cassette tapes and send them to everyone in the business, from Molly Meldrum to Denis Handlin, the then president of Sony, to the president of Warner/Chappell Music – the publishing label whom Daniel had initially approached with Red Edge. The demo features early versions of 'I Want You' (the 'chica cherry cola song') and 'To the Moon and Back'. We also send a copy to Tina Arena's manager, Ralph Carr, along with music industry veteran

John Woodruff, who co-managed Icehouse, The Angels, Baby Animals and Diesel. John was also a successful booking agent and co-founder of a booking agency called Dirty Pool.

We received approximately 150 rejection letters.

You'd think this would be discouraging but it wasn't! I believed so strongly in the music and what we were doing, it wasn't a matter of if but when we were going to be discovered. Amid the avalanche of rejections, Ralph Carr and John Woodruff expressed some interest. By this time, Ralph was very much in demand, having been associated with one of the biggest albums in Australian music history, Tina Arena's *Don't Ask*. The album was a personal favourite of both Daniel's and mine. Ralph phoned Daniel and said he 'wanted to hear more'. John Woodruff meanwhile had a similar reaction. By this stage I was working full-time as a substitute pre-school teacher and part-time at the video store. Because Daniel's phone number was on the demo tapes any time I had a break, I'd check my brick-sized mobile phone to see if there was good news. Usually there wasn't any, but one day Daniel left a very excited message saying that he'd had a further conversation with John Woodruff and he felt like it was time to 'make a move'.

We devised a devious strategy to get the ball rolling and generate some competition between Ralph and John. Since neither seemed ready to offer us a deal, we decided we would tell them both, 'thanks very much for your interest but we've decided to go with someone else'. It was a risky move, but it worked and motivated John to meet with us in person. He flew up to Brisbane the following week and booked into a hotel for the day. Daniel and I arrived for the meeting and John introduced himself with his hand outstretched.

'G'day, Stanley,' he said.

Shit. I forgot.

Above: My mother's mother, Jean, and her husband, Clarry, or as I called them, Nana and Poppy. They were so in love.

Left: My beautiful mother, Judy, holding me in front of our rented home in Buranda, Queensland, in August 1972.

Peter, Tracey, Mum and me in front of our bright red Mini. I loved that car. I have a bandage on my middle finger to stop me picking my nose (my mother's ingenious idea, haha).

1976, in the dog pen with Peter and our beloved bull terrier we named 'Snake'. We also had a pet snake named 'Dog'. I'm not kidding.

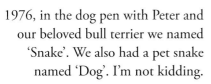

1977, barefoot with Peter (left) and Tracey (middle), on the roof of a run-down shed that would become the beginning of our failed family business, The Sand and Gravel Supermarket.

Christmas Day, 1983. With Tracey (far left), my cousin Michelle (second from left) and Peter (far right). I'm wearing my favourite E.T. T-shirt.

Eight years old at a local fairground. I see an anxious little boy lost, afraid to trust.

Caught doing my hair in 1982. The eighties were my favourite decade. Check out the 'spider brush' and aqua shirt!

Comfort-eating vanilla ice-cream with Milo sprinkled on top, after school. I'm thirteen years old here. The bullying at Mabel Park was just beginning.

Playing hooky from school with Nathalia (pictured) and Tammy at the Gold Coast, 1988. We felt rebellious and beautiful.

Man of Steele curtain call. Nathalia's to my left in her perfect eighties pencil skirt. We felt triumphant.

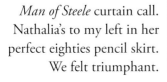

At my high school graduation formal. Note my rebellious use of eyeliner and hair mousse. I love that this photo looks like it could have been taken in the fifties.

After our school formal at Brisbane's The Pancake Manor. We had previously sneaked into Sybil's nightclub for one dance before we left, petrified we'd be thrown out for being underage.

The outside of Woody's Music Store in 1994. When you approached this window display, music was blasting from the speakers, enticing you inside.

December shopping time at Woody's was always incredibly busy. Claire (far left) and Gary (far right) after closing on Christmas Eve.

Never before seen photograph of Daniel and me, then known as Red Edge, taken by Nathalia in 1992.

My first year at Kelvin Grove, at a seventies fancy-dress party with my friend Anna.

1990. Nathalia (front) and me (background, second from right) in the house band of a production of *Ambulance*.

April 1995 after marrying Colby. My brother Peter was my best man. Daniel was a groomsman.

My first apartment with Colby. When I feel overwhelmed I sometimes miss the simplicity of a life like this. Everything I needed in one room.

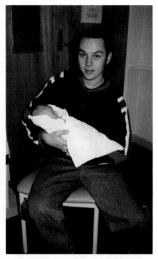

Singing 'Happy Birthday' to one of my beloved preschool students in 1996.

1996, holding my brilliant niece Sara Webb for the first time. She's now an award-winning astrophysicist!

NEWSPIX/GRAINGER LAFFAN

One of the first tabloid newspaper pictures taken of Savage Garden in 1997. We had no budget for hair, makeup or wardrobe. I'm wearing clothing I bought from a charity store.

The first Savage Garden tour. This was a sold-out sweaty club show on the Sunshine Coast. And yes, that is blue crushed velvet.

With the staff after the infamous in-store appearance at Woody's Music Store the record company initially didn't really want us to do, in 1997. It became one of our most highly attended.

Savage Garden performing at Westfield Shopping Centre in Carindale, Queensland the same week.

Singing 'I Want You' and sporting my infamous 'Monica Lewinsky' haircut on top of a Manhattan rooftop.

The first of many appearances on the *Rosie O'Donnell Show* in New York, 1997.

1998, the Future of Earthly Delites tour. I'm in full Madonna mode with Nicole to my right and Anna-Maria to my left. Boy, we had a blast.

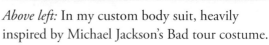

Above left: In my custom body suit, heavily inspired by Michael Jackson's Bad tour costume.

Above right: At a typical American state fair, right before going on stage.

Left: With the beautiful and talented Anna-Maria La Spina in Toronto. I'm wearing a Jean Paul Gaultier outfit, loaned to me by the designer. I used to smother myself in his cologne, so the first time I ever returned one of his garments he told my assistant, 'He can borrow my clothing anytime. The clothes always come back smelling divine!'

Astonished and slightly embarrassed by our success at the 1997 ARIA Awards.

In 1998 Savage Garden were honoured to receive the keys to Brisbane City.

Goofing around on a US tour bus in 1998. I loved sleeping in the bunk beds, despite how claustrophobic they might seem. I found it such a comfort to be rocked to sleep each night in my own private little cocoon.

In 1999, learning vocal parts with Walter Afanasieff at his WallyWorld studio.

With Dave Way, mixing the album *Affirmation* at WallyWorld.

Doing a press interview in a hot tub in 1999.

Loading the massive Affirmation world tour stage into an arena.

I'm still terrified of small planes, even if you call them 'private jets'. Here we are skipping between European countries.

Performing 'Chained to You' with the amazing Angie Bekker and Elisa Fiorillo during the Affirmation world tour in Brisbane.

Performing at the 2000 Sydney Olympics Closing Ceremony. I was so nervous to take my jacket off to reveal my T-shirt. Still one of my proudest moments in my career.

A rare public photo with both of my parents. This was taken at the launch of the *Affirmation* album in Sydney, in 1999.

A pensive feeling on the evening before shooting the 'Insatiable' music video in Australia.

A rare glimpse of the image I wanted to portray to the world as a solo artist, before the record label completely removed all trace of the music video.

At the Yatala Drive-In on the set of my solo video shoot for 'Crush (1980 Me)', 2002. Directed by Grant Marshall and styled and choreographed by his sister and my dear friend Claire Marshall.

Above and right: Another Grant Marshall music video, 'I Miss You'. I got to work with superstar Rose Byrne just before she became a worldwide name.

Signing autographs at the stage door after a show during my 2002 Too Close for Comfort tour.

Right and below: Polaroids taken on the set of the photo shoot for the album cover of *The Tension and the Spark*, 2004.

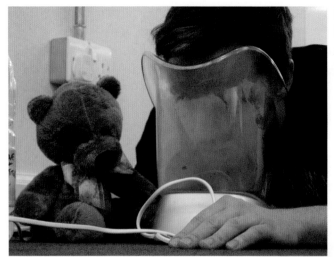

Steaming my voice backstage at the Apollo Theatre in London, 2007.

Good times in San Francisco with Claire. We were just about to go out to a gay bar. This was in the wonderful gap year after the band ended and I was feeling lost. She and her brother Grant came to stay and brightened up my world.

In 2005 with my darling mother in Hawaii. This is my favourite photo of us. I think we look so alike.

A Big Night In tour at the Sydney Opera House, 2006. The hair was quite big too.

In 2007 I launched what was probably my favourite and definitely my most expensive show – The Time Machine tour, again directed by the magnificent Willie Williams.

On the set of the glorious 'Black Out The Sun' music video, taking direction from Grant Marshall.

A wonderful on-stage breakdown during the 2011 Secret tour, directed by Willie Williams.

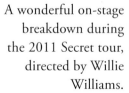

I love this photo of Gary Beitzel, taken in 2014 just before Woody's closed. His eyes are so vibrant and I can still hear his cheeky laugh.

I took this selfie in 2015 and published it on social media to show the reality of what depression actually looks like.

In the midst of artistic ecstasy performing the song 'Hey Matt' in 2023 during the Do You Remember? tour, directed by Willie Williams.

It was a dream come true to sell out the Wiltern Theatre in Los Angeles in 2023.

The man, the myth, the legend. Willie Williams and me seconds before the first show of the Do You Remember? tour in Perth, Australia, 2023.

Backstage with (left to right) Maddy, Trevor, Sharon, Virna, Karl and Lee.

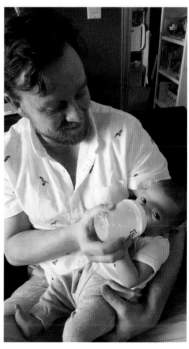

Bottle-feeding my goddaughter.

Real tears on the set of the music video 'Feels Like It's Over'.

I had decided that my stage name would be 'Stanley Hayes' – Stanley being my middle name. As soon as someone said it out loud I cringed, visibly, my face turning a bright shade of tomato red.

'Oh, it's Darren,' I said, not bothering to explain. John looked puzzled.

We spent the day together and the next thing I knew we had a contract for publishing and recording in front of us and were on our way to Sydney to record our debut album with producer Charles Fisher. It was that simple.

I quit my job at the pre-school and told everyone I knew that I had a record deal and was off to become famous. Colby and I had set a date to get married in April the following year. Surely we'd be finished recording the album by then. I'd managed to smooth over my relationship with Gary from Woody's. I gave him copies of our demo tapes and would visit the store often. He seemed genuinely excited about our future. I'd become friends with Claire Marshall too, by this stage, thank God, because Lord knows I'd put that girl through the wringer.

One day, shortly before I was to leave for Sydney, I was standing out front of Woody's. Claire caught me in a private moment looking sad. Up until that point, we'd only really been acquaintances. I'd just been inside the store while some of the record company reps and Gary had been talking about our demo tape. I had played a couple of the songs over the store's music system and the reaction wasn't great. It felt like there was a sense of second-hand embarrassment.

I started to cry and said to Claire, 'They don't believe in me. They don't think I'm going to be famous.'

Claire looked deep into my eyes. '*I* believe in you. I *know* you're going to be famous.' There was something so earnest in her delivery that it shocked me out of my self-pity. Claire Marshall believed in me and that was enough to hold on to. I think our friendship was cemented in that moment.

Finding Our Sound and My Sexuality

Signing a record contract and recording our first album was not quite the magical dream I'd fantasised about. To start with, John Woodruff was financing the whole thing, preferring to 'shop' the finished mastered album around after it was finished. This meant the budget was tiny. John mortgaged his house in order to raise some money and only later on, once he'd signed the songs to Warner/Chappell Music, did we receive an advance. In Sydney Daniel and I were put up in a tiny one-bedroom flat in Kings Cross, which back then was still known for its late-night bars rather than the gentrified neighbourhood it is today. I found living there alienating and a shock to the system. I'd never lived outside of the suburbs of Brisbane. I'd never travelled. And I'd never lived with anyone other than my family or Colby. It was challenging to find myself in close quarters to Daniel, who was not really a talker and who smoked indoors. With just one bedroom, we took turns each week camping out on the couch, rationing out privacy on a fortnightly basis.

Every day Daniel and I would take the bus from the industrial Kings Cross to the pristine seaside suburb of Rose Bay, where the producer Charles Fisher lived with his wife and daughter. Charles had a 24-track recording studio set up in his home and was a genius to work with. What he did to our songs was nothing short of transformative.

If you track down our leaked demos and compare them to Charles's finished productions you'll hear his masterful work. Daniel wanted to make sure his original keyboard sounds from his Ensoniq remained but all the other instrumentation like guitars, bass, strings and additional keyboards were recorded by session musicians or by Charles.

The vocals were painstakingly recorded over a long period of time and I got to the stage where I was able to operate the tape machine myself at times, which I loved. At first I was very nervous to sing for Charles, but eventually felt very comfortable in front of the mic. We were lucky in that Daniel's home studio was pretty sophisticated so my understanding of vocal production, double tracking, panning and laying down harmonies was well developed by this stage. This was a great advantage. The main thing Charles did for me was identify the unique, magical takes. He noticed things I did in a performance that I might have ordinarily thrown away as imperfect. He insisted they remain. That's a true ear. That's the job of a great producer; to identify hooks and remember them. Charles would listen to all of my takes and say, 'There was something on track five you did on the phrase "If you'll be" that was just heartbreaking. Let's hear that again.' And he'd be right.

We recorded for about five hours a day, Monday to Friday. This meant that Daniel and I had a lot of spare time on our hands. You'd think we would have leaned on each other and become close but we didn't. I was missing Colby terribly. I was missing my family, particularly my mother and my sister and my nieces and nephews. I imagine Daniel was missing his family and his girlfriend too.

One day, we were standing at the bus stop and my eyes filled with tears. 'I'm really not coping being away from home. I'm so lonely,' I said.

Daniel's response shocked me. He told me that he was not and could not be someone I could lean on. And that was the end of the conversation. I stood there in silence as the bus approached and felt so lonely. I was basically in a band with a person I couldn't talk to, I couldn't share things with. What was all of this for? I thought we were going to become best friends. Later I spoke to John Woodruff and told him that it was becoming a problem living and working in such close proximity and he agreed to move us to a hostel with single rooms so we could have our own privacy. Sadly, the distance between us only grew. I only really saw Daniel in the studio. He was pleasant enough but he was a work colleague. As soon as I got back to the hostel, I'd go to my room. In my spare time, I wandered the streets.

On the weekends, as a way to save money, I had 'no eating Sundays'. Basically, I would stay up as late as possible on Saturday, watching TV or playing Super Nintendo, going to bed around 7 a.m. and sleeping until 6 p.m. This eliminated the need for breakfast and lunch. I'd buy one small meal for dinner that night and that's how I survived financially and emotionally. It was a way to sleep away my life, a common symptom of depression.

In April 1995, recording stopped while I went home for two weeks to get married. Colby and I honeymooned in Tasmania, where we rented a car and drove around, staying in tiny cottages near the seaside each night and pretended to be adults. It was very quick and very rushed and leaving her felt abrupt but the recording had to go on. I was back in the studio before my twenty-third birthday.

Things were slowly starting to take shape and I was getting very excited about the album we were making. Songs like 'To the Moon and Back' sounded incredible with live drums by Terepai Richmond, bass by Alex Hewetson and otherworldly guitar by the legendary Rex Goh. Both the electric parts and the iconic acoustic solo are a credit to Rex's talent. Prior to Charles's production and Rex's performance, the demo was evocative and moody, but the addition of these bold musical statements made it really come alive.

When Daniel first gave me the instrumental backing track of the song, I knew *exactly* what it was about. It was so beautifully cinematic in scope. I started writing about Colby's sister and her tough exterior, but I was also writing about my own desire to be loved, in spite of what the world had done to me. I was obsessed with the movie *Blade Runner* and the Philip K. Dick novel *Do Androids Dream of Electric Sheep?* on which it was based. That's why there are all the science fiction and space references both in the song's lyrics and sound effects. Yet at its heart, it's really a musical poem about the desire to be loved.

Other songs were also sounding fleshed out under Charles's tutelage. 'I Want You' now had a chorus. Prior to the recording sessions it had a placeholder moment, a vocal throwaway line, but now it was a serious pop song. 'Break Me Shake Me' felt dangerous and real as opposed to the tinny sounds that Daniel and I had been able to produce on our own with just one keyboard and a few drum machines. I got to spend long periods of time recording my vocals, with Charles paying close attention to my sound, taking a lot of the Michael Jackson out of me and encouraging me to find my own, true voice.

The eight months in Sydney seemed to drag on, however, and I was always lonely. Luckily Colby and I had saved up enough money that I could afford to fly home for a visit.

I was counting down the days.

Shortly before leaving for Brisbane, while walking around Kings Cross one night, a discarded magazine caught my eye. At the time, the Cross was much more of a red-light district, with strip clubs and, I presume, prostitution and street drugs commonly available. I'd often see postcards of naked women and ads for 'gentlemen's clubs' but this was the first time I'd seen an image of a naked man.

I remember feeling terror as I kneeled down to pick it up. I rushed back to my room as quickly as possible, the magazine hidden in my jacket, petrified that someone might see me.

As I looked through the pages, some showing pretty explicit imagery, it was as though a part of my brain had been unlocked. It was so confusing. I felt the emotions of shame and sexual arousal simultaneously. I'd never seen another adult male naked before. It was like someone had flipped a switch and turned my world from black and white to technicolour 3D.

Over the next few days I pored over those pages like a teenager gawping at his first *Playboy*. I was only twenty-three, recently married to a woman, and I was realising that I was very, very attracted to men. It felt like some cruel joke God had played on me. I'd stood in a chapel and declared before my family and God Himself that I would stand by Colby forever. Why hadn't God shown me this part of myself before? But then again, I guess it had been here all along. I'd just refused to accept it. At primary school when I had a crush on a boy. At the movies every time I'd go back to visit my celluloid heartthrobs. On TV every time I watched *Battlestar Galactica*. I'd just never said it out loud and I'd never done anything about it. Now I knew this part of me existed, why couldn't I let it rot? It disgusted me and yet it dominated my thoughts.

My late-night strolls became a ritual. I found myself walking around Sydney most nights in a daze, troubled by my thoughts and tortured by these new feelings. It was on one of those walks that I stumbled upon a gay cinema. I stood outside, my heart beating fast. Remember, I'd never seen any images of gay sex at this point. There was no porn on the internet. I didn't have a laptop and I'd certainly never watched a gay VHS video. But now I could buy a ticket to see a movie of men having sex with men. It was dark, I felt anonymous and I decided to just go for it.

What happened next was like a horrible wonderful dreadful beautiful disgusting ecstatic explosion of sensory experience.

First there was the smell. Bleach. Disinfectant. Like a hospital. Why? I was about to find out. There, huddled in the rows of seats, were men, masturbating. It took me a minute to work out why. On the screen was an orgy. The most beautiful, handsome, muscular men, kissing and making love like it was the most natural thing in the world. I was repulsed and turned on at the same time. Then, somewhere out of the corner of my eye, I saw a group huddled together. I took a few steps towards them and my eyes widened. A really good-looking man with dark hair, a strong jaw and a midnight shadow of beard, had lifted his shirt up to reveal a perfectly muscled abdomen. Beneath him, three men were on their knees, taking turns pleasuring him. The man locked eyes with me and motioned for me to come forward. I wanted to. That desire alone terrified me. I stood frozen. As if locked by his stare. I could feel what it would be like to kiss him, or just touch his chest. It was a desire so strong, it felt like a magnet. Just as I was about to act, I snapped myself out of the moment. Like slamming an iron door shut, suddenly and without warning I ran away. I freaked out and bolted from the cinema.

Out on the street I started crying.

My first thought was that I'd cheated on my wife. My second thought was that I wanted to die. I literally wanted to commit suicide. I couldn't imagine how I could pick up my life from this moment and pretend to be anything other than who I was. I was certain I'd ruined my life. There was no difference between the physical act of cheating and the thought crime.

I walked home through the streets of Kings Cross, bawling like a five year old. My heart, broken. If I thought I knew anything of shame, nothing compared to this burden. It was as though every negative opinion I'd had of myself, every horrible thing the bullies at school had said, all the degrading comments my father had made, were true. I was disgusting. I felt lower than filth. I felt worthless.

I went to a phone booth, thinking I could call somebody. But who? On the glass was a sign for Lifeline. A phone number you could call in times of distress or emergency. I dialled the number without thinking twice.

A lady answered. She seemed kind. She got me to stop crying. She got me to confess what my heart was breaking over. I told her a brief history of my life circumstances and gave her a detailed description of what I'd just done, which, from my perspective, was absolute heresy; a world-ending action that had just destroyed my life.

She paused for a moment. Then, with just the slightest bit of necessary sass and an essential amount of humour, said, 'Oh honey, you need to go home and tell your wife you're gay.'

I was so taken aback by the simplicity of her advice. It was so obvious and yet obviously unthinkable to me at the time. I loved my wife. Telling Colby I was gay would end the marriage.

I hung up the phone, dismayed to say the least. But a weight had been lifted. This secret was out of my head and had been released into the ether. Like it or not, I was going to have to deal with the consequences of the part of me I had tried to starve to death. Somehow, it had survived and it wasn't going anywhere.

Being back home the following week was an exercise in anxiety management. When I was in Sydney I was consumed by loneliness. The inevitability of the looming admission of my sexuality seemed overwhelming. But around my mother, my sister, Colby and her parents, I felt comforted. I kidded myself that I could retreat to a place of ignorance again. I tried freefalling into the nurturing habits and warmth of my 'new' family – pizza with the in-laws, sleeping in on the weekend, brunch in the city at our favourite café. The 'tell your wife you're gay' mission was something I intended to do, but I kept putting it off.

None of my distractions were working, however. Every second I spent in our tiny basement bedroom (we were now living in Colby's parents' converted garage) felt like I was delaying the inevitable. The black sludge feeling of dread, so familiar to me as a child, the one that I prayed to God to 'not make me gay' – the sharp, thousand-toothed creature from a horror movie that stabbed my insides every time my father came home drunk – seemed to have woken from a coma and taken up refuge in the pit of my stomach. It dominated my every thought.

The night before I was due to fly back to Sydney, I told Colby what had happened in Kings Cross. I confessed everything in precise detail, right down to the call to Lifeline and the advice I received. We lay in bed, a mattress wedged neatly between a brick wall and a free-standing clothes hanger, and were silent for a few moments. Then Colby softly, confidently and calmly said, 'I think everyone is basically bisexual. I'm not worried about it at all.' She kissed me on the cheek and rolled over to go to sleep. I put my arms around her and silently wept. She either didn't understand the gravity of what I had just told her, or she didn't want to. Either way, my feelings of dread continued to grow. This was not going to end well.

Back in Sydney we began putting the final touches to the album. Since Charles only had a 24-track machine but we were recording 48 tracks of audio for most songs, we had never heard most elements of our songs together at the same time. This meant Charles was often blindly recording parts on 'slave' tapes – using his 24-track machine to lay down parts hoping that, when played back all together at the final mixing stage in a studio that could handle all 48 tracks, things would combine as he'd heard them in his head. What a genius he was. String arrangements and background vocals that had been recorded separately were sometimes roughly bounced down to a 'rough mix' so he could show us an example of what the finished product might sound like. Even using this rudimentary method it was clear that what we were making was going to sound incredible when all the parts were combined together.

We were almost finished tracking and there was just one song to go: 'Magical Kisses'. I loved the verses, but the chorus was disappointing. It was two words – 'magical kisses' – repeated over and over. Charles and John picked the song out immediately as a 'hit' and we'd placed it on the agenda to record. We all knew it wasn't quite right but nobody ever mentioned it.

The night before we were due to record it, I sat in the Bayswater Brasserie and thought about how much I loved Colby and how much I missed her. I thought about what was at stake in our marriage and how hard this time apart had been. I ordered a cappuccino, because that's all I could afford, and sat there for two hours with a pen and paper. I composed a new melody along with the lyrics to the chorus the world now knows as 'Truly Madly Deeply'.

The following morning I caught the bus to the studio with Daniel and showed Charles what I had come up with. They both liked it. I asked if I could record the vocals myself, since it was such a personal song. Charles agreed and for the next two hours I operated the tape machine and recorded the vocal that you hear on the record to this day. When I came out of the booth I told Daniel and Charles I felt like the song was too personal to be on the album and that it should be a secret or hidden track, as was common practice at that time on CDs. I didn't want it to be listed on the album, but for a few minutes of silence to pass and then for it to just appear at the end.

They listened to the song and both agreed that this was a crazy idea.

'This is a number one hit,' Charles said.

He was right.

I've always been someone who can write hit singles but prefers album tracks, if that makes any sense. I understand what it takes to write a hook, to include what we refer to as an 'ear worm', whether that's a buzz phrase, or a universal thought, or simply an infectious melody. But I rarely prefer those songs – by other artists or myself. It's not intentional, it's just my preference.

'Truly Madly Deeply' would go on to become a Billboard number one single in the US, number one in Australia and Canada and top five in many countries around the world. On the Billboard charts alone, it became the first song in the chart's recorded history to spend fifty-two straight weeks in the top thirty. To say it was a 'hit' is an understatement.

I never was good at picking singles.

Rollercoaster

With 'Truly Madly Deeply' recorded, our first album was done. We said our goodbyes and flew back to Brisbane, assuming that as soon as the record was released, we'd become popstars.

It didn't exactly happen that way.

A bit like how we couldn't get a record company to sign us despite sending out 150 demo tapes, John Woodruff was having problems getting major labels to hear what was so great about these two boys from Brisbane. John owned the rights to our recording contract, but he wasn't a record company. He needed to lease the rights that he'd secured from us to a major label record company so they could pay for promotion, music videos, packaging and so on. We also didn't have a manager – that's the person who takes care of the day-to-day running of the band and deals with the record company. At this point, John was performing all three roles, but he couldn't sustain that forever.

I went back to full-time work as a substitute teacher at the inner-city pre-school where I'd previously been. Daniel wasn't working at the time, so every day on my lunch break I'd check my phone to see if he'd received any good news from John. Every day, nothing. Friends whom I'd told I was recording an album and was going to be a star soon stopped asking questions. I'd made such a big deal about leaving my job but now here I was, back in the same place again. I assumed everyone was thinking I'd failed in my quest.

After eight months' recording, I had little to show for it. I had no money, and no university degree. I'd been literally one subject away from obtaining my Bachelor of Education when Daniel and I flew to Sydney. Because of a technicality, completing three years of the four-year degree allowed me to work in childcare and although it was better than shovelling dirt, I still felt like I'd failed. I couldn't finish the last subject because that was a six-week practice teaching placement and I simply couldn't afford any more time not working, as we were relying solely on Colby's wage.

The album wasn't mixed so I couldn't even play it to anyone. Also, and significantly, the band didn't have a name. At that stage we were calling ourselves Dante but it turned out there was another band with that name and they wouldn't let us buy the rights. I searched my mind for references I felt suited our style of music. I wanted to pay tribute to great duos like the Eurythmics. I wanted the name to conjure up the 1980s New Romantic influences that were evident in songs like 'Carry on Dancing' and 'Tears of Pearls'. And I wanted something that hinted at the darker, gothic undertones from songs like 'Mine', 'A Thousand Words' and 'Break Me Shake Me'.

For many years I'd been obsessed with the work of the American novelist, Anne Rice. In her *Vampire Chronicles* series, a phrase from the second novel, *The Vampire Lestat*, really struck me. The character Lestat sees the irony, sadness and tragedy of being immortal – having the gift of eternal life and yet watching everyone around him eventually die – and describes the world as a 'savage garden'. This resonated with the part of me that identified with my sexuality as being a blessing and a curse. I was so moved by these words that I suggested it as the name for our band. Both Daniel and John liked it. That said, I don't think any of us loved it and to this day I still don't.

199

If I'd had my way the band would have been named Heart of Glass not only in a nod to Blondie but also the emotional sound of our music. I always felt, as did the general public, that Savage Garden sounded like a death metal band. Regardless, it stuck.

John had promised that we'd probably mix the album in London and that Daniel and I would be attending. When you make a record, the mix is just as important as the actual recording. In the most basic of terms, when you record, you are getting down on tape each separate sound, whether that's a vocal, a backing vocal, a guitar, a kick drum, a snare – each on its own channel or fader. At the mix, you have control over the volume and EQ of every single one of those sounds and can arrange them in a myriad of ways. The difference between a good mix and a bad mix can make or break a project.

When Michael Jackson made his *Thriller* album, they mixed it quickly; too quickly, in fact. When Michael, producer Quincy Jones and mix engineer Bruce Swedien sat back and listened to the finished product, Michael wept. Not tears of joy. Devastation. All agreed it sounded terrible. Epic Records had set a firm release date and didn't really have the time to go back and redo everything and yet everyone agreed the record had lost its magic in their rush to finalise it. They all took twenty-four hours to sleep, then remixed the album from scratch, creating the masterpiece the world knows and loves today.

Mixing is a bit like seasoning food. Anyone can cook eggs but it takes a genius to make a Michelin-starred omelette. The difference can be infinitesimal – the amount of salt, or butter, or how long the eggs are left before they're flipped. Knowing what to do with the individual elements of sound is what a great mix engineer does and I couldn't conceive of being left out of that conversation. I'd also never had a passport or been out of the country so you can imagine my excitement at visiting London.

Then I got a call from John. Apparently, the tapes were being sent to London to be mixed – without Daniel or me. Up until now, I'd been pretty reserved and mild-mannered in all of our dealings. Daniel did most of the 'business' and I was the emotional but introverted one, rarely speaking up in meetings. Part of it stemmed from the fact that I didn't play an instrument. People assumed because Daniel played keyboards and a little guitar that his musical contribution was greater than mine. To be fair, I did little to dispel this myth. Later on my solo work and the validation of other collaborators would negate this, but in the early days I faced some stereotyping about my musical worth. I was about to explode this myth. I don't think John was prepared for my reaction.

'What do you mean I'm not going to be at the mix?' I roared. 'It's my album! I *have* to be at the mix!'

'Nobody attends the mix,' John said. 'You can have the tapes sent to you for approval.'

Without missing a beat I replied, 'Madonna, Prince, Michael Jackson. They attend every single mix session of every record they make. Fact.'

'Who the fuck do you think you are?' John said.

'An artist,' I replied indignantly.

'Well, don't be so fucking precious!' John yelled. Then he hung up.

The weird thing is, I knew I'd hit him where it hurt. A deeply caring and creative man, John was *all* about the art and I knew that he knew I was right. I wasn't concerned that I had damaged our relationship. In fact, I sat around and waited for his apology.

What came next wasn't necessarily an apology in words, but it was in actions. The American mix engineer, Grammy-award-winning Chris Lord-Alge (who had mixed Tina Arena's *Don't Ask* album and who was our number one choice), was suddenly able to fly to Melbourne. Daniel, Charles and I would join him for two weeks and attend every moment of the mix.

I'd won!

The album was mixed in the winter of 1996 and sounded extraordinary, a sonic wall of colour. At one point, John was standing in the control room, listening to the finished version of 'Truly Madly Deeply' and exclaimed, 'That's a number one single around the world, don't you think?' Chris shrugged his shoulders, as if to say, 'If you say so'. John was right, but he wouldn't be proven so for at least a year.

We left Melbourne with the album as the world knows it on cassette tape. I knew it was special. It sounded like a world-class product – as good as anything any of my idols had ever made. I was, naturally, expecting the next step to be artwork, a music video and world domination.

Not so fast. It was time to 'hurry up and wait'.

Our debut album, in all its perfection, sat on a shelf for the next six months. I went back to work at the pre-school and at the video store. This time it was less excruciating because I knew what we had up our sleeves.

One day, John called us and said the record had been signed to Village Roadshow: a *film* company, not a record company. Record scratch. A *what*? I remember being bitterly disappointed. I wanted to be signed to a 'real' label like Sony or Warner Bros. However, it turned out to be a blessing. John had inadvertently negotiated one of the most successful and artist-friendly deals in the history of Australian music. Because Village Roadshow were keen to make the fledgling arm of their record label a success, our royalties were really favourable. As was John's cut.

In August 1996, 'I Want You' quickly became a top five hit on Australian radio. I knew it was time to quit working at the pre-school when my four-year-old students told me they recognised me from the music video shows that week! I also had a very satisfying final experience at Rainbow video with a customer. A very rude one.

On Tuesdays, we had a promotion where customers could rent two films for the price of one. '2 for Tuesdays' we called it. They'd also get free popcorn. I'd always been good at customer service, thanks to the lessons Gary taught me at Woody's, and could usually turn a frown upside down. This day, one particular customer was a real grinch. I greeted him with a friendly, 'How are you?' and he grunted something inaudible back. Then 'I Want You' came on the radio. We always played the local FM station B105 if we weren't playing a movie. My face instantly lit up. I couldn't believe it. The grumpy customer noticed. 'How are *you*?' he asked, more curious about my change in expression than anything else. I grabbed his free bag of popcorn and his two movies, handed them to him with a smile and simply answered, 'I'm great!'

Things began to move at a lightning pace. There was no more time for the video store or any other day job for that matter. Before we knew it, we had a full promo schedule set up by the slightly pushy yet utterly charming Village Roadshow promotions and press person, Leonie. We'd already met when she was sent to see us in Kings Cross during the recording process and told to write our biographies for a press release. She arrived with a Dictaphone and smoking menthol cigarettes. Anyone who knows me knows I hate smoking, especially indoors. Leonie sat down in my hostel room, lit up a cigarette, turned on the Dictaphone and said, 'How do you want to be presented or perceived? What do you want people to think about you?' She took a big drag and exhaled, using her hand to waft the smoke away from me, as if that would make any difference.

'I'd like to be mysterious and shy, I guess,' I said.

Leonie burst out laughing. She knew, just from spending a few minutes with me, that Daniel was the outwardly shy one and that

I was the popstar. What she didn't know was that Daniel thought of himself as the Simon Cowell of the duo and that I was really a split personality. I had a performance side to me, that I showed the world, my protective mask that was confident and extroverted and showman-like. But inside, I was deeply introverted. I hated crowds, parties and meeting new people. I hated the situation I was in, with her, at this very moment. But I was learning to hide this. I was learning that what was necessary was the mask. The swagger. The costume. The person I escaped to in my fantasies at high school whenever I was bullied – that kid who'd survived all the humiliation and degradation. That kid who was singing these songs and who had wowed the crowds in the covers band. That's who Leonie thought I was.

Since she was our point person at the record label, we got to know each other quite well. She learned not to smoke around me and I learned that all she really wanted was to do a good job and to make us successful. Leonie genuinely cared about us, loved our music and believed in us. Over the course of a few months we became good friends. One day, over lunch near the Village Roadshow offices in Darlinghurst, she suddenly asked, 'Are you gay?'

I just about fell off my seat. Then I held up my wedding ring as proof. 'I'm married!' I cried with as much indignation as I could muster. If I'd been wearing pearls, they'd have been clutched!

'I know, it's just that, and forgive me if I'm overstepping the line here, but you blush every time Justin walks in the room.'

Now, this, 'Justin' she was referring to was a marketing executive at the label and I had the most outrageous crush on him. Her saying that to me was like someone reaching inside my brain and reading my most private thoughts. I felt violated and liberated all at once. I don't know why I trusted her, but I said, 'How did you know?'

'It's obvious. You're like a teenage girl around him. I haven't offended you, have I?'

I went on to explain my situation and what followed was a very serious and tearful discussion about coming out. Leonie was adamant that I had to be my true self but I was not ready to hear that kind of blunt advice. We parked the topic and life moved on. It had to. I wasn't ready to admit that I was gay and I wasn't ready to leave my wife.

Leonie wasn't the only one who'd been wondering about my sexuality. While walking down Sydney's Oxford Street one day, Daniel asked out of the blue, 'You know it would be okay if you were gay, right?'

That statement he made to me is one of the kindest things anyone can say to someone who's struggling with their sexuality. I'm grateful to him for being so progressive then. Over the years I've wondered if he and Leonie had spoken, or if our US management at the time had said something. I've had conversations in retrospect with Larry Tollin, who was one half of our US-based management, who said he could tell 'immediately' that I was gay.

Again, it was like the whole world knew before I did.

I struggled with the knowledge that this once toxic, shameful secret was slowly seeping into conversations with the people close to me and I was finding it difficult to contain. At the same time, there was no time to really deal with it. We had massive hit after hit after hit in Australia.

First, 'I Want You' reached the top five, then our follow-up single 'To the Moon and Back' went to number one and stayed in the Australian charts for thirty weeks. We couldn't get radio stations to stop playing it. 'Truly Madly Deeply', the third single, also went to number one and when the album was released it was mayhem. I'd seen international artists like Backstreet Boys and NSYNC performing in shopping malls across America and crowds going wild, but I never thought that kind of thing would happen to us.

That kind of thing *totally* happened to us.

We did appearances in shopping centres all over the country for each single release and as far as the eye could see there were screaming teenagers and their mothers, all waiting to catch a glimpse of us.

From our first live TV performance on the legendary *Hey Hey It's Saturday* to spending six hours signing autographs at Melbourne's Highpoint Shopping centre, the line between what I imagined Madonna's and Michael Jackson's lives were like and my very own waking life, was entirely blurred.

At this point in our journey, Daniel and I split our duties evenly. And you know what? We were close! We sort of trauma bonded over the frantic pace of what was happening. Nobody in the world knew what we were feeling but each other. We did every interview together, every radio station visit, every meet and greet. We were overwhelmed by the sudden success and fame. We couldn't walk down the street in Australia without being recognised. Anonymity, at least at home, was a thing of the past. But for a brief moment, we had each other. It didn't last long, however. I think by our third time around the country I could see Daniel was realising the scope of our success and began to retreat inward.

Leonie stepped up and became a rock back then. She worked so hard promoting our band and saw, firsthand, the emotional toll it took upon both of us. When Daniel couldn't be there for me, she was and I believe became a pressure valve for the strain we were both under.

I remember sitting next to Leonie, flying from city to city, crying from exhaustion. My body literally falling apart from lack of sleep. From in-store retail visits to local record company branches, all the press we were doing and the sheer volume of album covers we were signing, the job of being a popstar was not so much glamorous as it was hard work. And I loved it. Daniel, not so much. He was starting to show signs of strain. I felt for him. I could see the performance part of this job was something that came very naturally to me but the rush of attention was slowly making him unhappy and it worried me.

Let's Take This Thing International

While 'I Want You' was doing well at home, nothing short of a miracle was unfolding overseas. An American radio consultant happened to hear the song while at a radio conference in Australia. Impressed, he took a digital recording back to the US and started test playing it on select radio stations to see if it resonated with listeners. Unbeknownst to Daniel, John and me, it quickly became a top twenty radio play single – all without us having an actual record deal.

The amazing actor, comedian and at that time, popular talk show host, Rosie O'Donnell, would play a snippet every day on her show, nicknaming it the 'chica cherry cola song'. She would half-jokingly demand of her producers, 'When are we getting these guys on the show?' Word of her interest got back to us, via news media. Apparently, it also reached some of the major US record labels.

What followed was what's known in the industry as a bidding war. Clive Davis, the legendary music mogul from Arista Records, home to Whitney Houston among countless others, paid to have us flown from Brisbane to New York to play live for him. Not to be outdone, Don Ienner, the president of Columbia Records, one of the most prestigious Sony Music labels in history, requested a meeting as well.

*

November 1996. It's my first time in New York and it is mind-blowing. It's snowing, freezing cold, and I am determined to spend my first morning in the famous Bloomingdales café, eating a hot bagel with cream cheese and drinking piping hot coffee.

I haven't really slept. On the 23-hour flight I was in and out of consciousness. By the time we landed and were picked up by the limousine driver I was starving. It was close to midnight when we crossed the Brooklyn Bridge and I saw the Manhattan skyline for the first time. I was like Elliott seeing E.T.'s spaceship land in the forest. Eyes wide and full of wonder but with a tinge of sadness. This was momentous. This signalled an enormous change.

'Hey, I don't suppose there's anywhere open we could stop to grab something quick to eat?' I asked the driver in my broadest Queensland accent.

'Ya kiddin' me?' he replied in his perfect Brooklyn way. 'Dis is New York City. I can get ya waddeva ya want!' He stopped at a pizza joint and we got a couple of slices, before he dropped us off at our hotel.

The next morning, I was unprepared for the cold. But I was so committed to running in Central Park, I put on my black denim jeans, Doc Martens and a fake leather jacket and ran. I got blisters on my feet for my trouble. I returned to our beautiful hotel, showered, but it was still only 6 a.m. I made my way on foot over to Bloomingdales and proudly sat at the counter, eating my bagel and pretending to be a local.

By the time I got back to the hotel, Daniel and John were just waking up. We began discussing what lay ahead. First up, we had a whole day of rehearsals in a space downtown. When we got to the studio, I could hear Talking Heads rehearsing next door. It was surreal. We had a microphone for me, a keyboard for Daniel and a five-song set list to rehearse.

The following day we did our two auditions. First, for Clive Davis and his team of twenty or so robotic sycophants. We played just three songs. We were met with silence. Then Clive spontaneously applauded which seemed to be the cue for the robots, dressed in identical grey suits, to also applaud. Clive stepped up, touched us on the shoulders and said, 'Well done!'

At Columbia Records there was no audition. They just loved the music and were offering the better deal. Clive and Arista wanted us to include some cover songs on our album but Columbia were happy to let John Woodruff guard our creative control and simply let the album be what it was, apart from re-mixing a couple of songs for US radio. It seemed a no-brainer and we signed the deal with Columbia a few days later. They planned to release 'I Want You' in February 1997 to keep in line with the global release of the album in March.

On the way home to Australia we stopped over in Los Angeles, where we met with two different managers from two different companies. They had agreed to join forces to co-manage us. It seemed like a great deal for us, to have representatives from two different powerful firms. First was Larry Tollin, who had worked and had enormous success with Paula Abdul. Second was Bob Cavallo, who had co-managed Prince. Bob wouldn't be personally attending to us, but we'd have the weight of his power should we need it. He put forward as his point person the wonderful Rebecca Mostow, who had worked with Earth, Wind & Fire and, more recently, Seal. The meetings went well. We loved both Larry and Rebecca and even though we had some other options, they just seemed like good, decent people.

We had a day off, and got to spend it at Disneyland, when we came back and found gifts in our hotel rooms from Rebecca and Larry, to thank us for meeting with them. They had sent beer for Daniel and milk and cookies for me. They'd clearly done their homework. It worked. They were lovely people and we really needed their expertise. We decided to sign with both of them. Now we had a record deal in Australia and the world, and top US management for our day-to-day careers. John could take a step back and watch the success story unfold.

We went home for a short break before rushing back out to begin promotion.

I'm home and still feeling conflicted about my sexuality. I talk to Colby about it. The idea that I am to spend the rest of my life never expressing who I fully am is depressing me. I'm fearful of a future where I might be unfaithful to her at some point, or harm myself because of the depression I'm feeling. I'm devastated and think the marriage has to end. We decide to go to couples therapy but for reasons of privacy, the only option available to us at the time is a Christian faith-based therapist who gives me the worst advice imaginable. He basically explains his own marriage to me in a way he thinks I might understand and relate to. He says, 'Look, I'm a straight, married man and I happen to find Pamela Anderson attractive. My wife doesn't look anything like Pamela Anderson. Do I get a divorce? Do I cheat? Do I have affairs with blondes? No! I made a commitment. So I stay married to my wife. You made a commitment to Colby. So stay married.'

That was the end of couples therapy. Armed with that 'advice' we went home and that's when my depression really started to worsen.

Suddenly I was a celebrity, at least in Australia, and couldn't walk down the street or go to a shopping centre without someone recognising me. I didn't know how I was going to live with the knowledge of who I really was, on the inside, and still be the man who was married to this beautiful soul, Colby. It's almost as if knowing had ruined my life. At least before, when it was just my shameful secret, I could contain it.

We decided to take the drastic step of telling our families. But can you imagine coming out without ever having kissed a man? Or having held a man's hand?

We gathered the family around and I told them that I thought I was gay or bisexual but that Colby and I had decided to stay together. Colby's family were confused but grateful we were staying together. I spoke to my mother and father on the phone, purely out of circumstance, as I was trying to get everyone 'in one go'. They were incredibly supportive, even though there was some sadness about the marriage. I think the fact that we were staying together as a couple softened the blow. I definitely didn't receive any homophobia or negative kickback. My mother was adorably naïve, saying she had no idea. I remember saying, 'Mum! I styled your hair and picked your outfits at every wedding you ever attended.' My hilarious sister said to me, deadpan, 'I knew.' We burst out laughing. My brother was blindsided but supportive. He said, 'Do you realise how many kids I beat up at school just for calling you gay?' My father feigned concern about my 'lifestyle' being hard. I couldn't tell if it was genuine or just guilt on his part because later in the conversation he asked if it was his fault. I told him of course it wasn't. Long before the Lady Gaga song existed I reassured him, 'I was born this way.'

Meanwhile, the machine that is Savage Garden continues to plough through the pop charts.

In January 1997, our second single, 'To the Moon and Back', hits the number one spot and we announce a major tour of Australia. Tickets sell out so quickly, we have to add additional shows. The dates are so scarce that in some cities, the shows are months apart. We are a hot ticket, to say the least.

I remember hearing 'I Want You' on my local radio station in Colby's parents' basement on a show hilariously titled 'Hit or Shit'. Listeners were encouraged to call in after they'd heard a debut single and vote. Of course I phoned up, used a fake voice and declared this brand-new song a smash hit. So did my mother, my sister and all my friends. I wasn't sure if the song was going to make it but here we are six months later and we are a bona fide success story. Even though my internal life is falling apart, my career is soaring. I'm consumed with music and promotion and barely have any time to deal with the situation with Colby. If I'm not on a video set I'm on a photoshoot. If I'm not on a photoshoot I'm doing an interview. If I'm not doing an interview I'm on a plane to Germany. Economy, middle seat, back row, mind you.

Mercifully, we have the Christmas break off, but then we're immediately back to the US. In New York, we meet Marion, who deals with all the label's departments, whether it's artwork, radio, media or sales. She introduces herself by saying, 'I'm not going to lie, I hate pop music and I'm not a fan of your record but I'm very good at my job and I'm going to make your album a hit.'

Wow. Talk about blunt.

The first thing Marion did was make us watch our Australian music videos while she laughed at them in front of the other staff. She told us how awful they were and how she wouldn't be able to use them. To be fair, they were made on a shoestring budget. While the average US music video for a priority artist cost around $500,000 to $1 million, our Aussie videos cost about $25,000. That's why the original 'I Want You' video is essentially me, hanging off the back of a truck, trying not to swallow bugs while lip-syncing to the world's fastest lyric. But at 550 Madison Avenue, the big black tower that housed Columbia Records, Savage Garden were suddenly a priority and that meant we had to make a music video that could get on MTV. That resulted in hiring Nigel Dick – the famous British director of Britney Spears' video '. . . Baby One More Time' – to reshoot our first two videos. The budget for a Nigel Dick video back then was just under a million dollars.

Marion's 'makeover' of our image continued at lightning speed. She eyed us up and down and said our clothing simply 'wouldn't do' and took us shopping. She would walk us into stores and literally throw clothing at us. We had no choice in the matter. If she liked it, she bought it, and it all went on the company credit card – which, to be honest, went on the 'promotional spend' tab which would eventually come off our profits. This was all for a photoshoot for the album cover, and press shots because she deemed everything supplied to her via Australia 'unusable'.

We were lucky enough to work with the incredibly talented photographer Yelena Yemchuk, who had created imagery for the Smashing Pumpkins and other alternative artists. Yelena and I really connected and I felt safe in front of her lens. That feeling didn't last long,

During the shoot, I remember standing in one of Marion's chosen outfits – some kind of blue spacesuit – and from the opposite end of a very large warehouse full of people came her shrill voice, yelling 'Darren, suck your gut in!'

I wanted the earth to swallow me whole.

Columbia signed us for the rest of the world excluding Australia, so we are instantly and permanently, it seems, flown around the globe to meet with local record executives and perform our songs in local markets and at local radio stations. We performed the three singles hundreds of times, with the aid of an additional acoustic guitarist and a backing singer. John was strategic in his plan to ingratiate us to every single territory, no matter how small. This meant spending time in the Philippines, Taiwan, Sweden, Switzerland, Japan, Mexico and Spain – you name it, we went there.

As the album's release date edged closer, we had our second number one single in Australia, 'Truly Madly Deeply'. Our theatre tour sold out and I worked out that I'd visited more countries in a year than I ever knew existed. Savage Garden were popular on every continent. The US was having enormous success with 'I Want You' on radio and it was screaming up the charts. We performed on TV shows all over Europe and spend a lot of time in London and Paris as the European arm of Columbia Records was keen on replicating the American success. In fact, they were being pressured to, by the New York contingency. There was no time to stop and smell the roses, though. We had five days off in Australia then it was back on another Boeing 777.

There was huge competition between the UK and the US branches of the label. Back then Britpop was big in the UK and boy bands were big in the US. Neither understood the other's obsession. Every time we went to London the UK label laughed at the photos the Americans had given them. 'No, no, no, these will simply not do,' the product manager in the UK would say. They'd send me to a snooty hair stylist who'd cut my hair into some kind of bizarre Monica Lewinsky meets The Addams Family gothic bob. They'd then take their own promo shots of us that made us look like a shoe-gazing indie guitar band. Shots that, you can guess, the Americans hated. This back and forth never ended. Nobody seemed to care what Daniel looked like. Why would they? He was this perfect Aussie hunk. It was Wednesday Addams they all seemed to have a problem with.

*

In London my sexuality is confronted, again. This time by a very famous wardrobe stylist in the room of my very posh hotel. He's come over with a selection of outfits for me to consider for a performance on *Top of the Pops*. He's worked his entire career with a certain female pop icon but this time, he's working with me.

'You have very kissable lips,' he says. I'm taken aback. Mostly because he's so beautiful. He's young and pretty in that way all young people are: skin untouched by time, age or tragedy and eyes so blue they look almost painted by hand on a black-and-white photograph. He's my opposite in every way. Naturally dark hair, unlike mine that comes out of a bottle, olive skin and completely, outrageously and unapologetically out, loud, gay and proud. He leaves and I'm left in my hotel room, alone, wondering what the fuck just happened.

The next day I do the usual round of press and TV engagements and then it's time to get ready for a second styling session. The wardrobe stylist returns with another big rack of clothes.

'Can you feel the connection between us?' he says as he's showing the outfits.

I don't know what to do with that information. Is he flirting with me? Of course I feel the connection.

'I'm married,' I say.

'Okay, but surely you feel it. Come and have a drink with me tonight. I have to work but I'll be finished by 7 p.m. I'll call you.'

I convince myself that if I haven't confirmed I'm gay and I haven't said what 'having a drink' means I'm not cheating, right?

I sit in the hotel room all night and wait but the phone never rings. I'm stood up. Fair enough. I deserve it. Still, it's a lonely, degrading and foolish feeling.

*

215

Back home in Australia, the shopping mall appearances begin again, but this time for the release of the album. It's out on March 4th, 1997. The week of the release there are so many in-store appearances that I almost lose track of time and space. We have a promo band consisting of a drummer, a guitarist, a bass player and two female backing singers, with Daniel playing keys. We perform many 30-minute acoustic sets of songs from the upcoming album. The reaction is reminiscent of the feeling I had when I gazed around at the crowds in 1987 when Michael Jackson took to the stage. Daniel and I walk out and look up at the multi-tiered levels of these shopping centres and every single person seems to be a teenager, screaming. People overuse the phrase a lot, but it has hints of Beatlemania. It's one thing to watch but to experience it is entirely different.

The record company only wants us to do signings at major outlets, chain stores that existed at the time like Brashs and Chandlers, but I insist on doing one at Woody's. They think I'm crazy. They soon eat their words because the attendance ends up being one of our biggest. Of course it is. We're local heroes and hometown boys. So many people turn up the carpark has to be closed because there's a traffic jam around the block. We end up signing autographs for six hours. Gary is so proud of me. He's like a father. And the pride I see in his eyes is all the love and recognition I've been starving for my whole life. He's grateful I've brought so much attention to the store but he's also proud of me. I've done it. I feel like the prodigal son. Claire, Gary and his wife Carli and I spend a moment afterwards in awe at what we've achieved.

But such is the whirlwind, we barely have time to celebrate the album's entry at number one in the Australian charts.

*

Our first US television appearance is at the Nickelodeon Kids' Choice Awards in April 1997 and it's a massive deal. We have to leave Australia immediately after the album release to do US promotion, culminating in this huge TV performance. There's not much time to practise, but at soundcheck I just know it's going to be incredible. Soon, it's showtime and I'm staring at the red blinking light on the camera indicating we're televised live around the globe. I feel so at home with the massive production and the huge crowd. We're on an enormous black reflective stage, the size of a tennis court, and I dominate every square inch. Images of the performance are sent back to Australia via satellite and it makes us appear larger than life.

Something about those US TV production standards and the way television images look once they've been crunched down in size reminds me of watching Michael Jackson at the Grammys all those years ago. It really is starting to sink in. By the time we get back to Australia, two days after my twenty-fourth birthday, we learn that on May 10th, 'I Want You' has hit number four on the US Billboard Hot 100 and is certified gold.

Oh. My. God.

The reaction overseas, especially in Mexico, was off-the-charts hysteria. We were at a television station once, about to perform, and word got out. There was a large glass wall outside the waiting room of the studios and fans began to gather. Soon there was a mass of people as far as the eye could see. They began pushing up against the glass. Security looked concerned; management looked concerned. They made a quick decision to remove us from the situation and away from prying eyes because a crack began to form in the glass wall!

I loved performing in Mexico, Brazil, Thailand, Malaysia and India. I just remember the gratitude on the faces of the audiences, so appreciative that we'd taken the time to visit their countries. At each performance, I felt an overwhelming wave of sensations. First, there was the tsunami of attention coming from the crowd. I was acutely aware of the responsibility of the power I wielded. It felt corruptible, as in, if left in the wrong hands it could be put to terrible use. Perhaps it's because I was gay or perhaps it's because I distinctly remember what it was like to adore someone on stage, but I felt an enormous responsibility to take the adoration from strangers and turn it into something inspirational. That meant making sure my interactions with fans were memorable and inspiring. I've always known it's a privilege to meet a fan and to make their day. I learned this lesson in 1990.

EXTERIOR: Hilton Hotel lobby, Brisbane, 1990

My sister and I are lurking outside the Hilton Hotel to see if we can catch a glimpse of Stevie Nicks. Fleetwood Mac are touring without Lindsey Buckingham for the first time. We've been waiting near a café called Aroma's all afternoon and we just saw Christine McVie and another man leave the hotel. We stood way back but yelled out, 'We love you, Christine!' but she didn't acknowledge us. It was such a strange experience, having adored someone your whole life and for them to just ignore you. Our hearts are heavy as her car drives away.

But then the man who was with her comes over to us. 'Who are you here to see?' he asks.

Clutching copies of Stevie's *Rock a Little* solo album (the album that Chris Lord-Alge mixed, for those who read record credits) and some red rosary beads we shyly say, 'Stevie.'

The man tells us he is the tour manager then says in a hushed tone, 'Do me a favour. Stevie isn't feeling too great, but you'll really make her day if she sees you. The truth is, we aren't leaving for another two hours, at least. Why don't you come back here at 5 p.m. and I'll make sure she sees you.'

We can't believe it. This man is about to make our dreams come true. We rush off, so excited. We buy a copy of *Tango in the Night*, the last great Fleetwood Mac album, so we can get a copy signed for our brother Peter, and then we are struck with a thought. 'What if that was a tactic to get rid of us?'

We just have to trust this man is telling the truth.

We wait in Aroma's until they close at 5 p.m. and then return to the same spot. We can't believe it. The tour manager ushers a very frail-looking Stevie Nicks out the hotel lobby door and over to us. She seems so delicate and tired. But her eyes light up when she sees us. We give her a set of sparkling red rosary beads. 'I'll wear these tonight,' she says. Then she signs our albums, gives us a hug and walks to her car.

'I really can't thank you enough for this,' the tour manager says, and they drive off.

The car suddenly stops. Reverses. A window rolls down and Stevie says, 'Do you have tickets to the show?'

Of course we have tickets! We're massive fans! How sweet of her to even think of us. We tell her we do and off she goes, along with our hearts.

CUT TO: May, 1997

I learned how important it was to create a memorable experience for fans from my idols. When on tour or in public, I made sure I always smelled impeccable and looked recognisable. I wore the same cologne, perhaps too much, intentionally so that when people met me, they'd associate the experience on a sensory level as well. They'd walk away after hugging me and a part of me would linger for a while longer on their clothing. I took the time to hold people's hands at signings, look them deeply in the eyes and listen to their stories. I spent time in online chat rooms and read fan letters, responding personally whenever I could. It was a privilege.

The conflicting side for me was the sexual attention. Women mostly found Daniel to be the 'good-looking' one. I always assumed I was the weird, gothic, strange one. But now and then I'd feel this energy coming towards me that was sexual in nature. I never knew what to do with it. I found myself projecting a kind of asexual energy and taking on that persona as a way to deflect my own uncomfortable feelings around that.

Sadly, it meant that a lot of the achievements and the gratification coming my way didn't really reach me. It was as though I had created an avatar with dyed black hair and slick, slinky movement on stage. That's who they were screaming for, not this inwardly shy and secretly shameful kid who still felt like he was going to hell for being gay. I'd look around at our band members and backing singers when we performed and they seemed comfortable with all the attention. I compartmentalised it and made myself something of a wax figure. I felt fictional and otherworldly, and I wanted to project a sense of mystery, as though I looked, dressed and acted the way I did on stage twenty-four hours a day.

The promotion for the record was relentless. I can honestly say that I've never worked harder than those months leading up to the release of our first album. I was approaching the destination of fame at an alarming speed and could already feel the restrictive effects it was going to have upon my life and my choices. It was scary to think of the entire world knowing me when I barely knew myself. It felt a bit like being cast as a marble statue, in a specific position for all of eternity. I was being defined by my image, my looks, and the answers to questions I gave journalists. I kept my marriage a secret; nobody asked me to, but I felt an instinctive need to protect Colby's privacy.

But that meant a lot of journalists would ask questions about my love life. 'What kind of girls do you like?' was a common one. I tended to be vague and give genderless answers.

On the US trips we'd typically visit three cities a day. We would wake up in one town, do breakfast radio and sing an acoustic version of one of our singles. We'd then jump on a plane and fly to the next city and do a lunch performance to a radio boardroom. By 'drive-time' radio show hour we'd be in a third city singing for a whole new audience. The evening would be a dinner with a magazine, an inter-view or a photoshoot, followed by a few hours' sleep until the 5 a.m. lobby call to repeat the process all over again.

We did this across all fifty states.

As our star ascended, there was a major shift in my relationship with my father.

The man who told me I was never going to make it, who had shown zero interest in my career, who was the first person to ever call me a faggot, was suddenly my biggest fan. He turned up to every event, dressed to the nines. He got an earring. A diamond stud. His outfits become more outrageous – colourful ties and outlandish faux jewels. He started dyeing his grey beard all sorts of punk colours and insisted his name was 'Bobby' when we all knew this was a recent invention.

At concerts, he would take ownership of the friends and family ticket allocation and seemed to enjoy the power of doling out seats. My mother's side of the family didn't care about my 'celebrity' – they were just proud of me. But my father flaunted his self-appointed position and lauded it over them. He wore his access all areas pass like he was the star. Like a stage parent, he enjoyed wielding the power of controlling access to me. It infuriated my mother, who loved all three of her children equally, regardless of their occupations. My father, on the other hand, was suddenly showing a clear pride in and preference for one child: me. It made me sick and it caused tension between my brother and me. My father befriended fans, portraying himself as this gentle, sweet old man. We all knew the truth.

When the band did our first concert tour, we intentionally 'underplayed'. This meant John Woodruff advised us to be booked into small venues with limited numbers of dates, to increase the demand, thus resulting in the shows selling out within minutes. By the time we were ready to tour, the band was already successful and the excitement and atmosphere around our first dates were electric.

Playing in modest theatres in regional towns kept any potential mistakes out of the spotlight, but I'm proud to say every gig felt historic. In those days my wardrobe consisted entirely of patent leather pants and a velvet shirt which was drenched with sweat by the end of the evening. The success of this sold-out theatre run meant there was soon demand for us to start playing arenas. Up to that point, the only time we'd ever played a support slot was for INXS in Pennsylvania at a radio station concert in 1997. It was billed as the B94 Summer Stretch and featured Amy Grant, 10,000 Maniacs and the headliners, INXS. It was the last show of their Elegantly Wasted tour. It was also the last live performance Michael Hutchence ever gave, just two months before his tragic death in November of that year.

I distinctly remember playing our set to roughly 7000 or 8000 people and feeling very, very confident. We came off stage and saw the amphitheatre fill to almost capacity – around 20,000 people – in preparation for the legendary Australian icons to arrive. A humbling experience to say the least.

As I returned to my dressing room I looked out of the window and saw Michael Hutchence arrive at the venue. He got out of a car and it was like he floated on air. He didn't walk, he slid just above the surface of the earth. Inside our trailer, he introduced himself, thanked us for playing and gave us a cautionary pep talk about staying away from drugs and 'bad people' in the business. We were in awe.

When it came time for the main event, we joined the adoring crowd. I stood at the mix position. That's where I first met our lighting operator, 'Motley'. I stood there and just soaked in Michael's stage presence. He was, both on and off stage, a rock god.

The Future of Earthly Delites

When the album was finally released in March 1997 it went straight to the top of the Australian charts, spending nineteen weeks in the number one spot. After almost a year's worth of steady sales, it ended up selling over 12 million copies worldwide. In September of that year we were nominated for a record-breaking thirteen ARIA awards and invited to perform at the ceremony at Sydney's Capitol Theatre. It was an extraordinary honour and we were thrilled to be invited.

The day before the ceremony we were in Germany filming a live concert for a TV network. As soon as we got off stage, we were rushed to a hotel to shower, pack and then get on a commercial flight to Sydney. It was the first time in the twelve months since we started our journey that Daniel and I had flown anything other than economy. We sat up in business class, so we could lie flat and sleep. I wish I could say that the success had somehow miraculously changed our relationship, but the frenetic schedule only pushed us further apart. It gave us different purposes. Daniel was interested in the financial aspects of the business and the operational workings of touring. I disappeared into the creative side; costumes, set design, music videos and the fan dynamic. It was a huge responsibility having so much influence over such impressionable young audiences and I thought a lot about what I wanted to convey, thematically, visually and even on a one-to-one basis. My conversations on stage with the audiences often touched upon issues of self-esteem, reminding people that they were good enough exactly as they were.

As soon as we landed in Sydney it was straight from the airport to the theatre to soundcheck. What unfolded that evening was something historic. We ended up winning Album of the Year, Single of the Year, Best Group, Song of the Year, Best Independent Release, Breakthrough Artist, Engineer of the Year, Producer of the Year, Best Pop Release and Highest Selling Single. Ten awards in total – the most given to any act in one year and a feat that hasn't been repeated. I wish I could say that it felt incredible. What I remember was feeling embarrassed. I was aware of the impending 'tall poppy syndrome', whether that was real or imagined. I've watched footage of myself accepting the awards and I'm saddened that several times I began my acceptance speech by apologising for winning! In some ways, there was a feeling of inevitability, or a prophecy unfolding. I knew that everything that had happened, up to that point, was going to happen. That's not being arrogant, more a realisation of a dream and the crystallisation of a persona that had to exist in order for me to have survived my childhood and the bullying I'd experienced at high school. I made the decision that the only way I could continue was to become a superhuman. That night, I did. It was bittersweet.

Back in Australia our touring began for real. We had done that regional tour the previous winter, intentionally selling out small theatres. There'd been some friction in that band line-up. Eventually there was a shake-up and some members were let go. Our line-up for this tour consisted of Lee Novak on bass, who had been there from the very beginning, then additions Karl Lewis on drums, Ben Carey on guitars and Anna-Maria La Spina and Nicole McIntyre on backing vocals. Daniel would play a little rhythm guitar and some keyboards. We had laptops and synths running side of stage to fill in, adding to the mix to replicate the full, cinematic sound of the album.

This tour was called The Future Of Earthly Delites and it was the first and last time Daniel would be fully engaged in anything visually creative when it came to the band. For a short period after the ARIAs he seemed genuinely excited about the staging, the costumes, the set list and our chance to play arenas for the first time. We'd sit on planes and draw designs for the stage, come up with logos and colour schemes for backdrops and even colour palettes for our clothing. I loved that time we spent together. It was the first time since we'd written the music for the album and done the first Australian promo that I felt like we were collaborating and friends.

Meanwhile, my personal life was still crumbling. I was meeting more and more openly gay people. My definition of being gay was so limited, I hadn't realised how narrow a box I'd put myself into. We did a photo shoot with *Rolling Stone* magazine and the photographer, a really handsome guy, casually referred to his 'boyfriend' in between set-ups. Just hearing him say that broke me. I needed to leave the room to cry because the notion that someone could be free, happy, live a normal life and have a relationship with a man had, until very recently, seemed not only impossible, but life-ending. Here was someone whose life had not ended but who was thriving.

I went home to Colby and told her that I couldn't go on if I didn't know what being with a man was like. I didn't want to be a father one day and ruin our family by waking up and leaving because I'd met someone like this photographer, or like the stylist in the UK, and had 'fallen in love'. I was starting to have really dark thoughts because I felt trapped. I would never be unfaithful but at the same time, this essential part of me I was trying to suffocate was killing me.

How ironic. I wrote a song about it, a B-side at the time, called 'This Side of Me'. I was suffering so much.

Colby, ever the progressive and amazingly loving person that she was, suggested we could be in an 'open' relationship. I hated the idea of breaking the trust we had and couldn't conceive of ever being with anyone else while we were still married. Even though it felt like cheating, we agreed to try it for a short period. Being monogamous was a cornerstone of my belief system. Looking back, I think Colby was so desperate to do whatever it took to keep us together she was willing to give me any kind of freedom.

Having that permission in the back of my mind gave me some kind of peace, for a little while, and I did eventually have an opportunity to have sex with a man. It was with a stranger, and strangely, it was comforting even though I was terrified of being recognised but also of sexually transmitted diseases. We barely did anything more than foreplay. Given the circumstances, he was incredibly kind and understanding and afterwards gave me a big hug. It was all so oddly normal and comfortable.

I wish I could say it meant nothing or I regretted it but the truth is, it was life-changing.

I told Daniel and confirmed to him that I was in fact gay. This came with the unspoken understanding that, eventually, my marriage was going to have to end. It was strange that, although Daniel and I weren't close friends, I was able to confess this part of my life to him. I must say he was incredibly non-judgemental and accepting.

I called Leonie soon after and told her too. She was relieved. But my stomach was in knots. I felt terrible about what was looming: loss, change, loneliness. But I couldn't continue the way things were. The emotions were polarising to say the least. On one hand I was elated because I'd experienced for the first time in my life what my biological impulses had been craving, but on the other I was devastated because I was immediately overcome by a sense of shame and grief, twisted up for having been 'unfaithful' even though Colby and I had agreed to the situation.

Worse still, I was paranoid that my encounter with a stranger had exposed me to HIV. So paranoid that I set up an appointment with a free STD clinic under an assumed name. They took bloodwork, they asked questions. They swabbed and probed and eventually told me there was nothing wrong.

Then they asked me some questions.

'In this encounter did you . . .'

'No.'

'Okay . . . and did you . . .'

'Absolutely not!'

'No judgement. So, did you . . .?'

'God no!' I replied, offended.

The doctor looked at me and smiled with compassion and a sudden realisation. 'You do understand how you contract a sexually transmitted disease, don't you?'

'Um, not really.'

'Because you didn't do anything that was remotely unsafe, or even remotely approaching the possibility of contracting any disease, let alone HIV. Let me explain . . .'

I soon learned not only how gay sex works, but how viruses are transmitted and what safe sex is and isn't. I felt so stupid. It turns out I'd engaged in some very 'vanilla' foreplay. My fear of the disease had created an overly protective and unnecessary amount of anxiety over what was basically nothing. I left the clinic breathing slightly easier but knowing my life was still going to drastically alter.

I really didn't want it to.

*

The Future of Earthly Delites tour was a spectacle and it ended up being a massive financial success. I can't believe it now, but we essentially had no director. I had a vision for what I wanted it to be like – basically a throwback to the two tours that had influenced me most when I was growing up: Madonna's Blond Ambition tour and Michael Jackson's Bad tour. While Daniel rehearsed the band, I worked with our backing vocalists, Anna-Maria and Nicole, deciding which parts of the show would have choreography. I'd always loved the way Madonna had her backing singers Donna and Niki either side of her. I felt the triangle shape was strong, unifying and powerful.

I adored Anna-Maria and Nicole. Not only on tour, but through-out the following year they were my confidants, my dear friends and my shoulders to cry on during what was one of the most challenging and exciting years of my life. We laughed constantly on and off stage. And of course their vocal abilities were extraordinary. It was a real treat to sing with such talented voices and to bring to life the record-ings that were really just me.

Our bass player Lee Novak, the youngest of the group, was our little brother and the heart and soul of the band. He still is. Everyone brought a special energy. There was the amazing calmness and humour of Karl Lewis on drums, who was, even twenty-seven years ago, a zen and wise buddha; always loving, always calm and always full of joy. We had the lightning bolt of enthusiasm and talent on guitar, Ben Carey, who, bless him, had more energy than was sometimes required but it was an inspiration. He performed all the lead solos and the core of the guitar on stage. Daniel had free range to play rhythm guitar or switch between synths, which gave him freedom to roam the stage and join me in what I planned as very specific iconic visual moments that unified us as a duo.

The set and backdrop were sketched by both Daniel and me but fully realised by the ex-INXS lighting operator and long-time KISS collaborator Sean 'Motley' Hackett, whom we'd met at the INXS gig in Pennsylvania. Motley was up for anything. Satisfying all my favourite pop show criteria, I had a centre stage staircase and a catwalk. I worked closely with the costume designers to create bodysuits very much like the ones Michael Jackson had worn in the 1980s. I also came up with gags like wearing a silver cape that came to life with the use of smoke and wind machines and quick-change outfits that came on and off within seconds.

These were simple stage illusions but they worked. I'd spent my whole life studying the shapes that performers made and the impact of a good silhouette. I understood how powerful the first three songs in a set were, because that's when the press would get their image to run in the newspaper the next day, so I'd pay close attention to my body language as well as other critical theatrical moments. That's how I came up with the memorable image of Daniel and me back-to-back or me over his shoulder in the cover of the live DVD *Superstars and Cannonballs*. I would just stand there and hold that position until the photographers got the shot and only then would I move on. I knew exactly what image I wanted the newspaper to print and they usually did. In fact, I often wouldn't move until I was sure they'd taken the shot!

During the tour, Colby worked on a couple of shows in the costume department and was at the mercy of a very different side of me. In between songs she sometimes had barely five seconds to change a jacket or remove or add an accessory. I was used to the adrenaline and the pace. She was not. It's such a different world, backstage. My friend Claire is used to working with me and we barely speak during the milliseconds we have to transition between songs. Sometimes it takes four people to change one costume. Back then, my beautiful friend and hairstylist Troy Brennan would transform my sweaty brow and mess of hair into a slick pompadour all while I was frantically trying to get a jacket on, change my boots and make sure a battery pack was clipped in and operating. We soon decided it was probably best for our relationship if I wasn't barking orders at Colby in the dark. Seasoned professionals are used to the mayhem, but for a relationship as sensitive and warm as a marriage I would not recommend it.

Of course, my father was thrilled with his role as 'the father of Savage Garden'. He was at every soundcheck and took every opportunity to bask in the glory. Of course, I saw through his behaviour and knew it wasn't pride or love, but vanity. But the abandoned and rejected child in me still sought the approval. Somewhere deep inside was a little boy, relieved that 'my daddy loved me now'.

When I came out, my family were loving, supportive and understanding. However, I couldn't help but feel that my father's reaction would have been different had I not been a star. When I told him, he seemed understanding, but grief-stricken. Still, what was he going to do? I was a source of vitality and represented a whole new life for him. Was he going to reject me along with the fame, attention and money? Of course not.

Daddy issues aside, the Australian arena tour was a monstrous success.

On stage I had become so attuned to the audience it felt like I was touching one of those plasma balls, where the electricity is drawn to your finger. I had the ability to make any room seem like a stadium. Wherever I directed my energy, the atoms in the room would buzz. At the end of every show, there were hundreds of people who wanted to be around that energy, but I usually felt shy and withdrawn.

On March 7th, 1998, at the conclusion of the Australian leg of the tour, Daniel and I paid for a massive after-show party in Brisbane. It was pandemonium. I remember staring out into the crowd and there were people everywhere, most of whom I didn't recognise, getting drunk and having the time of their lives. I didn't drink and stood in a corner, on my own, drinking a glass of milk and hiding from the hysteria. It was in that moment that my friend Claire and her brother Grant first started their guardianship of my innocence. They stepped in and took me from the epicentre of my fame and back to the roots of my childhood.

We left the party, which was where anybody who was anybody was that night, and drove thirty minutes south to Logan, the suburb I grew up in. We went to a 7-Eleven, just like I used to as a kid. We got Slurpees and Killer Python jelly snakes, and we sat on the hood of their car and were just . . . children.

While everyone else was getting drunk, celebrating the success of the end of the Aussie tour, I was with two people who could clearly sense the impending danger of fame. They felt a duty to safeguard me and keep my feet firmly planted on the ground. Claire remains that person to this day.

The Power of Goodbye

The Australian and New Zealand leg of the tour began on January 29th, 1998 in Cairns, Queensland and the last show was in Auckland, New Zealand on March 14th. We had a month's break, then went to Japan and South-east Asia before embarking on a two-month run in North America. After that, it was across to Europe, finishing at the end of August.

Colby and I had been sent an advance copy of the latest Madonna album, *Ray of Light*. It was so new, there was no artwork for it yet. We sat in my dressing room in Auckland before the show and listened to the song 'The Power of Good-Bye'. It spoke of a relationship at the end of its life, with no options left but to say farewell. It was as though it had been written about us.

We looked at each other, tears welling in our eyes and Colby said, so gently and so solemnly, 'You have to go.'

'I know,' I said.

It was a heartbreaking moment of honesty. We both knew we had to separate, and I had to spend time away from her and begin my life as a gay man. I'm sure it sounds illogical and hard to understand, but it isn't what I wanted, but what I knew I had to do. We loved each other, we really did. Despite this, there was this one tiny thing that was really a monumental, fatal obstacle: I was gay and that wasn't going to change. Ever.

I set off to New York for a break in between legs of the tour. I rented an apartment on the Upper West Side and I lived like a single person for about a week. That's all it took until I met Jimmy.

Back in 1998, you could not get a more nineties aesthetic than Splash nightclub in Chelsea. It was a combination of industrial fixtures, exposed brick walls, with translucent 'shower' walls where go-go boys would dance. I'm no prude, but men dancing on counters has never been my thing, but it was exhilarating to walk into a space that was so absolutely unapologetically gay.

Meeting Jimmy was primal and instant. I entered the club and our eyes locked. Despite the chemistry, my self-esteem was so low at that point, I thought he'd just recognised me as 'the guy from Savage Garden'. As it turns out, he was actually checking me out. I thought he was incredibly handsome. He did the thing gay men do at clubs: averting his eyes and then finding mine at regular intervals until eventually I struck up the nerve to go over and say hello.

'How ya doin'?' he responded in his thick Brooklyn accent. He sounded like someone doing an impression of Al Pacino.

At that very moment, the DJ played Madonna's 'Ray of Light'.

'I *love* this song! Wanna dance?' I asked.

'Sure!' he said, and I grabbed his hand and dragged him onto the dance floor. We danced and halfway through the song I had another question for him.

'Can I kiss you?'

He smiled. 'Sure!'

We kissed. It was incredible. And that's how Jimmy became my first boyfriend.

He came home with me that night and we were inseparable for almost two years. It was snowing in New York and it all seemed so romantic. He wanted to stay and 'cuddle' which I thought was so sweet. Years later he would admit it was just because the trains had stopped, it was freezing outside and he didn't want to go home in the icy weather. So desperate for validation and to fill the void of losing Colby, I just decided in the moment that this one seemingly sweet and romantic notion was enough for me to trust this man completely. Having lived in New York, I don't blame him for not wanting to trek home in the snow! Thankfully, he was incredibly trustworthy.

Being with Jimmy was the perfect first relationship with a man; a montage of sweet moments going to the theatre, hanging out at his Soho apartment, discovering Manhattan through the eyes of a local and navigating my way through a same-sex dynamic. We slipped into a comfortable routine that distracted me from a gnawing grief and depression that desperately wanted to be acknowledged but that I sneakily avoided dealing with for as long as I could. We'd work out together at the gym and we loved binge-eating candy at the movies. Jimmy was older than me, more experienced and very, very calm, considering I was an absolute ball of electricity back then.

After a month or so of hanging out, I thought I loved him. Either way, I knew that if I could be with another person, my marriage was over. I had the difficult conversation with Colby over the phone about how our experiment to 'find myself' had sadly worked and that I was, indeed, gay.

The thing about coming out is, before you have a person to attach yourself to, it's just an abstract notion. But once I had Jimmy, everything made sense. *We* made sense together. All of those child-hood wounds that had been inflicted by my father were being healed in this safe and loving male companionship. All of my internalised homophobia was disappearing. Jimmy's was the hand I'd hold under a table. He was the wink across a crowded room to let me know he was thinking about me. He was strong but soft, dependable but cuddly. He was also reliable; *exactly* what I needed at that time in my life.

He used to wear the unisex Calvin Klein One perfume. When it was time for me to leave for the next leg of the tour, I was devastated. I didn't know what the state of our relationship was, but he gave me his polo shirt, sprayed with his perfume, and I kept it in a plastic bag to make sure the scent stayed fresh. I'd take it out at night and inhale his scent if I was feeling sad or missing him.

I spent a few days in London before kicking off the European dates, and through the stylist who had a crush on me earlier in the year, I met Kylie Minogue at a very trendy hotel. We sat in a booth and it felt good to be 'out' – at least in private. For a brief second I felt what it was like to be part of the 'in' crowd. Kylie was going through a transition in her career. The world didn't know it, but the megastar was a year or so away from having one of her numerous comebacks with the song 'Spinning Around'. At that point it hadn't yet been released. She looked perfect, ageless and the stylist was turning on his charm, but I hadn't forgotten being stood up the last time. Besides, I only had eyes for Jimmy. In fact, I left the table early, to go call Jimmy in New York. I was *that* besotted with him.

When I look back, I realise I hadn't dealt with the loss of the relationship with Colby. I had the liberation of a new life to distract me. I remember running down the aisle of a 747 when I met up with the band and crew in New York, telling everyone who would listen, 'I'm gay!' I was so full of joy and so utterly free.

I came out to everyone who worked with me and it became obvious that everyone at Columbia Records all knew because the next time I went to 550 Madison Avenue, the men in suits kissed me on the cheek, instead of shaking my hand. I found it condescending even back then, but I guess it was their way of saying 'we know and we're cool with it'. The local affiliates I worked with in every territory knew I was gay, as did the local US radio promo guys, who started trying to set me up on dates! If I'd known it was that easy for a celebrity to find a boyfriend I might have come out earlier. The point is, I was, in my wider circle, very open about my sexuality. There was never any attempt to have a 'fake girlfriend' or a 'red carpet plus one' to detract from my truth. The promotion carried on as normal and if anyone asked about my private life I just gave the stock answer, 'I'd prefer not to talk about it'.

I tried to see Jimmy as much as I could during the thirty-three-date US tour. We rarely had days off but if we did I'd fly straight to New York or he'd come see me if it was a weekend.

The shows were sensational and received rave reviews, but there was a growing gap on stage between Daniel and me. At certain choreographed moments during the songs, we were supposed to meet up at a specific spot on the stage or play off each other during guitar solos or instrumental breaks. Prior to the US leg, Daniel had mostly worked with me, as a duo, to the delight of fans. However, during the US leg, I'd find myself walking to my mark (a spot on stage marked by some gaffer tape), or walking towards him, and he'd blatantly turn his back and interact with the band or do his own thing. I'd be left looking a bit of a fool. I think it was his way of showing the audience that he was more of a musician than a showman, but it created the image that there was tension between us.

I was doing everything I could to present the two of us as a duo, strong and united like Bono and the Edge, or Annie Lennox and Dave Stewart, but it felt like I was being shut down at every turn. Eventually I accepted that the image of 'Daniel in the background' wasn't just a position he took in photographs.

It wasn't until the end of the almost year-long tour that reality set in for me about the end of my marriage and I officially applied for a Green Card and moved to New York to be near Jimmy. The tour bus ended up there – we had one last TV appearance on *The Rosie O'Donnell Show* – and after it was done, I remember saying goodbye to the band members one by one, not knowing when I'd see them again. Anna-Maria La Spina stayed behind and she and I shared an apartment for a little while. Thank goodness I had her. She was a ball of positivity and enthralled with the city.

That winter was freezing and we were living in Union Square – a terrible choice in the late nineties because it had no soul. Back then it was just a transit junction with a massive Virgin Megastore at the heart of it. It was a comfort to have Anna-Maria stay but eventually she moved out and I was left in this beautiful, sterile loft, alone most days while Jimmy worked. Without any distractions to ward off the pain, I was finally forced to deal with the grief that came with the end of my marriage and the festering trauma and anxiety that had been screaming for attention all these years.

INTERIOR: Bedroom, Lake Road, 1985

I wake up to the droning of an out of tune choir, as if played through a synthesiser and made to sound intentionally terrifying. It's coming from the hallway outside my bedroom and sounds like the soundtrack to a horror movie. I look over at my brother who's fast asleep. I get out of bed and open the door and that's when the blinding light hits me. It's coming from the end of the corridor. I shield my eyes from the intensity of the light but I can just make out the shape of a television, mounted in the ceiling above the doorway. That's where the light is coming from. It's pouring out of the screen with such brightness it can't possibly be natural. I'm petrified but drawn closer and closer to this portal, this strange static doorway to another dimension. I see now the television is a gateway and the light source is coming from the other side of the screen, from a massive place, impossible to fit inside a television. Electrical bolts, steam and stabs of laser lights shoot out from this gateway. The droning gets louder and there are screams now. I cover my ears because the sound is so piercing it's painful. I fall to my knees. I start screaming too. It's the end of the world. That's what I'm witnessing.

I'm woken up. Tracey is shaking me. 'Darren! Darren!' She's holding me in her arms. I look up at her face, then to my left. My mother is there too, in her nightgown. Peter is behind me. He's rubbing his eyes. There's no TV in the ceiling. No droning sounds. No portal to another dimension. I look down at my knees. They're bleeding from carpet burn.

'Are you okay?' my mother asks.

Bewildered, confused, I reply, 'I'm fine,' and stumble back to bed.

CUT TO: New York, 1999

I try to shrug off my anxiety by immersing myself in the relationship with Jimmy but without much going on in my life post-tour, it's a lot of pressure on my boyfriend. The end of a tour comes with its own form of grief. For the longest time, you are surrounded by a chosen family of strangers who form this incredible bond, perhaps through necessity. You start to rely on having that support system around you. Then it suddenly evaporates and you must work out how to live in the real world. That's hard to do when you've been removed from reality for, in my case, at least two years. There's a sense of purposelessness. I stumble around the city when Jimmy is at work, making myself look busy but I'm slowly realising I'm spending my days killing time.

INTRUSIVE THOUGHT: Any moment of any day, New York, 1999
I'm walking around the city. The ant farm of humanity. Everyone seems so busy, so fixated on their destination they don't notice the view. I feel invisible. I'm searching the faces of every stranger who passes by, trying to connect, but nobody looks up. I wish someone would look me in the eye and notice how sad I am and ask what's wrong. But nobody sees me. Maybe I'm a ghost. I certainly feel dead inside. I've been secretly crying for about an hour now. It started at the bagel shop. I got flustered when I didn't understand the store assistant's accent and she snapped at me and I left, bagel in hand, sobbing and I've been trying to recover ever since. There's no humanity here. There's no humanity here because this is my karma. I chose this, I created this when I left Colby. I had everything. Friends, family and a person who loved me unconditionally. Now I'm just alone. What does this remind me of?

INTERIOR: Kindergarten, sleep time
I hate the smell of the vinyl mattress cover. It's so unfamiliar and this sheet, this is not my sheet. I miss my mummy. I'm sobbing quietly because if I cry louder the teacher gets mad at me. I peek out from underneath the sheet and feel isolated in these unfamiliar surroundings. Everything smells like bleach. I look at the clock. I wish I could read it. I know when the hands get to the three Mummy will come get me, but I don't know the difference between the big hand and the little hand. My heart hurts so much it feels like it's broken.

INTERIOR: Mabel Park State High School, lunch break, 1986
I am so self-conscious of the fact that I don't know anybody. I'm walking around the covered lunch area pretending I have somewhere to go but I don't. I hate it here. I hate the uniforms and the lack of individuality. Everything feels so huge. It feels like only yesterday

I was a child and things were innocent. Now everything is serious and grown up and abrupt. There's an emptiness inside of me. There's no feeling of safety, of comfort. I turn the corner and see my pack of bullies. Luckily they don't see me. I slip into the library to avoid them and resign myself to forty-five minutes of hiding in this neutral zone. I sit behind a computer terminal. I'm so, so lonely here.

CUT TO: New York, 1999

My anxiety was constant. I tried to ignore it, like I ignored my sexuality. Like I ignored the fact I grew up in a home with a violent father. But it was ever-present. Jimmy would stay over some nights or I'd stay at his place. I was okay if I was distracted by the relationship, but in the moments where I was just sitting alone, watching reruns of *Where Are They Now?* on VH1, I'd become catatonic and overwhelmed with sadness. It made no sense. I'd 'made it'. I was a millionaire. I had a number one song on the Billboard Hot 100 charts.

So why wasn't I happy?

Loneliness Deep
Within My Bones

The pressure to come up with a new album, and the sudden shift from life in Australia to this new fast-paced solitude in New York – where I essentially sat around waiting for Jimmy to finish work every day – was slowly eating away at me. I must have been craving a normal life, to balance out the insanity of the rollercoaster that had been the previous few years, but I felt isolated, with few friends and no social life to speak of. I had developed a tendency to go inwards and retreat after huge periods of being 'on'.

Colby and I had made a pact that we should properly separate and have no contact. We felt it was the only way to allow ourselves the time to heal. But it was torture. I still wanted to be her best friend, and on some days, I wanted to be married to her again. I remember calling her one freezing winter's morning, begging her to take me back. Ludicrous, I know, but that's how lonely and sad I was. Thank God she was such a strong woman and could see the bigger picture and that it would only lead to heartbreak. She held strong and firm on our decision.

Daniel and I had started writing songs for the follow-up album but he wouldn't come to the US and I had no intention of flying back to Australia so we wrote remotely. I didn't realise it at the time, but it was quite an innovative thing to do. This was well before technology like Zoom or FaceTime. Emails could barely send a single photograph, let alone a song, so we'd post each other songs on tape via FedEx.

I had a tiny studio in my apartment with a small mixer, a DAT machine and a microphone. Daniel would send instrumentals of songs he'd been working on and I'd write melodies and lyrics, record them myself, roughly mix them and send them back. Everything I wrote was about either the breakup of my marriage, the fear of an impending breakup of my band, or my insecurities about my new relationship with Jimmy. Songs like 'Chained to You' dealt with the moment Jimmy and I met. A song like 'The Lover After Me' was my attempt to reconcile the pain and guilt I felt about leaving Colby. While a song like 'I Don't Know You Anymore' was almost a transcript of that wintery phone call when I'd begged her to take me back. It was shaping up to be a highly personal record from my point of view. By the time I wrote 'Crash and Burn' I was in emotional triage. I needed someone in my life to say those words to me, to tell me they'd be there for me. But nobody could. So I wrote them for myself.

Eventually my relationship with Jimmy fizzled out. I knew there was no long-term future for us, he wasn't out as gay to his family and it was painful for me to attend Christmas and birthdays or Thanksgiving and be introduced as his 'special friend'. I realised he was probably never going to come out to his family and that there were other things I wanted from life. Firstly, I didn't want to live in New York, and he was obsessed with the city. A born and bred, diehard New Yorker, he was never going to leave. Secondly, I wanted to have children but he didn't. How could I have a family with someone who couldn't even be honest with his own? I didn't blame him, he was older than me and from a different generation with a different set of family expectations. I couldn't judge him for that but I couldn't let his non-negotiables become mine.

Something else was going on with this relationship. I had begun to cause drama when there was none to be had. My friend Claire Marshall, now a dear companion and confidant, had come to visit from Australia and spent many a night refereeing rooftop arguments between Jimmy and me over the most inane things. It was clear that I felt more comfortable in conflict. Conflict was familiar to me, and the dynamic of having a man whose love was just within my grasp echoed the relationship I had with my father. When things were going well, it felt unfamiliar and that's when I'd rock the boat with my feelings of insecurity. I constantly feared Jimmy would end the relationship. I didn't need to. He was perfectly kind, sweet and faithful. I was just an open wound. It's fair to say he also knew how to push my buttons. So the sparks started making fires instead of romance.

During this time I went to my first therapist. I'd visit this man every week and describe the hollow feeling in my stomach, a flesh-eating feeling I woke up with every single day. In response, he would just shrug his shoulders and tell me I had unresolved childhood issues. No shit, buddy! I was fucking depressed and I thought about killing myself most days. How did he not diagnose that? He never once discussed or asked me about suicidal thoughts or depressive or intrusive thinking. The feeling of wasps stinging me had, over time, become a permanent, dull pain that woke from its slumber every morning without fail, to remind me there was nothing to look forward to. When I explained this to the therapist he seemed, himself, depressed. Perhaps he was just immune to New York living; perhaps I was not yet initiated to the cultural robustness needed to survive in the concrete jungle, but there was a huge disconnect. Talk therapy didn't work and the stiff upper lip needed to survive in the city was killing me.

I'd wake up most mornings, kiss Jimmy goodbye, and then cry. I used food as a way to push down my uncomfortable feelings. Oatmeal was the most effective. It was thick and sticky and it made me feel comforted. Eating oatmeal created a sensation like I'd laid a concrete tomb over my unwanted feelings. This would allow me to get out of the apartment and walk all day, seemingly without purpose, around Manhattan. While many of my favourite artists turned to substance abuse at their lowest ebb, binge-eating was my drug of choice. One thing that did help me get out of my head – at least for a while – was charity work. I volunteered for a wonderful charity called God's Love We Deliver which prepared and delivered food for people who were living with HIV.

I thought the charity work would give me a sense of hope and allow me to make new friends. It did neither. We would prepare food and often have to leave it with a caregiver or outside an apartment. There was no human contact with those who I felt needed it the most. Inside the kitchen, because I was new, I didn't know anybody and fell way outside the well-established cliques. I was not great at socialising so even the manual work was a lonely experience. I was glad to have served a higher purpose and not indulge my own privileged sadness on the days I worked there, but I didn't feel like I was contributing much. I had fantasies about making a new best friend while cutting carrots for a vegetable stew but that just never happened. I often stood at a table of ten or more people and worked in silence until my shift was over.

The weather mirrored my emotions. It was grey most of the time. I'd find places to walk, undisturbed, and cry, quietly to myself, until Jimmy got home from work. He'd ask how my day was and I'd lie and say it was great. I'd make sure that I'd worked out to keep my body in a shape he found attractive because the gym was his main obsession – he was fixated on his appearance. Not in a narcissistic way, just the way most gay men were in the late 1990s. There was this impossible beauty standard to uphold and it involved having zero body fat. Prior to coming out, I'd never examined my body so meticulously or worried so much about the shape of my torso or the number of abs I had. Now I was lying in bed each night next to a mirror, albeit a human one, full of the same insecurities.

When I first moved to New York I tried to use passive-aggression to change the day-to-day encounters I was having at the local bodega near my apartment. I'd approach the counter with a smile on my face and the items I was buying; usually a chocolate Yoohoo milk drink and a banana. I'd ask a polite question like, 'How are you doing today?' to which I'd receive a grunt. The person behind the counter would ring up my items, bark the amount due, I'd hand over the cash and they'd slam the change into my hand.

'You're *welcome*!' I'd then say, slinging my words back at them like some kind of sarcasm bomb.

My friend Myrna, a Cuban American who worked at Columbia Records and who'd grown up in New York, laughed at me after witnessing one of these interactions. 'What are you doing? You think you're gonna change the culture of the whole city by doing that?'

She was right.

I felt overwhelmed by all the changes in my life. Not just the sudden fame and then sudden silence between records, but also being torn from my native Australia and feeling isolated in a country and a culture I thought I knew from movies and television but clearly didn't. Eventually I stopped going to that shoulder-shrugging therapist and when the chance came to do some work in San Francisco – a one-off single with the prestigious Grammy Award winning writer and producer Walter Afanasieff – I jumped at the chance to get out of Gotham for a while.

Walter Afanasieff's credits read like the musical *Guinness Book of World Records*. He was responsible for co-writing and co-producing the first six Mariah Carey albums, and worked with Whitney Houston, Celine Dion, Barbra Streisand and countless other legends. He won multiple Grammy Awards including Record of the Year for producing the Celine Dion classic 'My Heart Will Go On' which featured in the film *Titanic*.

When I arrived at his home I felt an instant sense of calm. He lived in the beautiful city of San Rafael, about a twenty-minute drive north of the Golden Gate Bridge. It was cold, but the kind of cold where you were warmed by timber interiors, open fireplaces and cosy blankets. Walter had an enormous compound – back then known as WallyWorld.

In spite of his impressive reputation, I wasn't initially sure about working with him. I didn't think his style suited the direction I wanted to take the band. Daniel and I had been preparing songs for our follow-up album and I was intent on making a very progressive one. I wanted to move our sound forward and work with Marius de Vries and William Orbit – the team behind Madonna's *Ray of Light*. On our debut, Columbia Records had no say. It was already completed and while they made some minor changes by hiring Mike Pela to remix a couple of songs, it wasn't necessary, but rather a classic and strategic political move John Woodruff taught us. Sometimes in the record business, you allow the label to do something inconsequential – say, commission a new 'mix' of a song that really didn't sound very different to the previous one. Deny them and you'd have an enemy. Allow their suggestion, and they felt like they had more of a stake in the album, felt more invested and were more likely to promote your record. Vanity and egos. That's all it was.

For our second album, they were pushing for us to work with Walter. But I was concerned he was too commercial. Don Ienner, the president of Columbia Records, very cleverly knew how charming Walter was and that we'd likely hit if off if we spoke on the phone.

When Walter and I spoke, I sensed his approach was gentle and genuine. He started with compliments followed by assurances that we'd just try this one song and see what happened.

I remember falling into bed in one of the bedrooms in the luxurious guest house on his property after a five-hour flight from New York and taking in all this magical compound had to offer. The house was newly built in the style of a farmhouse. It smelled of spruce and new carpets and firewood burning softly in each of the guest rooms. There were gold and platinum plaques on the walls. A private gym and a massive blue tennis court. There were even golf carts to transport you around the complex and personal chefs employed to create healthy and delicious food. The huge chef's kitchen fridge was stocked with produce from a store I'd never heard of at the time, Whole Foods Market. It felt like everything was better in California.

Daniel arrived the next day and we began working on 'The Animal Song'. Hilariously, months earlier, Disney had asked us to write a song for a new film. There were two choices; *Runaway Bride* starring Julia Roberts and Richard Gere, or *The Other Sister*, starring Juliette Lewis, Giovanni Ribisi and Diane Keaton. I actually watched both films and decided the Julia Roberts film wasn't as appealing, and therefore wouldn't be a hit. Of course, *Runaway Bride* was a monster success, bringing in over $300 million at the box office. You've probably never heard of *The Other Sister*. I told you I was bad at picking hits.

Without a crystal ball, we put an incredible amount of work into that song. Walter took Daniel's simple drum sounds and keyboard programming and turned them into a symphonic orchestral jungle of wonderful noise, worthy of a film score. He took my simple vocal arrangements and turned them into a spectrum of colour – teaching me things about harmonies and recording that I still use to this day. The sheer amount of vocal tracks was in the hundreds and I was exhausted at the end of almost three days of singing. Walter brought in some of the finest musicians I'd ever heard, laying down live guitars and bass. He really took our sound to the next level. There was no doubt that he would be the person we'd use for our follow-up album. Quite simply, he made an astonishingly great sounding record. I still marvel at how good it sounds.

At the end of our time in San Rafael, I knew not only that my relationship with Jimmy was over, but so was my relationship with New York. I wanted to live in Marin County, the area that comprised the northern suburbs of San Francisco.

On the set of the music video for 'The Animal Song', I met a dancer, a woman, who seemed to have an otherworldly connection to me. I can't explain it, but she was somehow able to see inside my heart. She asked me if I'd ever experienced reiki. I hadn't. She offered to help. I didn't know what that meant but she said after the shoot, she wanted to do some work on my 'energy'. I knew the interaction wasn't sexual, but I was terrified all the same. After we wrapped the video, she came back to my room at the Mondrian Hotel on Sunset Boulevard. She moved her hands over my heart, floating them above me, and tears began to flow. Pain, from deep inside, poured out of me. I felt this ebb and flow between us. I could visualise a ball of dark energy being scooped up in her hands and slowly moved around in my body before being released. It seemed like hours went by. When we finished, I sat up calmly.

She stared lovingly into my eyes and said, 'You do know it's okay that you're gay, right?'

I cried all over again.

The Second Album

As Daniel and I had been working remotely – him in Australia, me in the New York – we only had a handful of songs for the second album: mostly instrumentals he'd worked on and I'd created melodies and lyrics for like 'Gunning Down Romance', 'Crash and Burn', 'The Best Thing', 'Chained to You', 'You Can Still Be Free' and 'The Lover After Me'. I'd pretty much written 'Hold Me' in my head and hummed it to Daniel from the guitar riff all the way down to the chord progression. And we had 'I Don't Care' – another song I'd written as a melody first, with the rhythm of walking to and from the train station.

When he flew into San Rafael, we started working methodically at WallyWorld with the wonderful programming assistant Greg Bieck and the lovely engineer Kent Matke. Walter would spend literally hours choosing the sound of a kick drum from a drum machine. His work as a producer was like nothing I'd known up to that point or since. He began his life in Brazil and learned to play piano as a child, by ear. I had no idea he'd played on Whitney Houston's first album and on most of her productions. He'd unknowingly taught me how to write music because I was listening to his incredible synth bass lines as a teen. A song like 'So Emotional', for example, is one of my favourite pop songs of all time, and although not properly credited, I can tell Walter is all over that production.

250

On our *Affirmation* recording sessions, Walter would take our basic demos, study them, then replace the original demo programming with his own keyboard work, diligently and impeccably taking the recording to levels neither Daniel nor I could reach on our own. He'd call in some of the most famous session players at the time, like bass player Nathan East who played for Michael Jackson and Eric Clapton, or guitarist Michael Landau who you would have heard on records by everyone from Luis Miguel to Joni Mitchell. When it came to drums, we were blown away to have the genius Steve Smith from rock band Journey. We were blessed to have that level of musicianship and it truly was a superstar backing band.

I cannot deny the alchemy Daniel and I had – the magic and once-in-a-lifetime songwriting chemistry. When we combined our creative talents, the results were undeniable. But neither of us would have described ourselves as session players and I certainly didn't think I was the best singer in the world. There was just something special about our songs. You can spend all the time and money in the world, and apply the latest technology available to an average song, but you won't make it a hit. Lyrics and melody are king.

I'd accepted the fact that our relationship was purely business, but I noticed during the recording process that he didn't seem to want to be there for very long. He was interested in other things, like building a house, investing money and getting back to Australia. I was obsessed with the music and its production. It was a happy period for me. It was like my life became magical again. Most of the sadness and anxiety seemed to go up in smoke now that I was back in a creative space. Soaking up time in the studio and being around people like Walter was like an apprenticeship. I felt more alive and inspired than I had in the year between making the two albums, but I could see that Daniel's enthusiasm was slowly fading; it was almost like a light inside him had switched off.

In some ways it was a good thing for our songwriting, because his disconnection led to boredom, and that boredom led us to the piano. And that's how the remaining songs on the album were written. My theory is that Daniel loved making demos at home, when he was in control of the sound. He also loved writing songs. But when the process was handed over to someone else, it was less interesting. Truthfully, we both got bored sometimes because once our parts were done, there was a lot of waiting around. But the process of being bored forced us to spend time together at a real piano and resulted in some of the best material we ever created. In between the formal recording sessions, he'd tinker away on the keys and I'd start spontaneously singing.

When it came time to write 'Two Beds and a Coffee Machine' I don't really know what came over me. Up to that point I'd never told anyone other than my close personal friends the truth about my childhood, and suddenly I was singing this song about an abused mother and her children on the run. It was incredibly raw and revealing and I cried the first time I sang it. I called my mother to ask her permission to put the song on the album and at first she said yes. I assured her I wouldn't tell anyone it was about 'me'. Then something happened. Either she got intimidated by the thought of the repercussions from my father or she simply felt it would be too exposing, but she called to tell me, weeks later, that she'd 'changed her mind'.

By that point the song was already recorded. We'd spent a small fortune on the orchestra and there were live strings. It was also one of the best songs Daniel and I had ever written.

It was a very tough position for me to take, but I stood my ground. With as much compassion as I could convey, I told my mother that I felt that putting the song out into the world would help more people than it would hurt. Denying her wishes felt cruel at the time but there was a part of me that also felt incredibly brave. There was a side of me that needed to be heard and I knew this song was the beginning of some kind of healing. Yes, my mother's abuse was her story, but it was mine too.

Ultimately I backed myself and decided to risk the wrath of family criticism and keep the song on the album. Unfortunately, doing so unlocked a level of sadness I had no idea was there. By acknowledging the pain and the trauma, in song, and seeing it in abstract – hearing it out loud – I was finally able to see how much grief I'd been holding all of my life. Up until now I'd done a pretty good job of surviving, using whatever coping mechanisms I had to get by. But now this cancerous memory was out of my brain and on the operating table, I was able to objectively study it. It was ugly, to say the least.

The introspection helped me form a more cohesive narrative for the album. I saw that I was writing a story about recovering from heartbreak but also about forgiveness – for myself but also for what had happened in my childhood. I started looking at the story being told and one day, while Daniel and I were waiting for Walter to choose a kick drum sound, Daniel pulled up a drum loop sample, the one that is now familiar to most people as the intro to 'Affirmation' – the fast 'garage' sounding drum pattern that runs the length of the entire song – and I started singing a melody and then writing lyrics that were single word affirmations. This was the birth of the album title and the lyric that you couldn't control or choose your sexuality. Declaring that truth was instrumental in the journey to loving myself.

Around this time, Leonie, the Australian publicist who first asked me if I was gay, convinced me that the band needed an 'assistant'. No sooner than I could blink, she was on a plane to San Rafael and had holed up in the guest house with Daniel and me. This arrangement would continue for many years, until I'd eventually meet and introduce her to the man she would marry. I ended up performing at their wedding.

But back in 1999 we were wrapping up recording the album with our new assistant documenting the process for the internet and our fanzine. We were all extremely proud of the work we'd done. Our managers at the time, Larry and Rebecca, felt it was a huge leap forward in sound and songwriting but for me, most importantly, John Woodruff loved it. His opinion meant everything.

We assumed we'd release 'Crash and Burn' as the first single and were all certain that 'Affirmation' was a massive hit. We sent the songs off to Columbia Records in New York via FedEx and waited.

And waited.

Nothing.

A few days later we received a message, via Larry, that the label were unhappy. To paraphrase, they said they 'liked' the album but they felt there was no hit on there. Apparently Don Ienner said something like, 'There's no "Truly Madly Deeply".'

Imagine the feeling of opening a vein, like I had, talking about my marriage, my childhood, my suicidal thoughts and having your efforts dismissed.

I remember being so furious I said, 'He wants a hit, we'll write him a fucking hit!'

Daniel and I disappeared to the piano room for maybe two hours, maximum. We started off thinking we'd write a very cheesy rip-off of 'Truly Madly Deeply' as a 'fuck you' to the record company. What happened took me completely by surprise. We wrote something utterly sincere and heartwarming. Daniel started playing and I sang, 'Maybe it's intuition . . .'

The incredible thing about 'I Knew I Loved You' is that I was not in love at the time. I felt very cynical about love. It's a song I now believe was a prediction about future love I would experience.

I remember getting a massive lump in my throat and it made me want to cry. That might seem weird, for a song that was about nobody and nothing, right? But it's true. It seemed to be deeply personal and touch on a need and a feeling I so desperately wanted; to be sincerely loved. However, at that point I couldn't conceive of asking for or even knowing how to invite love into my life. Somehow, there was a mystical process of creating something I did not yet know, yet I channelled something magical into existence.

We took the song into the studio and played it for Walter. He lost his mind. We recorded a demo and then Walter replayed the piano. His performance was magnificent and once again took the arrangement to a place much more sophisticated than our simple demo. I laid down my vocals and my backing vocals. Walter programmed some drums and percussion and some bass. A few days later we sent the final mixed song off to the label in New York with a handwritten note that said, 'Here's your fucking number one single.'

We didn't concern ourselves with their reaction. We knew we'd written a global hit. Of course the label loved it. It was strange the way power worked back then. Because the president had 'demanded' we write another song, it was like a demonstration of the power of his influence. Not only did it serve to inflate his ego but it was evidence to all that he was able to intimidate his artists into doing his bidding. He got his ballad. We got our second Billboard number one. Is it because the song was as good as or better than 'Truly Madly Deeply'? Or is it because the boss's fragile ego was stroked to the point he felt comfortable enough to threaten his staff to make it a hit? I'll never know. But a hit it certainly was.

We started mixing the album midway through recording. I did some of the vocals in New York and some in San Francisco. Before it was finished Daniel flew home to Australia. Again, it struck me that Daniel seemed more disconnected with the process than the last album. I was so protective of every little sound and questioned and studied every blip, bleep and high hat that went on tape. Daniel felt comfortable letting go of all of that and just leaving it to Walter and Dave Way, the mix engineer, approving the final mixes from across the world.

When the album was finally complete, I flew to New York to sit with audio engineer Vlado Meller who had also mastered our first album. I felt I had to see the record through to the end. It was an incredible experience hearing it in the highest possible fidelity in a room purpose-built for sound, in a way most people would never hear it. Once that was done, I said goodbye to New York, and goodbye to my first boyfriend.

I flew back to San Francisco to stay in Walter's guest house for a month while I shopped for my first American home – a condo in beautiful Sausalito, in Marin County. If you've never been there, let me try to describe it for you even though words could never do it justice. Discovering this gorgeous bayside enclave was like coming home. I'd looked at houses all over San Francisco but nothing reso-nated. I kept saying I needed a backyard because I wanted a dog one day. Every house the real estate agent took me to just didn't feel right. Then one day she phoned and said, 'I know you don't want an apart-ment, but I have a gut feeling about this one. Have you ever been to Sausalito?' I hadn't. I also didn't want an apartment. I didn't want to deal with neighbours, homeowners' associations and all that red tape, but I reluctantly agreed to go see the place on Bulkley Avenue.

As soon as we drove down Bridgeway Avenue I fell in love with the area. The ocean sparkled like Italy's Amalfi Coast. Fog was rolling in from the mountains. Little restaurants and souvenir stores were dotted along the edge of the touristy street connecting to the winding road that led up to the Victorian wooden building that would become my home for the next seven years.

I knew I would live there the second I walked in the door. Every window of the three-bedroom, split-level property looked out over the San Francisco Bay. It was like inhaling a sense of hope. I could feel the energy of a new life, a new era, rolling in, just like that mystical fog. Soon Leonie and I were working with a decorator, designing the space, choosing furniture, and making it my own. It was the first time since Colby and I had divorced that I'd actually bought anything really personal. The first thing I picked out was something I still have to this day: a blown-glass vase from Bridgeway Avenue, purple with flecks of green and gold and blue reminiscent of a Gustav Klimt painting. It was me. My taste. My new life.

Although my home was now settled, my heart was very much not.

As we were gearing up for the release of the album *Affirmation*, there was a lot of press and publicity to do, but also a lot of time off. We did the photoshoot for the cover with the renowned French photographer Stéphane Sednaoui. I'd always wanted to work with him because of what he'd done with U2 and Kylie. When we got to the set Stéphane had an idea to do a very long-exposure, colour photograph. Daniel and I would sit in a pose and he'd take coloured lights and move them around us, painting us with light. He ended up creating an image that was vibrant, modern and electronic, full of movement. Of course, the record company hated it. It got relegated to the inside insert and was printed in black and white. I heard a rumour they thought because of the pose we had been seated in we looked like 'lovers'; that is, 'gay'. So instead of the brilliant, artistic and colourful shot Stéphane had envisioned, they took two separate shots of us, stitched them together in Photoshop (and God knows what they did to my face – I still think I look unrecognisable)

257

and told us at the last minute that that was the album cover. No discussion.

During that period Leonie had noticed that if there was nothing on the schedule, I was sleeping in very late. If she didn't wake me, I'd stay in bed until 3 or 4 p.m. Some days, as the seasons turned to autumn, I would barely see the sunlight. She walked into my bedroom one morning, opened the shutters, and forcibly got me out of bed. 'It's a beautiful day and I want you to see it,' she said.

I reluctantly got dressed and joined her for our regular walk down the hill to the Starbucks, which sat right on the water, looking at beautiful San Francisco. Usually, I wouldn't see this view until after midday, but this was early for me at 10 a.m. We grabbed our coffees and muffins (I usually ate half of hers) and she confessed her deep concern over my wellbeing. She had lost her brother in a tragic traffic accident when he was a teen, and she told me that she couldn't bear the thought of losing me too.

Her words really sank in. Leonie knew, just like she knew about me being gay, that there were dark thoughts circling inside my head. She was right. Ever since my breakup with Jimmy I'd been fixated on suicidal thoughts, and they were completely irrational. I just felt dead inside. There were outside factors that were making me sad, of course, but I felt lonely, more than anything else. I'd been in some form of romantic relationship since I was seventeen and here I was, aged twenty-seven, single for the first time in my life, with all of my dreams having come true and yet a void inside me that I couldn't explain. Without the distraction of making the album, I was left with my demons.

I'd go out to clubs, trying to meet men, to no avail. Or I'd have disastrous encounters where I'd be fascinated with men who would treat me terribly, reject me, or just destroy my self-esteem. If I went out and I got a phone number, I'd feel happy. If I went out and I didn't get any romantic attention, I'd end up at a 7-Eleven buying junk food and binge-eating in my car, waking up the next day feeling terrible for what I'd done to myself and with a head full of negative self-talk like, 'You're fat, you're a loser, you're unlovable.'

'Have you thought of seeing a psychiatrist?' Leonie said. I was offended at the suggestion at first, but she continued. 'Maybe there's a pill you could take that could stop you feeling this way. If that were possible, wouldn't you want to find out?'

INTERIOR: Psychiatrist's office, 1999
The psychiatrist explains to me that it's possible I have a family history of a tendency towards major depressive disorder, given my grandmother's suicide, but also that my childhood experiences are a form of post-traumatic stress disorder. He says for some people, medication is a wonderful solution to a chemical imbalance in the brain; for others, it can be a tool to help the body and the mind tolerate the experience of revisiting those traumatic experiences as an adult, and unlearning the negative beliefs we associate with the experiences. He suggests that being on an antidepressant would be a helpful way for us to work together to go back and heal some of my earliest traumatic memories. It would allow my body and mind to make sense of what happened to me in a safe environment, without the brain's well-intentioned but ultimately unhelpful fight or flight responses that kept me alive as a child but were keeping me numb as an adult.

Many of us have heard versions of this because it's true – the brain has an extraordinary survival mechanism. My child's brain did whatever it could to keep me alive while I witnessed some of the most violent and horrific events imaginable. Some of the things I've uncovered in therapy, some repressed memories of things I witnessed between my father and mother, I have chosen not to make public. That's how horrific they were. So horrific that my brain had formed a 'partition' to stop me ever remembering them. But there have been times where the merest hint of a reminder would trigger a chain of behavioural responses ranging anywhere from feeling despondent and listless, to outbursts of extreme anger, or worse, self-hatred that resulted in suicidal ideation. All the while, seemingly without any cause.

My trauma responses weren't all bad. Sometimes they ignited and protected me and miraculously preserved some of my unique and innocent qualities, like my ability to express loving and kind emotions and of course, my creativity. Sometimes they made me childlike. Unfortunately, my mind had worked so hard at keeping me alive that by 1999, I was trying to live my life informed by experiences that my terrified eight-year-old self took as gospel. I was an adult on the outside but with an inner child making all of the most important decisions.

Underneath the numbness was something my brain didn't want me to remember. The hypothesis was there were feelings and beliefs about myself so painful, I had formed an almost literal protective wall in my brain to protect present-day me from experiencing whatever the hell it was that was lurking in my nightmares and sabotaging my life.

The notion that I should feel any empathy for myself, or the things that had happened to me as a child, had previously seemed not only self-indulgent but also unnecessary. It was my mother who was abused, I'd thought. The point of view of a child's experience, from my adult life, was now heartbreaking. Of course, I never felt safe. And now I was finally understanding, through the advice and objective observation of this very chilled man, that there were reasons why I felt so sad all the time.

'You've just told me that at least one person in your family committed suicide,' the psychiatrist said. 'You've explained that your mother experiences depression and from what you've told me, I think you experienced more than enough trauma in your childhood to be experiencing symptoms of anxiety and depression that are both inherited and a result of the trauma. I suspect your brain is not functioning normally. It's lying to you. With an antidepressant, you might be able to tolerate talking more about the things that hurt you as a young man, and by doing so, heal some of those wounds.'

He went on to explain that an antidepressant would help my brain produce normal levels of serotonin, the 'feel good' chemical that the minds of depressive people have trouble producing. In time, just by taking this medication, you can teach the brain to produce normal levels of serotonin on its own and the patient can be slowly weaned off the medicine if and when required.

'The medication isn't a cure. But it's helpful in therapy, allowing you to tolerate talking about your past,' he said.

So I decided to go for it.

After being on medication for a few months, I was sitting at a café with Leonie in San Rafael.

'How do you feel, now that you've been on medication for a while?' she asked.

I hadn't thought about it, which was a good sign. Things had been really calm.

'You know, it's like, all of the worries, the anxiety, the negative self-talk; all of that stuff is still there, but it's sitting in another room. I can go in there if I want and deal with it, but it's not overwhelming my thoughts anymore.'

'That's how the rest of us feel,' she said, smiling.

It felt good. It was a relief. I felt like a version of my old self for the first time in a long time. In therapy I was able to understand that

261

a lot of what was hurting me was ancient wounds and behaviours I had developed in order to survive. Most of my suffering involved memories of my father and protective walls I'd put up to prevent anyone or anything hurting me like that again.

Little did I know there was no pill to prepare me, or any of us, for what was about to happen next.

Trouble in Paradise

The first sign that something was wrong came during the US summer of 1999 while we were doing a photoshoot in Walter Afanasieff's guest house. Daniel had flown in from Australia to do some promotion and advance press and shoot the music video for 'I Knew I Loved You' which was scheduled to be released in September. But immediately I noticed there was something off in his mood, his behaviour, his mannerisms. Midway through the shoot, he asked if we could take a break.

I followed him into the living room and asked what was wrong. He told Leonie and me that he was unhappy getting his photo taken and was miserable being away from home. He seemed genuinely sad, so we brainstormed ways to alleviate his pain. Could I do more of the press? Could I be the face of the band to take some of the pressure off him? How could we make this easier for him?

Talking seemed to ease the strain and we went back and finished the shoot. The cover of the tour book and poster were taken by the front door of Walter's guest house, just a few feet from where we'd had our conversation. I hated seeing Daniel upset. I remember my heart genuinely breaking for him and vowing to do as much of the heavy lifting as I could.

*

263

The first single was released as planned on September 21st, 1999 in the US, September 28th in Australia and slightly later in Europe and Japan. The album was due out on November 9th, 1999. It took only a few weeks for 'I Knew I Loved You' to reach the top five at home, and fifteen weeks to reach number one on the US Billboard charts, where it stayed for four weeks. It remained in the Billboard Adult Contemporary charts for seventeen weeks and was the most played song on that chart for the entire 2000s. If you're into statistics it also stayed on the Hot Adult Contemporary Chart for 127 weeks, the longest time ever, beating the previous record holder, Savage Garden, with their little song 'Truly Madly Deeply'. I remember being concerned that 'I Knew I Loved You' didn't hit number one in Australia and hearing criticism that it sounded 'too commercial' and 'too American'. Thus began the tall poppy syndrome. To confirm this feeling, at the 2000 ARIA Awards, we received just three nominations, and won only one award, for Highest Selling Album.

Regardless, the advance critical reception seemed positive and we were hearing good things about the forthcoming singles, 'Crash and Burn', 'Affirmation' and 'Hold Me'. Music insiders agreed the album was a leap forward musically. To coincide with the pre-launch, we lined up a few small promotional gigs. In late October, we did one in Japan.

INTERIOR: Hallway, Tokyo hotel, October 25th, 1999
I'm in my hotel room wiping the sweat from my dyed blue-black hair with a white towel. We've just done a show Sony Japan had promoted as a 'secret'. The band and I were making jokes about it all day because it was a sold-out gig at a small theatre and there was nothing remotely secret about it. We played for about thirty minutes, showcasing songs from the new album as well as a couple from the first album. Attendees – I believe they were contest winners – were given a promotional gift bag containing the album art, the album,

the CD single and some literature about the project. Even though we only played a short set, I'm exhausted. We have to do the same thing in a few days somewhere else. After that, it's back home again for the official album launch on October 29th.

There's call to my room. It's our co-manager, Rebecca. She asks if I'm with our assistant Leonie and I confirm that I am. She seems very serious. She asks if we can come to her suite.

I have the sinking feeling in my stomach. Like someone has died. I'm not entirely sure why, but I just know I'm about to hear bad news. This feels like the night my father abducted my mother and brother when I was a kid.

We follow the hallway of the luxury hotel to Rebecca's room and she opens the door to her suite. Daniel is inside and seems to have been crying. It's obvious I've come in at the end of a conversation. A long conversation. The mood is thick. I assume someone has died.

'What's wrong?' I ask, my heart thudding in my chest.

'The two of you need to talk,' Rebecca says and she leaves the room with Leonie, to give Daniel and me privacy.

It feels like an eternity until Daniel speaks.

'I'm going home. I can't do it anymore,' he says.

'What do you mean?'

I'm trying to process what he's telling me. Is he skipping the promo we have planned? Is he leaving the band?

'I'm sorry, man. I have to do this for me,' Daniel says. He explains how he's just seen himself, an image of the two of us, actually, on the side of the promotional bags that Sony Japan has made. 'I'm not a shopping bag.' He keeps repeating this phrase.

'So, what, you're taking a break?'

He explains that, no, it's not a break, he's so unhappy being away from home; that he wants to leave the band, permanently, beginning now.

I'm trying to process what I'm hearing. Our album hasn't even come out yet. We're in Japan and are supposed to be in Australia in just a few days to launch the album. We've just released the first single and have a year's worth of arena dates about to go on sale.

'I'm sorry to do this to you, but this is just not for me.'

This part of the memory is crystal clear because I lose my temper. I take a room service tray and throw the contents across the room. A glass of water smashes and spills all over Rebecca's laptop, ruining it.

Leonie and Rebecca come back into the room. I plead with Daniel, with everyone. Doesn't he want to *think* about this? He's just *decided* this? This monumental decision that will affect not just my life but the employment of hundreds of people in our care? This decision that will not only destroy the release of the album but will permanently destroy our careers? I explain with deep passion that *maybe* there's a less drastic solution. I suggest, since we're headed to Australia anyway, he could go home, get some rest, and I could do the promo we have upcoming and he could just turn up for the live shows. He can leave the band if that's what he really wants when our commitments are completed, but rather than burn down the house we took years to build, perhaps he could take a minute to think of a solution that doesn't have irreversible consequences for everyone else.

There's silence.

'So am I going home tomorrow or are we headed to the next country?' I scream.

Rebecca offers some much-needed guidance and suggests we four sit down and talk things through. She's so warm and maternal. Thank goodness for her instincts in this moment because she manages to defuse the hysteria with her calm wisdom. She orders some room service and we agree to sit down and hash it out. It's explained to Daniel how easy it would be to just do the live parts of the job and none of the press. After about an hour of talking and all of us crying at various points, the mood is lighter and Daniel seems calmer. He seems to like this new idea. Instead of quitting tonight, he'll follow through with the live dates we have planned and I will take up the slack, basically do everything else. Promotion is the most exhausting part of the business and taking this off his shoulders seems to have taken the option of his leaving tonight off the table. Slowly a plan starts to take shape of how we can salvage things. We agree that Daniel will do the live shows, Darren will do the press engagements and at the end of the world tour, Daniel will leave Savage Garden, as requested.

There's a strange atmosphere in the room. People are now happy-crying. I'm numb. I tell Daniel that I love him. That I care for him. That I'd never want to see him suffer. He seems grateful and, most importantly, happier. I leave the room traumatised but relieved I know what is going to happen tomorrow. That's all I need.

Everyone in our entourage will eventually be told the news in confidence. There's no question in anyone's mind that Daniel is leaving. A couple of my closest friends in the band are sure their careers are over. They're understandably depressed and I do my best to reassure them that we'll all be okay. We have a year to work out what the future beyond Savage Garden will look like.

After we leave Japan, Daniel and I have extensive conversations about how, because of our six-album contract with Sony, it's probably a good idea not to tell anyone outside of our families, management, band and crew. We need time to work out the legalities if I'm going to continue on as a solo recording artist. John Woodruff, who is and has always been intrinsically tied to our record deal and is our go-between person at Columbia Records, will need to re-negotiate. We also don't want any negative news swirling around with a full year of press, promotion and a world tour still to do. We might as well use the next twelve months to celebrate the success we've had and make our second album a hit.

Privately, I ask Daniel for two favours. I explain that, historically, when bands break up, the singer usually gets blamed. Everyone thinks it's the frontman with the big ego who wants to go it alone. I ask that when the time comes to go public, that he'll take responsibility. I don't want to be blamed for killing off Savage Garden. This is his choice and I want him to own it. 'Of course,' he says.

Great. I'm thankful.

The next favour concerns our personal management deal. When we first signed it, there was a clause in the contract that said if one of the key people who originally signed us at one of the firms, left, we could, at any time, also leave the management company. That did in fact happen, almost a year into the co-management deal. However, since we both liked the day-to-day person who was taking care of us, we left things as they were.

Now that Daniel has no plans to continue as a performer, I ask that he join me in exercising our right to leave the management company at the end of the year so that I can look at different options for my solo career. Again, he says, 'Sure.' All it'll require is to send a letter notifying the company of our decision, together.

Two favours in exchange for doing a year's worth of promotion on my own.

'Yes,' he says. 'Of course.'

A few days after that momentous night in Tokyo, we flew home for the official album release. We performed in a church, near Surry Hills in Sydney and it was magical. My entire family was there, including my nephews and nieces and my now ex-wife Colby. Naturally, my ever-present, gloating father couldn't get enough of the attention. He swanned around the room like he was the creator of the band.

While in Australia we did some really special TV spots, including a rendition of 'I Don't Know You Anymore' on Network Ten's *The Panel*. It was just Daniel on a keyboard and me at a desk, sitting next to the hosts. Such a raw song performed in an unadulterated manner in a pretty humble setting. It's one of my favourite performances we ever did.

The album debuted at number one in Australia, reached the top spot in Canada, top five in most of Europe and top ten in the US and the UK. Not bad for a follow-up that would eventually match and then eclipse the sales of our debut.

I flew back to the US and soon after, so did Daniel,

The tour was announced. We were to start in Japan on April 2nd, 2000 and end in Johannesburg, South Africa on December 17th. The initial response was really positive. I remember being in a board room with the touring agents in Los Angeles and watching in real time as the ticket sales came in. It was electrifying.

When the US promotion began, the band was flown over to make things even in terms of Daniel's and my travel. We rehearsed near my home in Sausalito, did some television performances and more promotion, and then flew all over Europe, often in a terrifyingly small private jet. Our world tour included over eighty shows in Australia, Canada, North America, Europe, Asia and Africa. And it looked like we'd have our second number one single on the Billboard Hot 100 by the new year. We could not have been in a better position for the year-long promotion of our follow-up album.

The beginning of 2000, the new millennium, was an incredibly positive exciting time for me. I was settled in my new home in Sausalito. It was fully decorated and I was finally able to enjoy being there during the brief holiday break. Soon enough, we were on the road again, as we had promotion booked seemingly all over the world in locations such as Rio, Spain, London and Malaysia. There was so much at stake we had to make sure we got it all out of the way up front, because once we were on tour and performing, the live dates were pretty much back to back.

I was thrilled that we'd be working with the legendary show designer Willie Williams, who had now become a good friend. I found it surreal that as a teenager I'd been to see U2 and marvelled at his work. It turned out Willie had been living in San Francisco this whole time and, get this, was openly gay. Not only that, he'd once been married to a woman! He was fascinated by my knowledge of stagecraft and my enthusiasm for putting on what I wanted to be 'the greatest show on earth'. I was in awe of his every utterance. Working with him was a masterclass in art. His knowledge of the history of stage shows was intimidating and, never one to repeat himself, it meant we were getting the most original and genuinely exciting ideas available at the time. He and his lighting operator, Bruce, would come to the Gold Coast in a few months' time and set up our entire arena show inside a film stage at the Village Roadshow studios.

After a few more weeks of promotion in the US, we headed down under in February and set up shop in Oxenford, where we'd spend two weeks doing technical rehearsals. I was grateful to have so much time at home with my family and loved rehearsing on such a large scale. Everything seemed to go well. The set was *huge*. I remember my little nieces and nephews coming to run-throughs and being terrified of Uncle Darren because when I got on that monster set I really was ten feet tall!

After putting together what I felt was the ideal show, the equipment was locked up and loaded into cargo containers and we all went our separate ways. We'd meet up in Tokyo in April where we'd start the tour in earnest.

Resentment Builds

My heart truly broke when I found out about the extent of Daniel's pain at being in the spotlight. When anyone in my life is in crisis or having a period of unhappiness, my first thought is always, 'How can I make them happy?' But it's one thing to offer to do double the work and receive the same pay. Another thing entirely to see it play out.

I honestly felt no animosity towards him when the promotion for *Affirmation* began in New York and I started doing twelve-hour days of back-to-back interviews. I didn't mind making excuses for why he wasn't there. 'He's shy,' I'd say. 'He's more of a behind-the-scenes kind of guy.' Or, 'He's back in Australia rehearsing with the band.' The excuses started to wear thin once we were on tour, however. I was doing the same amount of shows, but on top of that, I was also doing press before and after the gigs and on my days off. Meanwhile, unbeknownst to me, Daniel was using his free time to form his own record label, Meridien Musik.

At the beginning of the tour, we agreed to let a film crew make a documentary about us. They filmed most of the Australian leg and all of our backstage banter. Nothing was off limits but none of Daniel's excitement about his life after Savage Garden made it into the finished documentary *Parallel Lives* because we were still terrified of the consequences of Sony punishing us for splitting up and derailing my solo aspirations.

After a scaled-down opening in Japan with a minimal set, we regrouped in Australia and debuted our most extravagant show to date. The staging, lighting and costumes were world class, thanks to the efforts of Willie Williams and his team of brilliant light magicians, not least of all, the gentle genius Bruce Ramus who had also come directly from U2. Of course it was also incredible to work for the first time with my friend Claire Marshall, who had by that stage graduated with a university degree in choreography. It was a beautiful feeling to be able to share the enormous scale of the adventure with someone who had grown up in my home town, with the same idols and inspirations as me. We had to pinch ourselves sometimes to remember that all of this was really happening.

Willie Williams is the master of a show opening and the Affirmation World Tour had one that blew my mind. Imagine an entire arena suddenly exploding into life with a burst of colourful neon lights in every single direction as far as the eye can see. From the second the concert began it was a technicolour sensorial overload. There was choreography, catwalks, shadow gags; I even paid homage to Elvis and Michael Jackson in a gold, custom-made leather suit. It was quite simply everything I had dreamed a concert could be.

The Australian leg of the tour went really well and we ended up playing multiple nights in huge arenas. I remember proudly taking my oldest friend, Nathalia, to soundcheck in Sydney, holding her hand as we walked in the back entrance of the now extinct Sydney Entertainment Centre in Haymarket and seeing the thousands of fans waiting outside just to catch a glimpse of Daniel or me. It was surreal.

*

After Australia, we had a short break before the US leg of the tour so we could go to Europe to do some promotion and ship across the stage and equipment. In June, I was invited to perform a duet at a very special concert in Modena, Italy with none other than the late operatic icon, Luciano Pavarotti.

As part of his series of 'Pavarotti & Friends' benefit concerts, we would perform 'I Knew I Loved You' and then I would sing a duet of the Neapolitan classic "O sole mio' with the maestro himself backed by a thirty-piece orchestra and a choir of local children in front of a live audience of thousands. And all in Italian! Even the rehearsals for the event were extraordinary. I can't explain it, but the maestro treated me like an equal. Now, don't get me wrong, I'm completely aware I was *not* his equal – but that was the beauty of the man. He had a joy for singing and when he heard my tenor voice, his eyes lit up and he began talking to his conductor excitedly. From what I could gather, the key I had chosen for the song was 'way too low'. So he raised the key. And then raised it again. And again! Each time, he'd wink at me with a smile, as if to say, 'You can do this!'

He gave me tips on how to breathe, how to hold myself. How to hit the notes.

Then, with a hug, he left! The experience with Pavarotti might be my most cherished memory from my career to date.

I also got to meet my idol, George Michael, who was performing as well. I'd recorded a cover of his Wham! Christmas classic 'Last Christmas' and was so nervous to see him face to face. He sat me down at a small booth and said, 'You recorded a cover of my song.'

There was an uncomfortable silence.

'Yes, I did,' I said.

After what seemed like an eternity he offered a cheeky wink and said, 'I quite liked it!' and I saw that beautiful smile. George was shy, humble and adorable. That was the first of a few cherished times

I would spend near him before his premature passing. He was such a gentle soul and an absolute angel. I miss his voice so much.

The night before the concert all the guest performers and crew spent the most beautiful evening at Luciano's own family restaurant with other stars like the extraordinary Annie Lennox and another favourite artist of mine, Tracy Chapman. When I performed the next evening in my custom Dolce & Gabbana tuxedo, I felt like I belonged on that stage. I was confident and proud and if you watch the footage, I got a rare 'bravo' from Luciano for my efforts. I was elated. Later that evening I sat on the roof of the hotel, drinking wine until the sun came up with Tracy Chapman, chatting about life and how crazy this adventure was.

We began our US dates in Augusta, Georgia, snaking up and down North America and in and out of Canada. We would go on to perform over thirty-five shows, doing a pattern of two in a row, one day off, then three in a row, one day off. It was gruelling physically but I loved the audiences. This tour we sadly lost the talents of our previous backup singer, the phenomenally talented Anna-Maria La Spina, who had just been signed to a publishing deal, but instead worked with the amazing Angi Bekker and Prince protégé and all-round legendary popstar, Elisa Fiorillo. Boy, those girls could sing! And the fun we had. I would give anything to go back in time to hang out in a suburban American mall on our days off, or experience my first-ever Chinese meal from P. F. Chang's with them. It was just pure, goodhearted fun. It was like being a teenager again.

Before the North American leg concluded, I flew my parents over to see a handful of shows. My father, ever the preening peacock, was devastated when he found out the band was breaking up. We were in Las Vegas and he gave me a lecture about what an 'idiot' I was.

He didn't care that the matter was entirely out of my hands, he was just worried about how the situation would affect him. He'd no longer be the 'father of Savage Garden'. He didn't see that, even on stage, the dynamic between Daniel and me was worse than it had been on the first tour. There was no collaboration after the first month of shows. Although we started off polished, precise and beautifully choreographed, by the end of that summer, Daniel mostly had his back to me and was jamming with the band. That left me interacting entirely with the audience or with our backup singers. We were no longer a duo and it saddened me.

I was getting anxious about what would happen at the end of the tour, but John Woodruff was very supportive. He was confident he'd be able to convince Sony that four more Darren Hayes albums would satisfy our original six-album deal we'd signed with Columbia. He told me to keep my head high. John had encouraged me to do the solo projects, like that duet with Luciano Pavarotti and the cover of 'Last Christmas' for a charity record for Rosie O'Donnell, and we looked at how George Michael had handled his departure from Wham! as a template for how I'd transition from a duo to a solo career.

Towards the end of the US leg, we paused to fly to Australia for another important honour. We'd been invited to perform 'Affirmation' at the closing ceremony of the Sydney Olympic Games on October 1st.

It was a wonderful time and an unforgettable experience. We were able to take some much-needed downtime and recover from the gruelling touring schedule while we stayed at the Ritz Carlton in Double Bay. Staying with all the other performers and attending rehearsals we found a real sense of community. There was no attitude or snobbery between any of the 'stars', probably because we each had to sit around and spend countless hours while this massive machine was being built around us. I became somewhat friendly with Kylie.

At the time, she came across as less 'popstar' and more sweet, unguarded Aussie girl. We exchanged phone numbers and talked about music and boys and producers and real things.

At the same time, Midnight Oil's Peter Garrett became a real hero of mine. I was aware that the Olympic Committee had refused to allow the Indigenous flag to be displayed during the opening ceremony, when the flags of participating nations were paraded around the stadium. This infuriated me. Now, bear in mind, the Olympics are an entity unto themselves. They have strict rules and they approve absolutely everything you do and wear on stage. I confided in Peter that I was going to wear a T-shirt featuring the Australian Aboriginal flag underneath my denim jacket. He warned me that if the Committee saw that, they'd make me change my costume, so I made sure that during rehearsals, I buttoned my jacket up. I did that right up until the last second of live television.

As I stepped out onto the white podium, I listened to the last few bars of Christine Anu singing 'My Island Home' and had a lump in my throat. I felt so proud to be Australian. I was aware that around 2.4 billion people were watching as I prepared to take my place. I proudly unbuttoned my jacket to reveal the flag I felt was missing from the festivities. Afterwards, heart thumping, I left the stage and got a high five from Peter. It meant the world to me. His activism has always been an inspiration.

I woke the next day to mixed reactions on the radio and for days after in the newspapers. There was more than a fair share of bigoted, racist comments from readers who complained that my costume was 'inappropriate'.

I didn't care. I'm so glad I did it.

After the ceremony, we were booked to do a free show in The Domain, a large park in the Sydney CBD. On our way to the venue, we watched fireworks explode over the Sydney Harbour Bridge in a spectacular celebration. I'm not sure of the exact numbers that night but I'm told that we played to over 50,000 people. I could not see the end of the audience. We performed the full Affirmation tour show for our home crowd, and even hired extra production, extra pieces of stage and extended our lighting rig to turn our arena show into a stadium-sized extravaganza. Unfortunately, I started losing my voice towards the end of the performance, and the next day I could barely speak. Thank goodness we had a short break before moving on to Europe.

The European leg was hectic. We were in a different country every day and the energy of our tour 'family' was naturally winding down. It was a bit sad. I've toured enough now to know that this often happens with a seasoned crew. Towards the end, they emotionally start to disconnect to prepare themselves for the grief of saying goodbye, and to connect to the new circus they'll soon have to join. Apart from the sadness, it was also tense because a faction had formed within the touring party. Daniel and one particular production manager had formed a small group of mostly men. Then there was me and everyone else. We'd find out at the last minute, for instance, that 'Group A', as we called them, had booked a ski trip or a day out or had gone to a restaurant without inviting anyone else. After a while we stopped taking it personally. But it still hurt.

Things were also tense between Daniel and me because I knew he'd been using the time that I was spending doing promotion to take meetings with record labels. While I was at a local radio station, or doing press on 'days off', Daniel was meeting with local Sony affiliates, playing them demos of his new act.

One night, I heard the now familiar music of Daniel's protégé blaring from the room next to mine. I recognised the voice. It was a backing singer from our first touring band, way back in 1996. I realised, in disbelief, he was playing the finished recordings they'd been working on. I can't explain the feeling of betrayal. I thought we would continue to write songs together, even if we were no longer a band. Up until that point, I had naively intended to be loyal to him and our songwriting partnership. I had no illusion about 'who was more talented'; I knew that we had a special chemistry *together*. I was going to honour that chemistry and write my album with him. But he clearly had other plans.

I've often said that songwriting is so incredibly intimate, it's like a relationship. In that moment it felt that, artistically, I'd been dumped. My heart broke. From that moment on, a shield went up. I fully understood who I was dealing with. I realised if I was going to continue in the music business, I had to toughen up and realise I had been underestimated by the one person I thought had always believed the most in me. Perhaps I really was just the monkey out the front all this time.

Our last show was in December in Johannesburg, South Africa. The gig itself was marred by a bad taste 'joke' by the male production manager I previously mentioned. He got the crew to hold up what he felt were funny signs in the crowd. Only they weren't funny. They were just mean-spirited insults about each of us. And of course we couldn't see who was holding up the signs so we thought they were being held by fans. I remember reading one of the signs written about our guitarist Ben Carey and wincing. I looked over at poor Ben and saw his face. It seemed to momentarily strip all the confidence from him. I felt the same way about the things on the signs about me. And it derailed the show. Afterwards, some members of the band were upset, I was upset. 'Group A' went out for a private dinner.

It was a sad way to end a year-long tour and, essentially, a band.

The next day, Daniel, Leonie and I had a pre-planned farewell dinner. It was bittersweet finishing things off this way with the three people who had been there at the start of it all. I had accepted that Daniel no longer wanted to be in the public eye, and I was prepared to go back and start my career from scratch without the Savage Garden name or Daniel's involvement. At that dinner we discussed everything truthfully. We all knew what had happened. We all knew what was going to happen next. It really was over. But there was gratitude and a sense of peace that night and I was thankful for the sense of closure.

We flew home and after a few weeks, released a statement on our website stating that Savage Garden was going on an extended 'hiatus' while I worked on a solo record. This would give us a buffer to navigate the legalities of our deal with Sony. Once John resolved the contract, we'd be free to expand more on what 'hiatus' actually meant.

In the short break after the Affirmation tour I had a conversation with Willie Williams, our stage designer and tour director. With his years of industry wisdom, working not just with U2 but R.E.M, The Rolling Stones and David Bowie, to name just a few, Willie gave me some of the best advice I've ever received. He told me to accept that what I had experienced with Savage Garden was likely the most commercial success I was ever going to achieve. He told me to start my solo career off as though I was a brand-new artist. If I could do that, I'd be able to enjoy every tiny bit of success, instead of comparing myself to the past and feeling like a failure if I didn't meet or beat those expectations.

I don't know if it was some magic spell but it really did work. I'm not saying that I haven't over the years felt other people's disappointment that I have not sold as many records or played to such large crowds as I did in a duo, but drawing a line in the sand freed me from the comparison game. I often felt with artists like Michael Jackson, that his tremendous success was often a curse. Imagine the pressure to better the biggest-selling album of all time. I remember people calling his *Bad* album a failure because it *only* sold 26 million copies. Can you imagine *only* selling that many copies of an album today? You'd be thrilled, forgive the pun.

Once we had spent some time decompressing after our marathon, year-long Affirmation tour, I phoned Daniel to discuss the first of those two promises he'd made. I was about to write a letter to one of our management companies exercising our right to leave under the existing clause but Daniel said he'd changed his mind following advice from our mutual accountant, a man whom I'd brought to the band six years earlier. This man was a small business accountant and used to work for Colby's parents. When Savage Garden started making money, I asked him to come and work for us.

Daniel explained that the accountant said there was no reason for him to break the management agreement because he wasn't going to be performing anymore. This took me aback.

'You realise if you do this, you're going to fuck me, right?' I said.

He apologised but said he had to protect himself.

It turns out Daniel had been told there was a tiny chance there could be a legal pushback and he didn't want to risk that.

After all we'd gone through, after the exhausting rounds of promotion and press where I'd done the work of two people, not asking for more money, Daniel breaking his promise felt like a huge betrayal of trust. I immediately went into self-protection mode.

I hung up the phone and didn't imagine we'd ever speak again.

Solo

The truth is I was lost. I had no idea what Darren Hayes sounded like. I hated my name, to begin with. If I'd known, or ever had aspirations of being a solo artist, I would have created a stage name. Darren Hayes is a fine name for your uncle, or a plumber or a newsreader. But a popstar? Hell no. But that's what I had to work with.

Then there was another crisis of identity. My hair for the entirety of Savage Garden was dyed blue-black. This had started to eat away at my confidence and my fear of being loved for something I wasn't. I stopped dyeing it towards the end of the tour and let my natural dark-blond curly hair grow out in an attempt to be authentic. The part of me that felt the audience would hate me if they knew I was gay was probably testing them to see if they'd like me without the costume of 'the guy from Savage Garden', as I was often referred to. That guy was a carefully curated superhero – an amalgamation of all of the popstars who had come before me. Hair by Elvis and Michael Jackson. Body by Michael Hutchence. Stage moves by Madonna and Bono. Clothing by Jean Paul Gaultier. Everything about me was armour to protect me from being seen. For this solo album, I desperately wanted to be seen, and that meant I had to begin from scratch.

I'd never written a song with anybody else other than Daniel, and I suddenly had to find a co-writer I felt would be the right fit.

Writing a song is like going on a date. It's ruined if there's no chemistry and you know immediately if you have it or not. The first person I called was one of the finest songwriters in the world, in my opinion, Patrick Leonard. He had co-written most of my favourite Madonna hits including 'Live To Tell', 'Like A Prayer' and 'Frozen'. Maybe I caught him on a bad day but we didn't click. That was disappointing.

I grew up studying album sleeves and scouring the credits and another hero of mine was Rick Nowels. Rick had worked on the Stevie Nicks album *Rock a Little* which had meant so much to me as a teen. He was incredibly successful, having written most of Belinda Carlisle's albums and worked with Dido and Celine Dion – and for me, most importantly, on songs on Madonna's *Ray of Light* album. I phoned him and we hit it off immediately. We soon began writing the first songs of my solo career. The process was effortless and I grew to realise that, although finding a co-writer I clicked with was rare, my songwriting ability had survived the breakup. What a relief! We worked on about eight songs and they all had a very folksy, dreamy, electronica sound to them. I was about to hit 'go' on the recording process with Rick as co-producer when I had a sudden change of heart. I began second-guessing myself and wondering if the songs were 'hits'. I was also petrified about what the record label would think. Rick's demos felt so different from anything I'd ever done before, I decided he might not be the right producer, after all.

By this time, John Woodruff had convinced Sony to allow me to fulfill the existing Savage Garden recording contract as a solo artist. With one caveat . . . If the band ever got back together we'd owe them four more Savage Garden records. It seemed fair – and also highly unlikely. Daniel and I weren't even speaking. I couldn't imagine us recording together again.

After giving it a lot of thought, I decided to go back to Walter Afanasieff, who had produced the *Affirmation* album. I had about ten songs under my belt at that point and figured maybe I'd write a couple more with Walter, even though we'd never written together.

What followed was a really amazing, exciting adventure.

I can honestly say making my first solo record *Spin* was an absolute joy. Walter is a music genius. Collaborating with him was like being let out of a cage. I was singing in keys I never knew existed and finding my way around chords and inversions I'd never heard before. We were incredibly prolific in the studio. He would be searching for a sound on a keyboard and I'd just start humming a melody and he'd excitedly say to one of the assistants, 'Quickly, put up a mic!' Within an hour we'd have a finished song. It got to the point that we always had a tape running in the studio because our songwriting chemistry was so spontaneous we never wanted to miss the moment a song revealed itself. Everything was documented. Tracks like 'Heart Attack' were wonderful, spontaneous creations. Whereas Charles Fisher had 'taken the Michael Jackson' out of my voice, Walter loved that he could hear it, buried deep within. He sensed what I loved musically and he'd start playing these jams, these really angry jams, and my subconscious mind would just free flow. A song like 'Good Enough' reached back to my love of Motown and was a love letter to my mother. By the time we recorded 'Like It or Not', a song I'd co-written with Rick Nowels, I was in a really great headspace. It's a song about messing up in a relationship with someone I met after Jimmy. We broke up and I called him to tell him I was in Germany and had just booked a ticket to Brazil to come see him.

'Don't bother,' was the response. Ha! Good for him! Rarely did anyone say no to me back then, but this man knew his worth, knew I'd done him dirty and made me repent. I did eventually get on that plane and apologise face to face and we remain friends to this day. Bonus: I got a great song out of it.

One of the things I most remember about these sessions with Walter was the improvement in my voice. He was used to working with truly gifted musical divas and he expected vocal excellence. He wouldn't let bad pronunciation or a flat note remain on tape. He pushed me further than anyone had pushed me up to that point. Then there were his vocal arrangements. Although challenging, it was heaven to learn and record his otherworldly harmonies – a process I've kept my entire career. I also got to hire Chris Lord-Alge – the man who crafted the final version of the first Savage Garden album – to mix the recordings, and it was a fun reunion to sit and turn the album into a sonic supernova of sound.

The craziest thing, and something we still laugh about, is that I also hired my school friend Nathalia to be my assistant. By this stage, Leonie had moved up to co-manage me, along with Larry Tollin. All I can say is if you love someone, you should *never* put them in a position of subservience! Nathalia had been working in the film industry in production and we both felt it would be 'fun'. But there is nothing fun about getting your friend's dry cleaning. It's just awkward. I might be projecting but Nathalia had so much more to offer and should have been in a management role.

Although she only worked for me for a while, I have fond memories of driving around Marin County in a convertible, listening to burned CDs of the latest mixes of my first solo album, and getting her opinion on them. She had been there from the very beginning and here we were, two kids from Logan, hanging out in a multi-million-dollar recording studio in the US of A. That in itself felt like a win.

Saved For a Reason

Midway through recording, in September 2001, I received an invitation to perform on a charity single produced by Bono and Jermaine Dupri to benefit AIDS programs in Africa. The tentative name of the collective was Artists Against Aids. The project was a 'We Are the World' type initiative to bring together as many big names as possible on one song, to raise money and awareness. We'd record a version of the great Marvin Gaye song, 'What's Going On'. It felt almost like fate. I'd grown up listening to Marvin my whole life and I knew that song back to front.

Around the same time, Michael Jackson was getting ready to perform his first full-length live concerts since 1996, a filmed event at Madison Square Garden called the 30th Anniversary Celebration. It was advertised as a reunion with all of his brothers and special guest stars including Whitney Houston, Liza Minnelli, Elizabeth Taylor and Marlon Brando. Claire Marshall and I were practically fused at the hip when it came to Michael and I knew this was something we had to attend, so I invited her to the US to both be my chaperone at the charity recording and to witness the return of our childhood hero, on stage where he belonged.

Claire, always keeping an eye out for my money and always on the hunt for sharks in my orbit, agreed on one condition: that we

285

fly economy to New York. She often did things like this to ground me and to remind me of where we'd come from. Of course I agreed and soon we were headed off to New York to meet Bono and see the King of Pop.

When we landed, there was an amazing energy in the city. I never loved living there, but I have always loved visiting. I could feel the magnetic pull of Manhattan the second we disembarked the plane and I couldn't wait to get to our hotel and start our adventures. The recording was to take place the next day and we had Michael's concert on Friday September 7th to look forward to. We were due to fly home on Saturday, September 10th. There was time to explore, reminisce about my old life in the Big Apple and have fun. We were both single and it felt like our worlds were just about to blossom.

During the recording session, I was nervous at first. The hallways of Battery Studios on West 44th Street were jam packed with celebrities like Justin Timberlake, Michael Stipe, Beyoncé and Jennifer Lopez. I was shocked to see Bono manning the huge SSL recording desk, actually producing the recording. When Justin Timberlake finished his vocals, we exchanged a quick hello and then it was my turn. I sang the song from top to bottom three or four times, then did a bunch of ad libs in front of all of those people.

Afterwards, Michael Stipe took a second to pull me aside to say, 'You have a really beautiful voice.' It felt surreal. Claire then came over and said, 'Did you see how everyone reacted when you sang? You silenced the room. People were literally in awe.' It's hard for me to accept compliments, but it was so kind of her to remind me of that, because in a room full of the best of the best, I wanted to make a good impression and leave with my head held high.

Also at the recording – in a studio owned by Sony, for a song that would be released on Columbia Records, my label at the time – were a few friendly faces. My friend Myrna, whom I'd first met in marketing but ultimately ended up becoming a wonderfully talented freelance photographer, introduced me to her friend, Miguel, who was the publicist for the charity single.

It was crush at first sight. Miguel was absolutely beautiful and had that kind of aura where you just wanted his sunlight to dapple upon you. He had that rare personality where I'm sure everyone felt they were in love with him because when he gave you his attention, you felt like you were the source of light in his eyes when in fact it was your own soul being ignited and simply reflected in the object of your desire. That was Miguel.

I mistook this flurry in my heart for a mutual attraction. Big mistake. But also, as it would turn out, a blessing. I'd been sad about my non-existent love life for a while and it was fun to have a crush. After the recording session I spoke with Myrna and she seemed happy to play cupid. We conspired to have some kind of group gathering where I might be able to spend more time with Miguel.

The next evening she invited me to a bar where Miguel and a few of her work colleagues were hanging out. I tried but couldn't get a read on him. He was a burst of sunshine, but he also seemed guarded and elusive. He left early and I stayed on, pretending I wasn't obsessed with him. But I was. Myrna suggested we organise a small group dinner another night. I loved the idea. I called Leonie, who was back in San Francisco, and asked her to extend the trip, so that we'd fly out on September 11th. Why not? The album was basically finished and it'd be fun to spend more time in New York. Leonie got back to me and said the only flight she could get us on was United Flight 93, leaving at 8 a.m. from Newark. Because of Claire's 'economy only' stipulation, our options were limited.

'That's really early for you,' Leonie cautioned. 'Are you sure you want to take that flight? It'll mean getting up at the crack of dawn.'

'Absolutely,' I said, still giddy from my encounter with Miguel.

The following evening we saw Michael Jackson in concert and it pains me to say I witnessed the fall of a giant. History has since revealed that Michael was struggling with an addiction to painkillers at that point in time. Claire and I had no idea. What we saw was a once magnificent performer in a state of confusion, apparent physical pain and in a situation that felt beneath him. He was two hours late, he was missing dance steps and he reminded me of a circus lion that had been beaten. I watched him reluctantly attempt to perform his old tricks, not out of a place of joy or desire, but out of necessity. It was hard to see my hero stumble. We left with a hollow feeling in our hearts. What had they done to him? We didn't know we had just witnessed one of the last times Michael Jackson would ever perform in front of a live audience.

The next morning the city felt different. Angry, on edge. We walked around Chinatown and I saw a cinematic montage of rage. A man screaming into a payphone and slamming the receiver into the side of the booth. A woman punching a taxi that almost clipped her as she stepped onto a pedestrian crossing. A cacophony of car horns and police sirens. Everything felt hostile. It was almost apocalyptic.

I'd been feeling on edge myself, waiting to hear back from Myrna about that dinner with Miguel. He'd been vague and non-committal. That was enough information for me. I wasn't going to embarrass myself by pursuing something that probably didn't exist anywhere else but in my mind. I asked Claire if she wanted to change our flights back to the earlier date and she enthusiastically agreed. She too had been experiencing a dark energy in the city. I called Leonie.

'I never changed your flight,' she said.

'Why?' I asked, a little annoyed.

'Because I know what you're like. You *always* change your mind.'

She was right. People had long figured out that I was sponta-neous and that often I would set in motion something I would later change my mind about – often at great expense. Leonie was smart to hold off on changing the flight.

Relieved our original flight was still booked, Claire and I said farewell to the city. We went to the top of the Empire State Building and looked out at the incredible view. She pointed to the Twin Towers and said, 'They're going to fall one day.' We both looked at the massive structures and shivered at the thought.

The next morning we boarded our original flight to San Francisco and thought nothing of our premonitory fears. We were leaving the city, headed back to the foggy, green Pacific comfort of Marin County.

On the morning of September 11th, 2001, I woke from a horrific nightmare to the sound of a phone call. It was an ex-boyfriend. A nice one.

'Hello?' I answered, half-asleep.

'Thank God you're okay,' he said, relieved.

'I just had the most horrible dream,' I started to explain. 'I was standing in a field, with all my friends and family, and we were watching this hot air balloon above us. Suddenly the balloon hit this stone structure, like an ancient Greek ruin, and burst into flames. The structure started collapsing and sandstone blocks fell to the ground. People were screaming and crying but I looked around and thankfully everyone was alive and okay. It was so real.'

There was silence at the end of the line, then, 'Darren, turn on the news.'

I had a TV in my bedroom and a remote right next to the bed. I'd got into the habit of falling asleep to *Star Wars* movies or old Hollywood films on Nick at Nite. I turned the TV on to CNN and saw the footage of the World Trade Center on fire and a montage of all of the carnage that had occurred that morning. Images of Flight 93, crashed in Pennsylvania, filled the screen. It was the field in my dreams.

'I'm just so glad you're okay. I thought you were in New York,' my ex said.

'I was . . . but we decided to come back earlier.'

I hung up the phone, in a daze, and went to find Claire.

The next few days were a blur. We experienced what I believe to be survivor's guilt. My friend Myrna had an uncle who worked in the World Trade Center. We spent time online trying to help her find any information about him from the little information we had access to. Since most of New York's mobile phone and web access had been either damaged or flooded with activity it was almost impossible for folks on the ground to work out what was going on. Eventually we would discover he was in one of the Twin Towers when they fell.

The aftermath changed America forever. There was the immediate loss of innocence. Even in Marin County, where I lived, the entire world stopped. Flights were suspended for two days and the effect was a deafening and morbid silence. The Golden Gate Bridge was closed for fear of a further terrorist attack. We lived in a quiet state of petrified mourning. In the years since I have often wondered if I now live in an alternate parallel universe; a universe where I survived. In the other universe, it's possible Claire and I would have perished and I wouldn't be writing this book. I think about what I've experienced in the twenty-three bonus years I've had on this planet since September 11th. In my dark moments, I've felt that I shouldn't be here, and I attribute the feelings of uncertainty and lack of purpose to imposter syndrome. I think, 'Maybe I was supposed to have been on that plane.' I only let myself think that for a second, because if I let myself go down that rabbit hole, my life can feel like a highlight reel of sadness, betrayal and heartache. I compare my life pre and post 2001 and it can be hard to see the joy in the latter. The loss of innocence – from the fall of Michael Jackson to the fall of the Twin Towers – felt so permanent. It was as though my American Dream had died.

That's in my dark moments.

In my moments of clarity I have to believe I was given a second chance. I have to believe that I have a purpose, and that even when it's not clear to me, I am here for a reason. I'm a survivor. I've been in survival mode since my first memories of being conscious. Surely I was saved for a reason.

When the world started up again, my focus returned to my solo album, which was now finished. We began to plan how we would market the record to the world. Since Savage Garden were, by that time, an Australian national treasure, we knew the news of the breakup was going to upset the fans. Although Daniel and I weren't speaking, out of respect, I knew I had to call him to let him know that my album was going to be coming out soon and that I was going to be doing press. I wanted to make sure he was prepared for it and that he would hold true to his promise to tell the truth that it was his decision to break up the band. It was important he was given a heads-up before any promotion started even though he was already promoting his own act, a duo called Aneiki.

By this stage, I had changed my management team slightly – I'd kept Larry Tollin and promoted Leonie from assistant to manager and the two were co-managing me. Leonie decided it'd be a good idea to do one in-depth interview with an Australian news outlet, rather than hundreds of little ones, to announce the news of my solo record and the breakup of Savage Garden. I would discuss for the first time the fact that Daniel had left the band and we would make an agreement with the journalist that the interview would be held until the release of my solo album, which was three months away. In media terms this is called an embargo. The journalist we trusted, Cameron Adams, was a long-time supporter and fan. We flew him to San Francisco, put him up in the guest house at Walter Afanasieff's studio, and he agreed to the restrictions. In return, he would hear my album in its entirety, get the world-exclusive interview, and we'd do a photoshoot for the piece a few weeks later. Sounds great in theory, doesn't it?

I played Cameron the album, talked through the meaning of the songs, and had a sincere conversation in which I admitted Savage Garden had actually split up the previous year in Japan when Daniel broke the news to everyone. It was a relief to finally be able to tell the truth. There was no malice in revealing this. I was sympathetic to Daniel's new life trajectory and careful to speak kindly of him, in spite of our falling out, aware that our fans wouldn't want to take sides.

Afterwards, Cameron joined Leonie, some of the studio staff and me for dinner. I distinctly remember telling Leonie that although I wasn't looking forward to it, I was going to call Daniel the next day to let him know that I had started doing long-lead press for the solo record so he could be prepared for when the news broke. She agreed that was essential and we all went to bed early knowing the next day was going to be another busy one. I was off to Los Angeles to film the music video for the charity record I'd sung on earlier in the year, 'What's Going On'.

Cameron Adams and I are friends now, but he knows what he did after that dinner dropped a bomb on my life. Instead of holding the interview until the agreed time, he broke the embargo and called his Australian editor that evening and posted the news that Savage Garden had broken up. By the time we woke it was world news. Tabloid news. Breaking news.

It was absolute chaos. Worse than we could have imagined. Daniel was at a radio station with his band and the DJs naturally asked him for his reaction. In the heat of the moment, I can understand that he was surprised to hear anyone outside of our team talking about the breakup. He said on the record, 'It's the first I've heard of it.' A lie to protect me? Maybe? I'll allow that. Sure. He's flustered, we're not speaking, he's been questioned by a journo and he's gone to the default answer we've been sitting on forever, which is that we were on 'hiatus'. But he knows the truth.

This statement becomes a headline that, to paraphrase, becomes a storyline making me the evil guy who broke up the band and who didn't even have the decency to tell his partner! The press love it. They run with it. It's my worst nightmare and it's *exactly* what I feared would happen if Daniel didn't admit it was his decision.

I'm on the airport runway about to board a plane to Los Angeles when I hear what Daniel has said. I call him straight away and ask him why the fuck he said what he did. He says he was taken by surprise and didn't know what to say. 'I'm about to have a press conference now, actually,' he then tells me.

Excuse me, a *press conference*?

The man who left the band because he hated all the attention has somehow arranged a press conference on his own. How? I still wouldn't know how to arrange a press conference and I own my own record label and have been doing this for twenty-eight years!

'What are you going to say?' I ask, sheer panic in my voice.

'I'm going to do what's best for me,' he says, repeating what he'd said during our last argument.

'I hope that's to tell the truth.'

There is a brief silence and then he says, 'I have to look out for me now.'

By the time I landed in Los Angeles, it seemed Daniel had not used the press conference to clarify his first remarks. In the news articles his quotes did not admit that ending the band was his idea. The news articles suggested he thought we were just on a break! That he mused that he had always wanted to leave the door open for a reunion – which was in complete opposition to everything he had said to me and everyone we worked with. I couldn't believe it. He had never discussed any of this with me.

I called him again in disbelief. He told me he'd been taken out of context and that he had in fact taken ownership about the breakup but that the press didn't print those parts of his statements.

'Then put out a new written statement, clarify your words!' I urged.

He wouldn't.

That was the moment we stopped being friends.

While Daniel eventually made it clear that he left the band, public misunderstandings continued as late as 2022 when I appeared on *The Kyle and Jackie O Show* in Australia and still had to clarify that I hadn't left, Daniel did.

In hindsight, I wish we had both planned how to tell the public the band was ending, with a dual press conference at the same time. It would have saved years of mindreading and unnecessary blame for each party. The truth is, bands break up all the time. We just handled ours badly.

The Fallout

I filmed my parts for the 'What's Going On' video in Los Angeles but my mind was distracted by the absolute shitshow of how my debut solo record was being launched. The first sign of trouble was when I was summoned to an emergency video conference call to discuss my 'image'. In the meeting the men in suits at the US record company had the cover of George Michael's *Faith* up on the boardroom wall. They were comparing it to test images we'd sent them of me with my longer bleach-blond naturally wavy hair. There were so many people sitting around the boardroom it looked like one of those images you see from the White House when the US is taking out a terrorist cell. The mood was similar too. Apparently they wanted to give me a unique memorable image, just like George Michael's 'Faith' era.

Bear in mind, at that time, Sony had essentially put George's career on hold for five years when they disagreed over the style of his music and his image. He had sued them to get out of his contract, and famously lost the case, but the damage to his career was fresh in my mind. I tried to explain to everyone that, as a fan of George, I knew there was nothing 'styled' about the cover of the *Faith* album. It was *all* George. He was a beautiful man, standing in profile, holding a leather jacket. They disagreed. They felt it was all about the gold crucifix earring he wore in his left ear. They too wanted me to wear some piece of 'iconic' jewellery in the music video and for the album shoot that audiences would instantly identify as 'Darren Hayes'.

We did the photoshoot for the album and of course someone tried to get me to wear a topaz crucifix necklace. I had been working for months with a US-based choreographer, practising simple dance moves, mostly salsa-based hip movements and so on, so I'd feel natural when it came time to perform the loosely Latin-inspired song, 'Insatiable'. My costume, a beautifully fitted black leather jacket and faux black snakeskin pants, was chosen by a stylist who worked with Mick Jagger and Aerosmith, at the request of and approval by the label, I might add. There was not a thing about the video or my look that didn't get run past them. This was in sharp contrast to the Savage Garden days where I basically wore whatever I wanted. Sure there were arguments over the cover of the *Affirmation* album but overall, aside from the initial humiliation by our US product manager, my image was never policed. When you look at those images, I was very androgynous, to say the least. Heavy makeup, lip gloss, eyeliner and always walking the edge of masculine and feminine in my choice of clothing. It was all intentional and the label loved it at the time.

The video idea I approved for 'Insatiable' had a simple storyline: a beautifully photographed performance, much like George Michael's 'Careless Whisper', where I'd perform the song on a regal Victorian theatre stage with massive jade green walls of light behind me. This would be intercut with footage of me making my way through a crowded nightclub, searching for *someone*. That was it. That was all that was written on paper, or the 'treatment', as it's known in the music video lexicon.

We shot the video over three days in Sydney and I left the set feeling happy with what we'd filmed. We took still photographs and some of those ended up being used as the cover for the single and as press images. The lighting was incredible and I was thrilled with the styling and overall look.

Weeks went by while the footage was assembled and edited. More time than usual passed and I became worried when I hadn't heard any feedback from the record label or seen a rough cut. My universe imploded when I did eventually see the first edit. Unbeknownst to me, a third part of the video had been shot, a part that was never run past me. This footage was of a woman, naked underneath a leather trench coat, running through the same nightclub I was filmed in. The way the edit was spliced together, it appeared as though I was looking for her. My dancing had been cut out completely. It was all just close-ups and beauty shots. Any time the camera seemed to suggest I might move my body the edit cut to something else.

I hated it. Apparently so did the label, but not for the same reasons. A trusted friend within the company told me the consensus was that I looked too feminine when I moved. The insinuation was that I looked too gay. Someone very high up hated my natural curly hair, and since they'd seen some images of me from the album photoshoot where the hair stylist had straightened it, decided that we should reshoot the video with my hair straightened, with me not moving at all, and in a scenario where I was observing some romantic situation. I was basically to appear as a third-party narrator to a heterosexual love affair. With dead straight hair.

At the same time, all of the TV shows I'd expected to appear on were suddenly not booked, or not available. The same label insider told me the fear was when I moved, you guessed it, I came across as effeminate. It was like a reverse Elvis Presley situation; instead of looking too sexual, I just looked too gay. What had changed from four years earlier when I was wearing neon-blue nail polish, skin-tight see-through shirts, gothic makeup and eyeliner on every

American TV? I believe what changed was the fact that I was openly gay and this terrified the bigwigs. They were afraid I might publicly come out.

This was around the time Ricky Martin had just ruled the charts with his first English language album. He was also signed to the same record label. I remember being in those boardrooms, with those men in suits, listening to them openly mocking how feminine Ricky was and joking about his sexuality. That's how I found out Ricky Martin was gay, by the way. Not when he eventually came out to the world, on his terms, but from listening to the homophobic 'jokes' and slurs made about him, in front of me, in a boardroom of my US record company. You can imagine how terrified I felt.

So here I was, about to launch my solo album in the US after selling 26 million albums with Savage Garden and I had none of the essential tools. No live performances. No TV appearances. And with a music video that had essentially neutered me. The label booked one media meet and greet in Manhattan: two hours of shaking hands with journalists.

When 'Insatiable' was released, it landed with a fizzle in Savage Garden's two biggest markets, the US and Australia. Both were Sony territories now, unlike before when we had Village Roadshow, the independent and fierce underdog fighting for us. Thank God for the UK, where the single was getting number one radio airplay. It'd go on to become one of my biggest hits ever, and that was including the Savage Garden singles. But in America, the song that the men in suits had told me was 'Grammy worthy' and a number one hit was now apparently 'not connecting' on radio. So what did they do? They dropped it like a hot potato. Literally dumped it, stopped all promotion and spending, and shelved the idea of launching a second single. Before my album had even been released, my solo career in the US was effectively over.

Something similar happened at home. The head of the Australian label answered to the US and it appeared that I was not a priority. It didn't help that the breakup of the band had been handled so badly – most Aussies still thought I had left without telling Daniel. I remember a particularly low point in Sydney with a radio station who were refusing to add the single to their playlist. I was in the middle of a photoshoot for my tour program and the station called Leonie and told her that another artist had cancelled a drive-time interview. They asked if I would come and do the interview instead. I had no ego about the fact that the very people who had once been Savage Garden's biggest supporters were now refusing to play my song. I didn't care that the very same station who wouldn't have me on as a guest had suddenly asked me to fill in because someone else had stood them up. This was business. We dropped what we were doing and raced through the peak-hour traffic to the station as fast as we could. When we got there, I remember Leonie was on the phone in tears. 'You can't do this to him. This is so humiliating. We're already here. Can't you just let us up and have him do a pre-recorded interview or something?'

'What's happening?' I asked.

'They said we were late, so they've cancelled the interview. They won't even let us in the lobby.'

Everyone was embarrassed. I sat with the feeling. It wasn't shame, exactly, but echoes of the sensations of being excluded at high school. Of being bullied. I'd spent fifteen years building up a persona and a self-belief that the world was a safe place and I could create a protective barrier around myself that would shield me from those feelings of rejection and ridicule. But I might as well have been back at Mabel Park State High School waiting for an invitation to a birthday party that was never going to come. Waiting for the laughs as bystanders bent over in stitches as they saw the look on my face. Did I really think these people loved me? How foolish I was to think even for a second that any of this was real.

But rather than spiral into a self-pity party, I recalled the words that Willie Williams had said to me about my solo career. I tried not to take it personally. Everyone in my team was expecting the media to treat me exactly like they had when we'd won all of those ARIA awards or when we were one of the biggest-selling bands in the world. They didn't. In some ways this felt a little bit like the public shaming that I knew would come, the obligatory tearing down of an idol after having built him up. I took it on the chin and held my head high. But inside I was devastated and humiliated.

It was also a difficult time in my personal life. I had been single for a while and was used to it. But just before the album was released, I had met someone, a person in the entertainment industry. While all of this nonsense with the record label had been going on, I had fallen into the relationship effortlessly. He was a hard person to love, and looking back now, I realise he was really just a version of my father. Freud referred to these types of relationships as being based in a condition he called 'repetition compulsion'. It was a sort of wish fulfilment to choose someone who vaguely and subconsciously triggered some of the wounds I had from childhood, and a desire to make the relationship work, in an attempt to retroactively heal pain from the past. I thought if I could love this man and fix him, maybe it would fix me. It didn't.

I was at New York Fashion Week, about to do one of the only live performances the label had arranged, and my boyfriend had joined me. He was never really supportive or encouraging of what I did. I was starved of both affection and approval so in the rare moments he did show me love, I felt like the luckiest man in the world. I got dressed in my suit and I came fresh from the suite where the hair stylist had groomed me and went to our hotel room to show him my finished look.

'How do I look?' I said.

'You look like a fag.'

It was the beginning of the end of our relationship. I'd fought my whole life to recover from the horror and pain of being called that word and here was the person who was supposed to love me just casually slinging it at me. No. I would not put up with that.

Later on, my friend Troy, his partner Shane and Leonie planned a surprise thirtieth birthday party for me in Sydney. My boyfriend knew all about it and had been told to get me to come to a small dinner with a handful of my closest friends and where they'd surprise me. The day before the 'fake dinner' we had a huge argument. The day after, he apologised, and said, 'Instead of going out to dinner with your friends tonight, how about we just stay in? Just the two of us?'

I had such little self-esteem at that point, I was willing to do anything or see any of his actions as romantic and loving. 'How sweet,' I thought, 'that he just wants to be with me.' So I called Leonie and told her we weren't feeling well and that we were going to spend the night in. Leonie was outraged. 'You *have* to come to this dinner! Put your boyfriend on the phone!'

I heard them talk for a few minutes and he hung up.

'They really want you to come,' he said, reluctantly. 'So let's just go for like an hour.'

'Okay!' I said, happy to please him.

We turned up to the 'dinner' and, to my surprise, it was at a warehouse filled with at least a hundred people. My entire family was there. Old school friends. They'd flown in from all over. My friend Troy and his partner Shane, who, although none of us knew it at the time, was very ill at that point with cancer, had spent days decorating the space. Someone was filming my reaction as I walked in the door.

I'm sad to recall when I watch the video the first thing I did was turn to my boyfriend and mouth the words, 'I'm so sorry.'

I apologised for being the centre of attention.

He turned to me and said grumpily, 'Don't worry about it.'

I spent about thirty minutes at the party, hugging, kissing and thanking everyone for coming before my boyfriend pulled me aside and said he wasn't feeling well and wanted to go home. So we went home.

When I was ready to tour the new album, he was off making a film and I was zero priority to him. I had spent so much time putting him first, massaging his ego and watching him literally pull his hair out stressing about his impending film shoot. I made myself so tiny for him, played down my success, made my own career less of a priority. I had the legacy of my band balancing on my shoulders and a multi-million-dollar tour in the balance, and yet I flew to Europe to be with him on the set of his movie. Despite that, he was so busy I barely saw him. I waited around his apartment all day for him to return and remember lying on the floor of his beautiful flat, staring at the ceiling strumming my guitar and writing the lyrics to new songs. My health was at rock bottom. My immune system was barely coping and I'd risked it to be with him. It made no difference.

When the tour started in Melbourne, I sat in my dressing room thrilled to have received flowers from my family, from the record company – even from my ex-wife – all wishing me luck. There was nothing from my boyfriend. That was the wake-up call. We broke up over the phone and soon after I came down with viral laryngitis. I took the breakup very hard. I thought I loved him and I hadn't really felt that way about anyone in a long time. I got sick and was forced to cancel some shows. I was heartbroken and depressed. It did, however, give me plenty of material to write about and my follow-up album, *The Tension and the Spark*, was mostly about that relationship.

In the UK, *Spin* debuted at number two and I sold out three nights at London's Apollo Theatre in Hammersmith. It was a massive kick-start and to this day it's the reason I'm so grateful to UK audiences. It's safe to say the country saved my career by embracing me when the rest of the world's media left me for dead.

I toured from the end of August through to November 2002, performing forty-three dates throughout the UK, Europe, Japan, South-East Asia, Mexico and Australia. I even performed inside the Kremlin. Well, I performed one evening inside the Kremlin; the government cancelled our first show because of the Moscow theatre crisis on October 23rd when Chechen operatives kidnapped 912 audience members at the Dubrovka Theatre in protest of the Russian–Chechnyan war. It was a terrifying time to be in the country because we saw the entire operation play out in the news and the resulting death toll of hundreds. We played our second scheduled show as advertised, but the feeling was extremely tense, as you can imagine.

At the end of the tour I was exhausted. I flew home to Sausalito for a week or so and got so sick, I could barely speak. I think my body just needed to fall apart. Unfortunately, I had a long string of UK promotion pre-booked. One was a live performance at Capital Christmas, a huge concert with lots of international stars for Capital Radio, one of the biggest pop stations in England, and some TV shows including a very popular morning show.

I managed to make it through the Capital Christmas performance and then I lost my voice. I went to see an ear, nose and throat specialist surgeon on Harley Street and the doctor looked at my vocal cords and said if I sang, I'd risk damaging my voice forever. I was in a conundrum. I didn't want to cancel the promotion the record company had booked or pull out of the various TV shows, but I couldn't risk injuring my voice.

The only way we could get through the next few engagements was if I lip-synced on TV. I reluctantly agreed to do that, but was worried that I'd be expected to talk to the host after the performance. I was under strict orders to be on complete vocal rest, which meant not making any sound.

The day I was meant to do the popular morning show I woke up and my eyes were glued together. Conjunctivitis. I was so rundown, my body was falling apart. When I cleaned the gunk from my eyes, my lids were bright red. There was no way I could appear on television. I looked like a demon. We did some quick thinking and it was decided I could wear some lightly tinted sunglasses. I was worried it would look rude, but my team said, 'You're a rock star. Liam Gallagher wears glasses. Bono wears glasses. Just own it. Besides, we'll tell the team the truth and they all know you can't speak so they're aware you're very ill. They'll just be grateful you're doing the show and not cancelling.'

As we set up ten minutes before going live, a sound tech came up to put a mic on the lapel of my jacket. I knew what this meant. This was intended for me to have a chat with the host after the performance. I turned to my manager and just with a look, without a sound, conveyed my terror. Hadn't they told production about my voice? I can't speak! There was nothing we could do. Suddenly we were live and I mimed the song wearing my light-blue tinted glasses. Immediately afterwards, the beloved host came over for a chat. I responded to the questions but every sound I made felt like razors were slicing into my throat. I was worried I was damaging my voice, just by speaking, but I had no choice.

The segment finished and we went to an ad break.

We cleared the set and so the strange legacy of my morning show reputation was born. The next time my people tried to book me on the show, I was refused. The reason? The booker said the last time

I was on I was 'rude, wore sunglasses during the interview and refused to speak to the host'. Essentially, I was banned!

This misunderstanding happened at least three more times. It became so bad that every time a record company wanted to have me on the show, they would have to arrange a lunch with the production staff to prove to them I wasn't some arsehole. I would have to casually repeat the story about how, one time, an eternity ago, I'd had to wear sunglasses because I had conjunctivitis. Then they'd let me do the show. A year later, the same thing would happen and I'd have to jump through all the hoops again.

Fame is a peculiar, fickle and very weird thing.

How to Lose a Record Deal

By the end of 2002 I was an emotional and physical wreck. I'd been working non-stop in the music industry since 1992. I'd spent a decade slogging away in sweaty bars in Red Edge, through the rollercoaster success of Savage Garden and sling-shotting into an unplanned solo career without a break. On top of it all I had wasted a frustrating amount of time defending the false accusation that I had left the band. It tarnished what should have been a joyous period in my life. Instead of being able to take Willie Williams' advice and just go with the moment, I was so concerned with keeping the momentum going and deflecting the bad press I never stopped to consider if I was happy.

I wasn't.

I was deeply unhappy.

In San Francisco I met a new therapist who would walk me through the pain and the torment of my childhood in a way nobody ever had. His name was David and he had a little practice on Polk Street, Nob Hill, a beautiful and historic neighbourhood full of Victorian buildings and old-world charm. Our first meeting was really the first time I felt safe and emotionally 'held' by a psychologist. In the past, doctors had prescribed antidepressants as a band-aid for my emotional scars. David was different. He was empathy personified wrapped in a blanket of kindness.

306

I saw him every Tuesday. Afterwards I'd go to this charming retro diner and drink coffee and eat lunch and let the session resonate for a while before driving back over the Golden Gate Bridge to Sausalito. I started making the connections about the desire I had to be loved and the conundrum I faced coming from the family I was born into. Bono has often described the emptiness of a performer as trying to fill a 'God-shaped hole', a phrase he may have borrowed from Salman Rushdie. Regardless, I was able to recognise that whether I wanted to admit it or not, I had a deep longing to be loved by a father, just not the one I'd been given. David encouraged me to identify the small child inside who was crying out for someone to protect him and love him in a way that only a father could. This required revisiting the ways in which I felt abandoned. It felt like an archaeological expedition into the darkest tunnels of my heart.

INTERIOR: Psychologist's office, San Francisco, 2003

I walk up the comfortingly familiar carpeted stairs of the Victorian building that houses David's practice. There's a smell to San Francisco, I swear. I've never been able to pinpoint it but I think it comes from within the buildings. I suspect it's due to the frequency of earthquakes which dictates that most structures aren't made of brick but of wood. This makes them pliable and flexible when terror reigns on terra firma. Whatever it is, the smell of pine or cedar or spruce is an earthy and grounding scent that permeates most homes in the Bay Area.

I enter the small waiting area and press a button to let David know I've arrived. Within seconds, I'm greeted with the warmest smile as he opens the door to his study. He has these deep brown, almost black eyes that radiate kindness. He's tall, trim and older than me. Maybe old enough to be my father. I'd be lying if I said I hadn't fantasised about what it would be like to have had a dad like him.

We sit down and we talk like friends until the conversation naturally sparks a question that leads us down a path of investigation. Today, I've mentioned something about feeling like nobody was ever really attending to me as a child. The attention was always on my father.

'Did you go on family vacations together?' David asks.

I laugh.

'Okay, how about family nights out together?'

'The only family nights we had were a period in the mid-1980s when my father was a regular at the Waterford Hotel.'

'Tell me more.'

'Well, it was a time in my parents' marriage where my mother had gone to meetings for partners of alcoholics. But nothing was working. So she tried to join him in his world. Rather than be left alone every weekend, we would, as a family, go to this outdoor pub and just watch my father get drunk.

'There were picnic tables and a swing set and it was next to a river, of sorts. So me and the other kids would play outside until well after dinner time. Then if we were lucky maybe we'd get some potato chips and a pink lemonade. We'd run around barefoot with the other pub children, making temporary friendships that lasted from 3 p.m. to 10 p.m. every Sunday. I'd either end up eating a meat pie or my mother would manage to drag my father home in time for a home-cooked meal. She usually wasn't successful because the drunker he got, the more belligerent he got. Sometimes we'd end up in the owner's own house, watching the adults drink after hours, as we kids fought off sleep. That was a good night.'

'And a bad night?' David asks.

I stare out of the window. I can see vague shapes walking up and down the street, obscured by the dimples in the vintage glass. They're like my memories. Distant enough they can't hurt me anymore. I don't want to pull them into focus.

'A bad night was watching a fist fight break out. Sometimes my father, sometimes strangers. Dodging broken beer glasses. A bad night was my father turning from sloppy drunk to mean drunk and having to worry about what was going to happen when my mother got him home.'

David explained that many children of alcoholics lacked a sense of consistency. A regular routine with a set bed time, for example, was just one of a myriad of ways a child could feel a sense of structure. The boundaries and gentle guardrails that a stable home life could provide help them make sense of a world that can seem chaotic.

I felt a sense of grief when I heard this. I thought about my sister and how she was often trying to provide that for me, even though she was just a teenager at the time. At what expense, I thought. The loss of her own childhood. And my brother Peter, so silent and often so angry. Of course he was. He was the middle child in a dynamic where his voice was often muted simply by the nature of our distinct personalities. My sister had to be loud and aggressive as the protector, while I was naturally emotional and verbally expressive. Peter seemed to go inward, perhaps as a form of self-protection. I know it must have been difficult for him because he shared a lot of common interests with my father. It must have been conflicting. He loved his parents and yet one of them was hurting the other.

Then there was the dichotomy of our relationship. I shared so much with my sister – music, fashion, movies. But being a young kid who was gay, I didn't share many interests with my brother. He was very physical, into rugby league, girls and typical things hetero-sexual boys are into. He had a brother who was more like a little sister. When I look back at our childhood, it's Peter that I often feel the most sorrow for, because it was he who was the most isolated emotionally.

I told David that my father loved hunting and from my earliest memories I recall him heading 'out west' to Gundagai, a town in New South Wales, about a twelve-hour drive from where we lived. When I was five he started taking my brother and me, along with a mate or two of his and some of my male cousins. This was not glamorous. Back then, children were allowed to ride in the back of a pick-up truck. My father and his mates would sit in the safety and warmth of the cabin while the two hunting dogs, our camping equipment, my brother, my cousins and me all sat in the back of the truck with the adults' eskies, or coolers as Americans call them, full of beer. When the men wanted a drink they'd knock on the window and one of us children would spring to life and hand them an ice-cold beer – all while travelling at lightning speed, often in the middle of the night.

If any of the men needed to go to the toilet, they'd stop at a gas station. If any of the children needed to go to the toilet, we were expected to pee out of the back of the moving vehicle. I remember once my brother was so desperate to pee, he banged on the back window. This request was ignored several times. 'I'm busting!' Peter yelled. From the cabin came the command, 'Just piss out of the side of the truck!' So my poor brother got up, steadied himself like a stunt man and relieved himself, enduring the humiliation of the entire contents of his bladder splashing back into his face at 80 kilometres per hour. The men didn't care.

When we got to our destination around midday – usually a sheep farm – we'd unload the truck and begin a weekend of animal cruelty. No hunting occurred during the day. No. That was reserved for watching the adults drink beer and boast and demonstrate such masculine qualities as 'men can swear' and 'men spit' and 'men have knives'. They'd cook a one-pot dinner by a campfire and then just when an eight year old was exhausted and ready to go to bed, the men, now fully intoxicated and armed with loaded 22-calibre rifles, would put the two deadly pit bull dogs and the children in the back of the truck, designate one of us as 'spotty' (the spotlight holder) and off we'd go in pursuit of feral pigs.

The truck would lurch and heave in and out of crops at break-neck speeds while the dogs would howl in anticipation of what was about to happen. One of my older cousins would operate the spotlight and one of the men would be up the back with a rifle. If they spotted a kangaroo they'd shoot it. No questions asked. If they spotted a pig, they'd unleash the now ravenous canines from their heavy chains. Saliva flew through the air as the dogs would scream and cry as they disappeared into the darkness to do what they'd been bred to do.

We'd then wait for the blood-curdling squeals. They sound exactly like a human would scream if two dogs had attached themselves to their throat. The truck would take off, like a rocket, in the direction of the noises of horror and we would be confronted with a large feral pig, often a pregnant mother, and two pit bulls with an ear each in their mouths, blood smeared all over their white coats.

To remove the dogs from the pig there was no verbal command. It was a fist or the shoulder of a rifle. So dedicated were they to the job, the dogs often found it impossible to unlock their jaws from their prey. The drunk men would beat the animals over the head before hog-tying the near-dead pig and throwing it into the back of the truck. On the way back to camp, we'd pick up any dead kanga-roos they had shot. If we were lucky, it too would be a mother, with a joey in its pouch and we were allowed to play with it for the duration of the trip.

All of this seemed like violence on cocaine. Murder on Adderall. And yet at the same time, entirely normal. Because it was all I knew.

When I finished telling David this story his eyes were wide. His face pale.

'You've seen so much violence in your life, Darren. And you were such a gentle child, desperately seeking validation for the emotional qualities you possess. You had a role model who not only actively tried to discourage those qualities, but who was also incapable of modelling positive masculine attributes. I'm so sorry that happened to you.'

I cried a lot in David's office. The tears were grief, I guess, for a childhood I never had. That I never knew I was entitled to. It's funny how a child only knows what they're exposed to and therefore thinks of as normal. I'm reminded of the analogy of the boiling frog. My repeated exposure to violence, in small but constant increments over time, made me unaware of, if not immune to, how extreme the conditions I was raised in were.

I told David about a picture of me taken on a hunting trip when I was around five years old. I'm standing with my brother, my sister and my cousins, proudly holding the almost fully formed embryos that had recently been inside a pregnant sow. It's barbaric and it haunts me to this day. Our hands are smeared with uterine blood. If I think about the context of the photo for too long my mind conjures up horrors. Presumably this animal had just been killed, bled and butchered. During the process the men had discovered the sac of babies and thought us children might like to hold them. This immersion in violence and the remnants of the physical act of violence all around us was barbaric. It was like we were some deranged members of a cult, a pseudo Manson family, taking a photo after a ritualistic killing. At the time, we smiled for the camera like we were holding a koala at the zoo.

Through our therapy sessions, David helped me gain distance from the shame that was imprinted upon me and the simple fact that

I had one male role model and that person was full of rage, unable to contain his emotions and lacked any kind of restraint. It came out when he got drunk, when he lost his temper, when he hit my mother. When he hit his children. It came out when he went hunting. He proudly displayed his knives, his guns, his ability to use them to take lives and the skin of animals. He proudly displayed his rage like I displayed my *Star Wars* toys.

I admitted to David that my father's behaviour towards us, though frightening, just seemed like normal parenting at the time. It wasn't until our therapy sessions that I'd been able to revisit some of the 'spankings' that I received and view them in a different light. My siblings and I weren't just spanked. Sometimes we were slapped in the face. Sometimes my father used his fists on my brother. Sometimes the bruises he left remained for weeks. We believed we deserved it, I guess. I certainly had an inner monologue that said, 'I am a bad person. I deserved this. This is normal. This is what happens to bad little boys.'

David explained that what I experienced was not something I deserved and certainly had nothing to do with me as a person. He helped me understand that it was my father who was unable to control and contain his own shame, self-hatred and rage, and that he projected all of that onto the people around him. He was unable to host those feelings. I, on the other hand, had made a career of hosting and expressing feelings. One could argue that was why my lyrics and performances connected with so many.

I remember asking him, 'Am I a bad person?' This came up because I'd fallen out with many people and my love life was a shambles. 'I guess I'm afraid I'm like my father.'

David smiled at me with those eyes that were like a pool of never-ending kindness and acceptance and said, 'Do you think your father ever asks himself if he's a bad person?'

The revelation was instant. Of course he wouldn't! He believes the entire world has wronged him.

I told David about how our family life really did revolve around my father's ego and his hobbies. Firstly, there was the collecting of exotic, rare and I must stress *illegal* birds. My father was obsessed with parrots. Rainbow lorikeets specifically. He'd somehow trade goods, money or services for them and sooner or later we'd have half our backyard sectioned off as a bird sanctuary.

Next was his cowboy phase. That was interesting. It began with outfitting the entire family in Wrangler jeans from head to toe. I don't know where we got the money for it but you can imagine a tiny Darren wearing a felt cowboy hat, plaid shirt, denim trousers, cowboy belt with western buckle and actual cowboy boots with spurs. This was to match the adult version of the costume my father wore, while he embarrassingly dragged us around various state rodeos where he would compete, riding bulls.

This performance art certainly required commitment. Up at dawn, driving to God knows where, listening to country music on cassette tape to get us in the mood. When we arrived, the entire family would sit on bales of hay while 'Bobby Hayes' (his brief cowboy name) waited for his turn to be thrown from a bucking bronco. The second-hand embarrassment I felt was palpable. My face got so red I felt it would explode like a tomato in a microwave. Bobby Hayes barely lasted a second in the saddle, and the laughter in the crowd was not subtle. I don't even know if his bull made it out of the gate before his sweaty hairy cosplay cowboy body was flung into the blue sky and slammed down onto the red earth with a mighty 'that'll teach you' crunch. Every time it happened I hoped he'd die or get seriously injured. But he always dusted himself off and got back up again.

I remember getting lost at one rodeo. Come to think of it, I got lost a lot as a child. But this particular western-themed one really stung because not only was it announced over a giant PA system but I remember feeling ridiculous in my outfit. I sat swinging my legs on a massive decorative old-time wagon filled with, you guessed it, bales of hay, while concerned adults looked with pity at the abandoned child in the country and western outfit complete with a bandana so big it threatened to take over his entire face. Honestly, at the time I wished it would.

Fantasies of my father dying were common. I remember him taking us on a camping trip where we stayed by a river. First of all, I hated camping and I still do. I think it stems from the fact that my introduction to the great outdoors was via a gateway of violence that was pig hunting. This particular near-patricide memory involves the whole family swimming in a crystal-clear river, while my mother, who is a nervous swimmer, sat tentatively at the edge not wanting to get wet. So of course, we three children and our father used our hands to splash water playfully towards her. This escalated to skimming pebbles on the surface to try to get her wet and entice her into the freezing but invigorating body of water. One by one, we each ducked below to fetch a river rock to toss in her direction. My father dived to the bottom of the river and swam breaststroke. I picked up a massive rock, almost as big as my head, and hurled it towards the riverbank, near my mother, hoping it would make a massive splash. Uh oh. My toss was miscalculated and the rock missed the bank by six feet and hit my father's bald head underwater with a subsonic 'thud' we could all not only *feel* but see. Blood began to billow in a red cloud in the water.

'I've killed him!' I thought, partly in shock and partly in relief.

To my disappointment he leaped out of the water, placing both hands on his head, clutching his wound in pain. 'What in the hell did you do that for?' he cried, clearly too dazed and confused to summon the energy to punish anyone.

315

'It was an accident,' I said. 'I was trying to splash Mum.'

Probably because of the headache already forming and the bruise that would eventually take over most of his head in a few days' time, that was all the explanation that was needed. He went and got a towel, some ice and eventually a beer. I sat wondering if I'd meant to hit him. What would have happened if I'd killed him? The thought was too much to bear and I quickly pushed all manner of motive or guilt aside. It was an accident and he was fine.

In the therapy sessions in between albums, I worked through an enormous amount of guilt, responsibility and shame for many relationships in my life. I still felt terrible about leaving Colby all those years ago. I was still financially taking care of my friends and family in ways that were unhealthy. I presented this as a way of expressing my love, but at the root, I was able to see I was terrified of being abandoned. As a result there were a lot of people on my payroll. I began to question my sense of self and it brushed up against my deepest fear, which was that nobody really loved me for me. They either loved the character I'd created in Savage Garden, being in my weird, strange fame orbit, or that I always picked up the cheque. I own the fact that I put myself in that position. I wouldn't allow people to split a bill or even buy me a cup of coffee. I always felt responsible for everyone around me. If a friend was depressed, I'd pay for their therapy. If someone passed away, I'd feel it my responsibility to pay for the funeral service. My heart was in the right place but it created an imbalance of power and I know that was not fair on anyone. In the long term, it took agency away from those I loved, or it allowed people to take advantage of me. Either way, it was confusing.

When I first made millions of dollars, I did what most people with a guilty conscience about becoming suddenly rich do – I paid off the mortgages on my family's homes. It relieved a feeling of guilt in me for a little while because I couldn't fathom the concept that my own siblings owed money to a bank at a time in my life when I could buy a house with cash. This also allowed my mother to leave my father and a few years later, my parents mercifully separated and then divorced.

At first, I felt a strange rage about the situation.

Why hadn't my mother left him all those years ago, when we were suffering so badly? I feel selfish for having that reaction. Obviously I see now that my beautiful mother, like me, was a victim of domestic abuse. My father's first victim. She was stripped of her self-worth from the minute she met him. She endured decades of physical and psychological abuse all the while having to make huge decisions about her safety and her ability to feed and clothe her children. When she finally had the courage to leave him, it was because her children had grown up, were safe and she didn't care if she lived in poverty.

I couldn't let that happen.

I bought her a little seaside home so she and my father didn't have to stress about dividing their assets.

But it wasn't enough for my father. The only time he ever wanted to speak to me was to ask me for money. At that stage, I was paying all of his bills. He had some emergency credit cards in my name but he seemed to have so many emergencies the cards would max out constantly and he'd call me to pay them off. And I did. He never spent money on anything urgent. It was lavish gifts for women he was pursuing, equipment for his hobbies, or travel. It got to the point where I just couldn't afford, literally or emotionally, to keep giving him money.

Therapy helped me see how my previous relationship was an attempt to fill the void I felt was missing from my fractured relationship with my father. I was repeating the same patterns, choosing emotionally unavailable men, or men who would belittle me or take advantage of me. To put that behaviour in language where I'm not a victim: I had zero self-respect or self-esteem. I allowed men to treat me that way and it was destroying my life.

Slowly but surely David encouraged me to love myself. To connect to the little boy inside who was so terrified of being abandoned, and to remind myself what a wonderful job the adult version of me had done to protect my child-self all these years. I was littered with behaviours designed to help a five year old survive trauma and was still living as though my life were in danger. But my life wasn't in danger. I was just terrified to confront the pain.

I was able to channel the lessons I learned about myself and turn them into songs and they became the basis for the album *The Tension and the Spark* – a record that would receive some of my finest critical reviews and yet get me dumped from Columbia Records. It was a deeply personal record, with no filter. I spoke about my broken romantic relationship. And I spoke about my family. I was brutally honest. In the song 'Unlovable' I practically wept into the microphone.

> You made me feel like my father never loved me. You made
> me feel like the act of love is empty. Am I so unlovable? Is my
> skin untouchable? Do I remind you of a part of you that you
> don't like?
>
> – 'Unlovable'

When the record was completed, I took it to Mark 'Spike' Stent, who had mixed all of Björk's albums but had recently started working with Madonna. I had approached him to mix my *Spin* album years before and he was notoriously blunt. He didn't like the music. So he said no. This time, he was beyond enthusiastic. I knew the music I'd made with my collaborators on this album was raw and cutting edge. I wasn't pretending to be anything other than who I was. I was a man in pain and this was the sound of it.

Columbia Records hated it. 'Do you have another single? Can you write a single? We need a single,' was their response. Reluctantly I wrote a song called 'Shit on the Radio' and sent it to them. Needless to say they said they didn't like it and the album was 'fine' the way it was. But they made it clear they had no intention of promoting it in the US.

My spirits were lifted when I got a phone call out of the blue from Elton John. At first, I missed the call and he left a voicemail. It turned out we had a friend in common, a publicist at Columbia Records. Elton's message said he loved my new album and please could I call him back. I was speechless. I did, of course, and was treated to the kindest, most supportive pep talk about how much he respected my work on the album. He invited me to Las Vegas that next week to see his show. When I arrived, there were probably fifty people in his dressing room and he stopped all conversation and said, 'Everybody, this man has just made the most incredible record.' I will never forget Elton's kindness during a time of great uncertainty in my life.

In the UK, the album received an entirely different reaction: the label loved it. The president at the time was obsessed with the song 'Darkness' but I wanted to release 'Unlovable' as the first single. A compromise was made to put out the deeply ironic and cynical pop song 'Pop!ular' instead. In context, the song made complete sense. It came halfway through the record and was a retrospective jab at the artifice and fake image machine I'd been put through. Out of context, it didn't really serve as a true indication of how deeply serious and emotional the album was. Still, my team was thrilled that one part of the world was excited about the record.

The decision was made to relocate to the UK for six months to promote the album.

I'm sad to say that, although the local Sony affiliates in Sydney were incredibly supportive, Australian radio was not. It had now been almost five years since a top forty station had officially backed my music. With no radio support, I didn't have the promotion or the sales to bring my tour to Australia, my home country. The UK and Europe seemed to be embracing my sound and that's where I had to head.

I didn't want to leave Sausalito, my therapist, David, or my dog, Wally, who was only two years old at that time. But I had to go where the sun was shining and ironically that was London.

London Calling

The truth is I never wanted to leave San Francisco, but the situation with my record company in the US was so untenable there was no choice. In 2004, my entire entourage – and it *was* an entourage – including my dog, Wally, moved temporarily to the UK into a rented house on Ossington Street in Notting Hill. There was my manager at the time, Leonie; her husband, Robert (who was also my main co-writer and musical director); my hairdresser, Troy; my trainer, Sharon; and finally my manager's nanny, Michelle, who took care of their son. All, bar the nanny, were on my payroll. And yes, it was as dysfunctional and crazy as it sounds. Thankfully that period of employing my friends was slowly coming to an end.

My mental health was spiralling yet again. I had just careened out of another relationship disaster where I'd given all my self-esteem and power to a man, only to find myself a hollow shell afterwards. I was confused about my sexuality. So far, nothing about being with men had brought me any peace or joy. I found myself longing to become a father and live a simple life. I saw a psychiatrist who put me back on antidepressants and I constantly fought the urge to go to sleep and never wake.

I was working a lot, doing a tonne of promotion and appearing literally at the opening of an envelope. One television show

I was convinced to appear on, against my better judgement, was called *Popworld* hosted by presenter Simon Amstell. At that stage, my lyrics were beyond ambiguous – I was using male pronouns about my objects of affection, and was not hiding the fact that I went on dates with men, but in the media, I had never been 'outed' and nobody had ever directly asked me about my sexuality. In the past, there had been vague allusions, questions like, 'People speculate about your sexuality, does that bother you?' to which I would always answer, 'Not at all.' I never had a fake girlfriend or did anything to present myself to the media or my fans as being heterosexual. One would think that after five years of being divorced to a woman and never ever having a public relationship with a woman, it was blatantly obvious that I was not straight. There'd always been this tacit agreement with journalists that we all knew who I was, but because I didn't lie about my sexuality, they seemed to leave me alone.

That was until I met Simon Amstell.

Popworld was based around the kind of comedy I hate: it punches down, often to humiliate or dig up the dirt on guests. If it didn't manage to achieve that through the live interview, it did it in the editing suite. The premise was that popstars were vacuous idiots who weren't aware they were being mocked. Unfortunately, the show was one of the few outlets at the time for live performances and nabbing a spot was considered incredible exposure. So I went on and performed the song 'Pop!ular' and then sat down for my interview, most of which never made it to air.

The first question Simon asked me was, 'You're obviously gay, why don't you ever talk about it?'

I felt a rage fill my body. This man, who was gay just like me, thought he had the right to out me, without knowing a thing about me, or my life, or my circumstances. It was such a betrayal of community and even back then, so utterly inappropriate. Instead of reacting in anger, I let the rage simmer within. My eyes became two slits.

'You want to know how I like to fuck, Simon?' I said. 'Is that it? If I'm more of a top or a bottom? Is that what you'd like to know? Actually, I'm kind of versatile. Are you interested in me? Would you like me to fuck you?'

The entire room stopped breathing.

Simon was speechless for the first time in his life. Someone yelled 'cut'. A producer came over to me and said, 'Are you okay?'

I was frozen. Traumatised. Just like I felt in high school. I was 'vibrator' all over again. I was a 'faggot' holding my face after my father had thrown a watch at me. I was a thirteen-year-old kid being spat on, eyes glazed, dissociated, devastated and cold as steel.

'I'm fine,' I said in a deathly cool tone.

'Let's just start this again,' the producer offered apologetically.

I never broke eye contact with Simon, who was squirming in his seat.

They yelled 'rolling' and Simon began a benign and harmless interview that I honestly can't even remember, I was so catatonic. As I was led out of the studio, I got put into a van and that's when I broke down. I felt the years of bullying take their toll. I felt my armour crumble from three decades of survival. I was a snotty, heaving, bawling mess, crying from the depths of my soul.

'I can't do this anymore,' is all I said.

The idea that anyone felt they had a grip on a rug underneath me that they could pull out at any time was never as prominent as it was then. I felt utterly ashamed and totally powerless.

I spiralled into a deep depression after that interview.

Still, there was work that would not wait, a tour booked and the reality of life in the UK. All I wanted to do was curl up into a ball and run back to Sausalito. But I couldn't.

Although I was thrilled with the music I'd released and the tour Willie Williams and I were putting together, the sluggish album sales triggered a war between my management and the record label. Columbia said they didn't want to release the songs I wanted to and on the eve of the second scheduled single, 'Darkness', they cut all spending on the campaign. The official explanation was they didn't want me to have a low-charting single. It was baloney. Sony were merging with BMG, people were losing their jobs left, right and centre and nobody really cared about my artistic integrity. The situation was dire.

One day, I was complaining to my dear friend Troy about my disastrous love life and feeling very sorry for myself. He pointed out that the love of his life, Shane, who had now been diagnosed with cancer, was dying, and that if it took me the rest of my days to meet someone, so be it. 'Just choose to be happy,' he said, understandably furious with my self-indulgent misery.

His tough-love approach woke me up from a depressive coma.

I met my future husband, Richard, the next week and a year later we got 'married' in a purely ceremonial wedding in the backyard of a house I'd bought in Notting Hill. It didn't come without some sacrifice, however. I had to sell my beloved sea-side home in Sausalito and surrender my Green Card to become a British citizen. It was a testament to my love for Richard, at the time. I used to say the only thing I loved more than San Francisco was him. A year later, when civil partnerships became legal, we officially recognised our relationship. Prior to that, I was invited to attend Elton John's wedding, and the one piece of gossip I'll share was that there were more Diptyque candles (the expensive $100 French kind you see in most *Vanity Fair* celebrity home photoshoots) at that wedding than I've seen in my entire life. So many that guests were stealing them as they left! Elton was, and always is, a complete gentleman, and greeted each and every guest as they arrived. There was no minder whispering in his ear, but he remembered me and told his husband, David, exactly who I was and how much he'd loved my album. That man is the real deal.

Once married, it was easy to come out. I loved myself and there was something tangible to point to. I was in a relationship I was proud of and being able to declare to the world my happiness in my own skin healed something inside of me. I didn't exploit our relationship, I didn't do the cover of *People* magazine with a 'Yep, I'm gay!' quote. I came out by writing a blog on Facebook, letting my fans know I'd married my boyfriend. I don't even think I used the word 'gay'. It was a very simple and quiet process.

The reaction was mostly kind and welcoming, but I did feel a change in the way the media perceived me. I was suddenly everyone's 'favourite, harmless, gay uncle'. Back then, you'd see this stereotype on television, where the only acceptable mainstream gay people were comic relief. Take a show like *Will & Grace*. Gay men, or queerness, was only okay in the mainstream if it didn't offend anyone. At the same time, gay men were rarely allowed to be sexual beings. That's a bit of a problem for a popstar when sex appeal is an essential ingredient.

I say the reaction was mostly welcoming. I remember coming home to attend the ARIA awards, where I hadn't been since I'd performed 'Lost Without You' for Delta Goodrem, when she was recovering from Hodgkin lymphoma in 2003. I hadn't been nominated for a single award, nor invited to the ceremony since, but I was attending that night as an independent artist, when a 2Day FM journalist asked me on the red carpet, 'Are you a top or a bottom?' Classy.

*

325

The next few years were wonderful creative times in the studio and I absolutely loved the work I was doing as well as the associated musical tours. My record deal with Columbia mercifully went away. They got two more songs out of me for a 'best of' Savage Garden compilation (although we initially did discuss the possibility of co-writing new material for the project, ultimately Daniel declined to participate) and when it was time to submit music for a follow-up solo record I was honestly ready to record three hours of tantric screaming if it meant they'd boot me from the label. Thank God they 'passed' on the option to 'pick up' my next record and I was free of the men in suits. It was liberating but also shocking that I made that record company so much money and in the end there was not so much as a thank-you note. Just silence.

In 2006 I had the opportunity to do a whimsical and completely bonkers 'best of' tour in Australia with Willie Williams called A Big Night In with Darren Hayes. Essentially a live game show – I'm not kidding – it came about after Willie had noticed that my in-between song banter was, well, funny. I had a habit of making light of my misery and very little was out of bounds. The night I confessed that I'd had recent troubles with haemorrhoids he came backstage in fits of laughter. He couldn't believe that a 'popstar' would say such a thing on stage. He said he wanted to lean into my theatrical and funny side next time. So we did.

Yes, I played all the hits, but we began the show by encouraging all the single audience members to call a certain phone number. We then built upon our concept of finding a date for one lucky person. With the assistance of my entire entourage, we then gave them the time of their lives. As soon as the red curtains opened it was like a scene from Broadway. Troy was on stage ironing. My manager was drinking martinis at the purpose-built bar. My assistant Lana was hanging around on her laptop. All had the task of finding a date for the lucky audience member, who was given a makeover and then pampered, live in front of the audience. Once we'd found them some suitors, we seated the couple at a table and I serenaded them. Each night we had a local restaurant deliver food. You can imagine the poor delivery driver's face when he arrived at the Sydney Opera House Concert Hall!

During a part of the show we called the 'Savage Garden Karaoke Challenge' I gave an iPod of instrumentals to an audience member and sang whatever they wished while they held up a video camera, filmed me and projected the images on a massive screen. It was funny, first and foremost. It also celebrated the history of Savage Garden in a way that was fan-centric. You could tell I enjoyed singing the songs as much as the audience enjoyed hearing them.

But like all good things in life, the tour had to end and I regrouped in London to dream things up again.

Grief is Patient

As the years went by my depression slowly crept back in. One day I realised I'd developed a ritual of jogging at sunset, alone, just so I could look at the sun and cry. There was so little light in London, especially during the winter, and I started wishing I was back in Sausalito. I bled all my sorrow out during those runs and returned home as though nothing was wrong. Sometimes I'd find myself in the carpark of a grocery store, sitting in my Mini Cooper with the engine turned off, crying, without explanation. I missed California. I was tired of feeling misunderstood in London. And I was lonely. Most of my entourage had disbanded and I had few close friends besides one darling who lived more than a two-hour journey away. And I didn't have David, the therapist who had been so helpful in San Francisco.

In the years since *The Tension and the Spark* as I slowly started to let my entourage go, it was disappointing to realise that some friendships seemed to fizzle when I stopped paying people. It was a hard lesson to learn that many of my longest friendships were actually just staff. There were some financial betrayals and I had to reckon with the fact that I had created a world of transactional relationships. This pattern began at the first band dinner I ever paid for and continued throughout my professional and personal life. I felt financially responsible for everyone and everything.

I remember being in Paris for my birthday in 1999. Most of the band and crew knew I was fun to hang out with because I'd always pick up the tab. This particular night, a group of close friends including Lee Novak and Karl Lewis declared they wanted the band to pay for my dinner. Everyone agreed. It was a touching gesture and it meant the world to me. When the cheque came, however, quite a few people at the table either looked away or put their hands in their laps. There was an uncomfortable silence and in that moment it was obvious to me that I was expected to pay the bill. Yet again. So I did. But I left the table with a heavy heart.

I recall these anecdotes not to criticise others, but to demonstrate how used I'd become to being in a position where I felt like I was essentially buying love. It was a brutal slap in the face, almost twenty years later, to realise that some of my deepest relationships were based purely on money. This cynicism affected how I viewed friendships. I became guarded and inward. I didn't trust people. I fantasised about moving back to my old house in Sausalito. I'd google it often to see if it was for sale. Once I even flew back to look at an apartment in the same building, with no ability to actually purchase it, just existing on the fumes of happiness that being in Marin County had given me before returning to London.

But as much as I yearned to move back to America, I couldn't imagine ever living that life again. I had to surrender my Green Card in order to move to the UK and I didn't know if I qualified for another one. Then there was the issue of my husband. Our union wasn't recognised in the US. I felt trapped.

Homesick, I decided to fly to Australia to spend some time with my mother. I arrived at the car rental facility at Brisbane airport and gave my driver's licence to the guy behind the counter. He looked at my ID and did a double-take.

'You look a bit like him too,' he said.

'Excuse me?'

'The guy from Savage Garden,' he said, as he continued inputting my info into the system.

It was an awkward moment. Do I confirm I am the person he thinks I am or do I just play dumb? Ah what the hell, can't hurt.

'I *am* that guy. That's me,' I said.

He stared at me. Then glanced incredulously at my driver's licence. 'Geez you've piled on the weight!'

I could have died of embarrassment. Yes, I had put on weight. Years of being on antidepressants has that effect. Doctors don't really know why. You lose urges. Like the urge to exercise. Or give a shit about what you look like. It's ironic. I used to want to kill myself every day until I started taking those pills. Now I'd look in the mirror and hate what I saw, but not enough to kill myself, thanks to the medication. Oh the irony.

I got in the car and sobbed. Drove to my mother's house and curled up in her loving arms.

That week, I'd take a solo trip to my old life. Time travelling I call it. I parked on Lake Road. I stood in front of the old tree where I used to climb its branches and hide and feel so safe. I looked at the house, almost unrecognisable from the horror stories of my memories. Then I walked, slowly, on foot to the Argonaut shopping centre. Step by step getting younger and younger so that by the time I reached the park on the corner of Lake and Reserve roads, I felt like a teenager again. At that very moment, hundreds of rainbow lorikeets chirped in unison until their calls became a frenzy. It was as though they were saying, 'The boy king has returned!'

I didn't feel like a king.

Things were strained with my family. I had, for a long time, employed my mum, my sister and my brother's wife to run my fan club. It was a hard job during touring and album cycles, but there wasn't much to do during the in-between times. It wasn't a necessity and it never made a profit. But it made me proud to be able to support my family.

Over the years, I'd been spending more and more money on tours and sets, and making less and less money. Essentially paying for the privilege of touring. One day, my accountant sat me down and said that my music career would have to essentially just be a 'hobby' from now on.

I was devastated. Humiliated. Embarrassed.

The fan club was haemorrhaging money. We'd have to shut it down. The first thing I had to do was stop paying my family. I wrote my brother a letter explaining this, which was a humiliating thing to have to do, and embarrassing because I felt like a failure. My sister's marriage had ended and she was now a single mother of two young children, but my brother and his wife both had full-time wages, so I felt justified keeping my sister employed for a while until the fan club could be wound down. I always intended to take care of my mother.

We had, mercifully, got back in touch with my Aunty Jenny and Uncle Colin once my father was out of our lives, and I discovered she'd had two more beautiful children, Todd and Daniel. Aunty Jenny was just like I remembered her; hilarious and loving. She reminded me of Cyndi Lauper. And she was so proud of me and my career. My nephews Matthew and Kim meanwhile were all grown up. Kim was married and pregnant with her first child.

Then something terrible happened. I got a phone call from my brother. We rarely spoke so I knew something was wrong. He told me that my Uncle Colin had died. On the way to visit his first grandchild in the hospital, my darling Uncle Colin and beautiful Aunty Jenny were hit by a driver who was texting. It was a head-on collision and my uncle was killed instantly. Aunty Jenny was in a coma for months. She awoke to a world without the love of her life and with a three-month-old grandchild. I still cry when I think about it.

Some of the events around this time inspired my album *This Delicate Thing We've Made*.

I was in a honeymoon period with Richard and was obsessed with Kate Bush and the fact that she used a Fairlight synthesiser on her 1985 album *Hounds of Love*. So I went on eBay and found one for a mere £5000. In the 1980s, they cost over $100,000. Mine was clunky and barely worked but when it did, it was very special.

My dear friend and musical director at the time Justin Shave and I set up camp in Primrose Hill to the north of Regent's Park. I became fixated on the past, specifically on travelling back in time, to change things. The album cover featured a paper origami bird – a visual metaphor about marriage. I knew, even back then, that the relationship was fragile. The 2007 Time Machine tour that accompanied *This Delicate Thing We've Made* was my most expensive as a solo artist but I don't regret a single thing. I wrote a song about my sister coming to save me in her yellow car and every night I'd stand upon this purpose-built, eighteen-foot animatronic neon origami bird and 'ride home' to her. On opening night I could barely get the words 'She's coming to rescue me' out before I started crying.

The tour came to Australia at great expense but, no surprises, made no money. Grant Marshall, who had filmed all of my solo concert tours, shot it at the Brisbane Convention Centre.

Afterwards I took time off to lick my financial wounds.

Back in London I moved us to Clapham in the south of the city, away from the bustling and exciting but honestly suffocating media hub of Notting Hill. I thought being close to some greenery and a quieter lifestyle would bring some inner peace. It did for a while.

I spent wonderful moments on the common with my dog Wally, lying on the grass, trying to disconnect from all things music business. I used the time to reflect on what I liked and what I didn't. I think I was jaded following my first attempt at being an independent artist on my own label. I felt discarded by the industry. *This Delicate Thing We've Made* had virtually no radio support anywhere in the world. The exception was a remix of 'On the Verge of Something Wonderful' which became a Billboard Dance Hit.

I was becoming cynical, something I never wanted to be, and I took that as a sign to step away. As a result, I had no real desire to make music, no creative urges at all. An industry friend encouraged me to do some co-writing for other people and I reluctantly did the rounds in London, pitching songs to other popstars. In the process, I spent time in Sweden with Carl Falk, a songwriter who at the time was unknown but would eventually become very famous writing songs for One Direction. He and I formed a special musical bond and before I knew it, I was writing a follow-up album, *Secret Codes and Battleships*. Recording that album was a rollercoaster. First of all, some of the songs were leaked before they were finished, which meant I had to hire a digital forensic specialist to track down the files and those who had them. It cost more money than it was worth. I was also trying to wean myself off antidepressants. Something I took upon myself to do for reasons I still don't understand. One song, in particular, 'Cruel Cruel World', is about that experience. 'Blood-stained Heart' was written for my sister, about her divorce. I just remember the image of her, always the strongest person I ever knew, suddenly sucker-punched. I wanted to step in front of the pain.

Then, one very cold June day in 2009 while in Stockholm, I woke to the news that Michael Jackson had died.

My phone had been going crazy with notifications, my email inbox was full. Tracey eventually got through and told me what had happened. I'm so glad it was her. I was numb. I didn't understand. How could this man who had inspired me to become a performer be dead and yet I was still alive? I had so little will to live anyway, why had the universe wasted it on me?

As I made my way to the studio, the newspapers were plastered with pictures of him in an ambulance. I went into the recording booth and saw a candle burning. I was getting ready to sing the song 'Black Out The Sun'. It was horribly prophetic and appropriate. My heart made its way through my vocal cords and onto that recording. 'There is an emptiness inside of me, since you've been gone, all the world has lost its meaning, all my colours run . . .'

As I left the studio I saw the candle, still burning. I thought about how inspiration is like a flame that gets passed from person to person. That fire had been extinguished in my idol but it still flickered within me.

Why?

I went back to London with that song in my pocket, intending to give it to the British singer-songwriter Leona Lewis. There was something magical about it. Even though her label loved it, I was secretly devastated I'd agreed to give it away. It felt like giving up a child. In the end, they slept on the song for almost a year before saying they didn't want it. I was happy about that. It now belonged to me.

I had long since started my own record label and released my own music that I adored, but the industry was becoming more and more affected by weak sales. Touring was expensive, I never made a profit, and sometimes I ended up in debt. Although I had a new team and a new sense of excitement from them about the music I had made, I was reluctant to return to the stage. I didn't trust the media, I didn't trust that anyone would play the music, or that any label or distribution partner could get it to my fans.

Secret Codes and Battleships was an intentional return to a more pop sound, and I'd partnered with a major label in Australia this time, which relieved me of a little of the financial burden, but not much. Right from the beginning of the project, however, it was clear that it didn't matter what kind of music I was making, radio just didn't want to play it. I got the usual excuses from the pop stations, 'We love Darren but this doesn't fit the format.'

Unfortunately, in the UK it was the same.

The first single didn't land at all. Just when I was about to give up there was an unexpected surprise. The song 'Black Out The Sun' seemed to please the gods at Radio 2, the most popular station in the nation, with over 14 million listeners. It was added to the station's A list, which meant it received regular daily airplay over a lengthy period. That decision – along with my legacy in Europe reminding people of my back catalogue – gave my career a much-needed boost and really helped the associated tour. Still, the process was expensive and exhausting. I employed so many staff, radio pluggers, publicists, artists and musicians. At the end of it all I was in debt again.

By the time I was set to get back on the road, I had made a secret pact. I was retiring. I didn't tell my audience or even close friends, but there were clues in the pre-show music I played each night. Each song hinted at a farewell, with either the words 'Goodbye' in the lyrics, or the theme of death. The penultimate piece of music before I took to the stage was Tchaikovsky's 'Finale' from *Swan Lake*, followed by a recording of the song 'Oh My Love' by Katyna Ranieri, as featured at the end of the film *Drive* in a scene where the hero drives away, surely bleeding to death.

I was deeply tired, in my bones. The years in London had just flown by. I blinked and ten years had passed. I spent my fortieth birthday in Paris, desperately sad.

'What's wrong?' Richard asked.

'I guess I always assumed we'd have kids by now,' I replied.

There was a brief pause and he said, 'But you never really wanted to have kids, did you?'

I betrayed myself in that moment and instead of screaming out with everything in my heart that I wanted to be a parent, I just agreed. I didn't know what was wrong with me. I was grieving for something that was still missing. Maybe a break from the industry was what I needed.

Back in London we continued the tour. I sang passionately and performed with abandon. I was performing for the last time, the audience just didn't know it. At my last show in Brighton, I left the stage, heartbroken. I felt like a failure.

The following night I drove around London on my own, utterly lost. I looked back on the past decade and felt completely drained and totally worn out. I thought back to seeing Michael Jackson's last performance at Madison Square Garden and shuddered at the thought of myself becoming a version of that type of performer: painted into a corner against my will, wheeled out to sing the 'chica cherry cola song'. I did not want that to be my future. But I too felt like a worn-out circus lion.

Weeks passed. Then I came up with a crazy idea.

There was still a one-year US work visa left on my passport. What if we just packed up everything and left? I didn't think the idea would appeal to my husband but to my surprise he agreed on one condition: he didn't want to live in San Francisco. He wanted us to have a new adventure in a city neither of us had lived in: Los Angeles. The only part of LA that I liked was Santa Monica. So we agreed upon that.

In 2012, we packed up our lives and left the UK for good.

Reinvention

When I landed in Los Angeles I thought it was the biggest mistake of my life. I knew nobody. What the fuck was I thinking? My career was mostly based in the UK. My long-term assistant and pretty much rock of my life, Tracey Turner, who had worked with me since 2004, lived in the UK. There was no infrastructure for my business in LA. I had nothing to build on. I immediately fell even further into a depressive slump. Richard was fine. He had a plan to study screen-writing. But I was emotionally and physically drained.

A friend of mine who was a life coach would later try to get me out of the slump by working on my self-esteem. In one exercise she asked me to describe myself as an animal. I said I felt like a once mighty lion, now old and wounded, lying by the side of the road, gasping for breath. That realisation led me to a ten-year journey in therapy. Ten years of going to the same therapist every week, trying to get to the bottom of why I felt such tremendous sadness in my heart.

The first time I walked into his office, I had a huge burden on my shoulders. I'd been depressed for at least half my life. I felt a gnawing guilt in my stomach and I didn't even know how to artic-ulate it.

INTERIOR: First therapy session, Los Angeles, 2013

I instantly love Matthew. He's similar to my therapist in San Francisco for many reasons. He has a background in the creative arts, he's not an alpha type personality even though he's masculine, he has real empathy, the kind you can't fake, and he's created an office environment that is warm and enticing. It's like the places I go to in my mind when I want to seek comfort. Retro furniture that reminds me of my childhood, plants, artwork that I get lost in, and a smell I can't quite place. It smells safe in here. Maybe it's incense.

We beat around the bush for a bit. Asking polite questions. Being polite. I give him my family history in short anecdotes but he sees there's something lurking below the surface. My lip is trembling, my eyes are filling with tears. I'm trying to hide that from him. I have a nervous tick: I pick individual hairs from my beard, one by one, from my cheek. It's become such a habit I don't even notice I'm doing it. It greatly concerns Matthew. It's an anxiety disorder, I explain to him, diagnosed by my shrink. He tells me he can see that I'm in a great deal of pain. That statement alone makes me cry. He tells me it's okay and hands me tissues.

'What is it you're afraid of?' he asks gently.

'I'm afraid my marriage is ending.'

The words come out of my mouth and I instantly want to take them back. But I can't.

'What would happen if your marriage ended?'

I burst into tears. The shame monster appears. The wasps in my tummy stab me. The endless pit of doom appears; this is a new one. It's just off to the left of me and if I fall into it I'll freefall endlessly. There's nothing inside but darkness. No oxygen. I'll be suffocated. I'll never be able to come back up for air.

'My whole world would end. I can't imagine a world without Richard in it,' I say. 'He's my life. My family. My everything.'

'Alright, well that's good. So let's save your marriage,' he says. But, he warns, rarely is a marriage ending about two people not being in love anymore. Usually it's about a loss of emotional intimacy. He wants to know what's hiding inside me, what am I not sharing with my partner. What is it that I can't seem to say to Richard that I'm so afraid of?

I don't think there's anything I don't share. I think it's that we find it impossible to discuss it together. I desperately wish we could talk openly about how devastated I feel about the distance between us. We just seem to avoid it. I think the thing I'm avoiding is saying that I'm afraid our marriage is in real trouble.

So that's where we begin. Working on building up my confidence and my communication skills to be able to talk to my husband honestly about our relationship.

Matthew gives me one word of caution. He tells me to avoid discussing my marriage problems with people outside. He says it creates an unfair dynamic. I take this to heart, literally. Until the day I talk to my friend Maddy almost a decade later, the only person with whom I discuss my marriage is my therapist.

My original plan, when I moved back to the US, was to curl up under a blanket and just grow old. I didn't understand what was happening inside my marriage. I didn't know how to fix it. But I didn't have the courage to end it because I had such love and a duty of care for the person I'd pledged my life to. It was inconceivable that there could be anything wrong with us, because we were such good companions, and yet I felt trapped by my secrecy pact, even before Matthew advised against sharing intimate details. I was so ashamed that something was wrong. It was just like my childhood all over again. I thought back to my high school musical and the schmaltzy ballad 'Put On a Happy Face' I'd sung. I wasn't particularly fond of the song but it showed everyone I had a good voice. I'd been putting on that happy face for as long as I could remember and it was exhausting.

Having stepped away from the music industry, I was dealing with a deficit in my life, but I didn't realise it. I had treated my career and my creativity a bit like a tumour. Instead of targeting the parts that were toxic, I had removed an entire limb. That meant the whole universe of performance and every outlet of creativity was now gone. Yet I still had a feeling of dread in my stomach most days. One of the most helpful and beautiful questions my long-term therapist posed was, 'What if the feeling inside your stomach, this feeling of dread, was not a tumour, but a pregnancy?'

What a beautiful thought. What if I'd been spending all this time preventing something from emerging that I thought was going to be catastrophic but was actually something wonderful?

Seeing how sad I was, Richard suggested I take a theatre improv class to get me out of the house and to stimulate other parts of my creativity. That led me to the Groundlings, an improv comedy school famous for its alumni who went on to work on *Saturday Night Live*. Comedy greats like Kristen Wiig, Lisa Kudrow and Will Ferrell are examples of legends who trained there.

When I auditioned, I felt like a complete idiot. It was the first time I'd done any acting, really, since auditioning at Kelvin Grove when I was eighteen. I thought I was terrible and I remember literally sitting in the gutter in Hollywood afterwards, with my head in my hands, thinking, 'What the hell did I just do?' I was surprised to learn days later that I had passed the initial screening and made it into the program.

I spent five years studying at the school and also moonlighting in outside acting classes. During that time I met most of the friends

340

I have in Los Angeles today. They are people who, when they first met me, did not know what I did for a living and were in fact shocked to discover I had this secret life as a 1990s popstar. It was an essential experience for me to feel what it was like to walk into a room and stand on a stage without any expectation or advantage. I failed and succeeded purely according to my performance.

Yes, doing comedy and facing fears of the unknown was great for my atrophied artist's brain, but the true gift was learning how to make friends without my credit card. It was so wonderful to realise I was lovable and likeable just because of how I treated people. My fractured heart needed to learn that lesson.

In the process, I became a godfather. My goddaughter is now seven years old. When I met her father, Johnny, he was the most talented guy in class, intimidatingly so. We ended up writing a musical together and during that process he and his wife became pregnant. I offered to babysit their child while Johnny continued his studies at the Groundlings. I'm so grateful for that experience because I spent one day a week with her, from the age of six weeks old, until she went to pre-school. I bottle-fed her her mother's expressed milk, I changed her, I bathed her, fed her, put her down for naps and washed her clothes. We went on stroller walks and I hung out with other parents in parks. I got to love her, and protect her, in ways I'd never experienced with my own father. I also got to feel, in a small way, what it might be like to be a dad. Loving her healed a part of me that needed healing.

I remember one day she woke from a nap and she was frightened. I heard her cry out for me on the baby monitor and I went up to her room in a hurry. I found her with her arms outstretched. She'd had a bad dream. I held her so tightly and told her, 'I'm here, darlin'. I'm here. Darren's always going to be here. You never have to worry because whenever you're with me, you're always going to be safe.'

My heart exploded with joy. It felt like a full-circle moment to be able to offer safety from a place in my life where I had come to accept I had never felt safe when I was a child.

During those years I also slowly found my way back to music, something I swore I never wanted to do again, thanks to the Groundlings and Johnny. I became the Groundlings' default 'music guy' whenever anyone had a sketch idea that needed a song. By the time I was putting together my final showcase, most of my sketches involved music in some comedic way or another.

Over a period of five years, I slowly built a home studio with the help of my friend Trevor Yasuda, who is a phenomenally talented musician, producer and songwriter and, at that time, was an engineer with the producer Rick Nowels. Trevor helped me put together a small mixing desk and two microphones when I started a movie podcast. Over time, I learned how to use Logic Pro, the professional recording software many producers use to make albums, and my podcast studio gradually transformed into a pretty sophisticated home recording studio.

By the time Johnny and I had finished writing our musical, I knew how to engineer, record, mix and pretty much write music on my own. Something I never thought I'd be able to do.

Nightmare

INTERIOR: Hallway, Lake Road, 1987

I'm woken by the droning sound again. The out-of-tune choir mixed with human screams. It's coming from the hallway and this time I know what's out there: the television with the portal to another universe. Peter has long since moved out of my bedroom. It's just me here now.

I open the door and the hallway is swirling with bits of paper and debris, animated by a massive industrial fan, the kind I've seen in a Duran Duran music video. Strobe lights blink so rapidly it makes my movement appear in slow motion. I look up to where the television is supposed to be – mounted on the ceiling at the end of the hallway – but it's not there. Instead, there's a glowing white light under the door to Peter's bedroom. I make my way slowly to his door. Open it. Peter is asleep and underneath his single bed is the source of the neon glow and dry ice, pouring out onto the floor. I can't see what's under the bed, it's obscured by his bedspread which hangs almost to the floor.

I get down on my hands and knees and crawl towards him. I half close my eyes and grab his bedspread and lift it up quickly, like tearing off a band-aid.

I scream.

There's a dead body.

My brother screams.

I've woken him up.

The bedroom light turns on.

I've been having another night terror. There are no strobe lights or neon fogs or eerie musical soundtracks. No dead body under the bed. Tracey and my mother have woken up. Everyone is looking at me. I'm dizzy. Confused.

'Go back to bed, love,' my mother says gently.

CUT TO: Santa Monica, April 2017

My family had long since ceased all contact with my father, having exhausted all avenues of kindness. As far as I knew, he was living in a trailer park somewhere or other.

One day, I got a phone call from my sister. She told me that my brother's son had died from suicide. He was only eighteen. At first I couldn't process what I was hearing. Ben was so happy. He was a jokester, a prankster. He was the life of the party and was just a baby.

I got on the next flight I could to Australia. As soon as I landed, I discovered the airline had lost my luggage. I remember being at the lost luggage counter when the situation really hit me. I was dealing with the airline agent who was telling me that my bags would arrive 'in a couple of days'. I broke down crying, telling her that they wouldn't arrive in time for the funeral. She didn't seem to care. It hit me in that moment that when somebody dies, the world just goes on. Shops open on time. Kids go to school. Luggage gets lost. You don't know when you walk down the street what anybody is going through. Somebody could be having the worst day of their lives and yet the world keeps spinning as though nothing has changed.

After travelling for almost twenty hours I finally got to my brother's house. I can't put into words the anguish I felt, seeing Peter in so much pain. I fell at his feet and wept.

As everyone does during times of crisis, my family did whatever we could to try to support my brother and his family during what was an impossible time for them. I was tasked with telling my father of the tragic loss. My nephew and my father had been close, in spite of his exclusion from our greater family. Although my brother had no relationship with him anymore, he wanted him to hear the news. There was one caveat: for the sake of the peace of all involved, my father was to be asked to please not attend the service. My sister and I set about trying to find him. It didn't take long. It was like falling back asleep into a nightmare that had been gleefully expecting my return.

My nephew Ben, or 'Benny' as we all called him, had been a spark of joy from the second he first opened his eyes. I've honestly never met anyone like him. He had a permanent grin and the first two words he ever said must have been 'but why?' because he questioned everything. He lived passionately and he loved passionately. He got into trouble at his strict religious school because they didn't understand he had a mild learning disability; a unique way of processing information, a condition my sister has and I suspect I may also have to some degree, although I've never been formally diagnosed. It can manifest as an attention disorder or simply 'bad behaviour' but it breaks my heart that none of Ben's teachers really took the time to see how brilliant he truly was. The rigid curriculum of a traditional school system isn't made for children as unique as Benny. As a result, he often struggled with self-esteem. On the surface he was exuberant and charmingly confident, but he was often self-deprecating about his intelligence. It's a shame because I thought he was a genius. He was also hilarious and had a brilliant sense of humour. Whatever I thought doesn't matter because when he took his own life, an act that devastated his immediate family and sent shockwaves of grief throughout his universe, all of that magnificence disappeared instantly, unfairly, prematurely. Forever.

In trying to notify my father of his grandson's death, my sister and I had put together various leads and pieces of information from friends of friends and whispered last sightings. We deduced the location of the trailer park where he might be living. We knew he'd been travelling back and forth between Malaysia and Brisbane with his new partner so it was unlikely he'd be at this location, but we had to try.

By now, my father's relationship with all of us was non-existent but he had, for better or worse, developed a bond with Benny. I thought at the time it was incredibly admirable of my brother not only to allow a relationship between the two of them, but to also have the moral decency to tell our father of his grandson's death. I certainly wouldn't have.

I hadn't seen my father in over ten years. The last time we'd spoken, he had asked me if I wanted to 'invest money' in his house. This is the house I paid the mortgage on decades before. It turns out he'd taken out loans on the house and was yet again in debt. At the time, I genuinely could not afford to loan him money, or anyone else for that matter. I was recovering from two drastically overspent tours and I was honest about that. He had two brand new Harley-Davidson motorcycles, racehorses, and all manner of luxury items. I suggested he could sell one of the many trophy items and he took great offence. It struck me as ironic because the one time I ever asked my father for money was just before Savage Garden broke big. I was behind on my rent and I got a traffic ticket for bald tyres on my very old car. I needed to get four new tyres and I was ashamed to call my father to ask him for money. When I did, he said no and told me, patronisingly, 'Maybe you need to adjust your lifestyle.'

When I declined to 'invest', again, in his house, his tone immediately changed and he hung up. About a week later I received an email eviscerating me. I couldn't believe it. I had been paying that man's utility bills, phone bills, credit cards, you name it, for years. I paid his home off. I flew him around the world. The one time I said 'no' – he basically cut me out of his life.

I was fine with ending the toxic relationship. He had demonstrated that all I ever was to him was a source of money. But his treatment of my siblings and my mother was unforgivable and so this showdown I was about to have with him was significant. It would mean knocking down a barrier I never intended to break. Yet here I was with Tracey, purposely seeking him out.

'That's it. That's his car,' Tracey said as we drove slowly along the gravel driveway of the trailer park. My entire body froze. I felt like I was eight years old again, sitting in a sandpit, playing with my *Star Wars* toys, seeing his Ford F100 pick-up truck arrive. Only this time, I was the one searching for him.

We parked the car and got out, walking gingerly towards his trailer. The door was open. I peeked inside and could hear a loud snoring sound. I smelled a rank odour of unwashed bodies and trash. 'Robert,' I called out. Inside, a figure moved underneath a sheet, barefoot, emaciated. He sat up and looked at me, startled. He was completely unrecognisable. No longer the overweight, bearded, bald, muscular and tattooed terror I remembered from my youth. This creature looked more like Gollum from *The Lord of the Rings*; wasted away by time and from years of ingesting his own hatred. Sinewy and pale, his skin clinging to its bones.

'Yeah?' came the reply. He looked right through me. Zero recognition.

'It's Darren,' I said coldly.

'Who?' he replied, confused, stumbling to his feet.

'It's Darren. Your *son*.' I couldn't believe he didn't know who I was.

'Jesus Christ, I didn't recognise ya. How are ya?'

He thought this was a social visit? And that we would just pick things up as if nothing had happened?

'I've got some bad news to tell you. Can you come outside?' In spite of my utter resentment towards him, I was not without compassion. I was aware my news was going to devastate him. I wanted to be as considerate as possible and give him time to digest things.

I averted my eyes while the stranger before me put some clothes on. My sister and I moved outside to a seating area, if you could call it that. It was one fold-away chair on a concrete slab. The ground was littered with cigarette butts. My father smoked two packets a day when I was a kid, but he'd given up twenty years ago. Apparently he'd taken up the habit again.

Tracey and I sat down on the ledge of the concrete slab and our father hobbled over to his chair. He smelled like he hadn't bathed in a long time. He looked tired. His grey beard was stained with nicotine.

'Do you mind if I smoke?' he asked.

Something came over me. All of those years of growing up in a house where living in a smoke-free environment was never an option. As a child my clothes always stank of cigarettes. The walls, the carpets, the curtains. Everything.

'I do, actually.'

My father stiffened, visibly annoyed. 'Why?'

'Because I don't like it,' I said firmly.

He was forced to extinguish the already lit cigarette. It was a tiny victory but it felt huge to me.

'Dad, I came here to tell you some very sad news. Benny's dead.' I conveyed this as compassionately and kindly as I could.

There was a pause and then my father said, 'Was it drugs?'

Rage filled my body. Ben had never taken drugs in his entire life.

'No, it wasn't drugs. He committed suicide, you fucking prick.' I was furious. Ben was a clean-living, good-natured soul. He drank beer but he was no junkie. The insinuation was so inappropriate, so cruel.

'There's more,' I continued. 'Peter has asked that you don't come to the funeral, to keep things peaceful for everyone.'

'Oh is that right?' my father said, with the sinister tone I remembered from my childhood. 'Well fuck this, I'm gonna smoke.' He lit up a cigarette. 'I bet you it's because of his father,' he added.

I couldn't believe, in this time of absolute sorrow and tragedy, he was trying to blame somebody. And not just anybody, he was blaming his own son.

'You're an arsehole,' I said.

'And you're a faggot,' my father snapped back.

At that moment my sister stood up for me, like she had my entire life. 'Don't you *dare* say that word to my brother!' she yelled.

With that my father got up and raised his fists to me.

'What, you wanna hit me?' I said. The adrenaline in my body was now the only thing controlling my actions. I stood up to meet his fists, my own raised and ready to fight. 'Just try it, you fucking prick,' I growled, holding my ground. I was no longer the scared little boy, watching this man beat my mother to a pulp. I was a man myself, and I was tired of running away from the monster that had terrorised my life since my brain had stored memories. It was a debilitating and conflicting feeling, being in a physical war with the man I swore I'd never see again, engaged in an act of potential violence as a sworn pacifist, feeling how rage could fuel a reflexive gesture so at odds with my gentle nature.

Every bully who'd ever struck me flashed before my eyes. I saw my high school terrorisers, I saw the random strangers from the past who had hurled homophobic slurs at me, I saw the record company executives in their pin-striped suits. The faces of a thousand tyrants cycled endlessly in front of me but instead of fleeing like I had every time I'd felt threatened in the past, this time, I held my ground. I stood in a boxer's stance, ready to do whatever it took to defend myself.

My father seemed frozen in thought, having never seen this defiance from me. For a second I saw a flash of the scared little boy in him wash over his face and then it was gone, replaced by a devious thought of escape. I saw him, in real time, weigh up his options. And then he bolted for the trailer, scurrying off like a cockroach. There was a commotion inside, the sound of drawers being opened, objects being turned over.

'Let's get out of here,' Tracey warned, 'he might have a gun.'

We knew that he owned weapons. I was not about to find out what he would do if there was one inside. We jumped in the rental car and got the hell out of there. We drove to the nearest police station to file a report. We knew from my brother that my father didn't have a licence for any weapon he owned and we were terrified that he might do something violent. As we sat in the interview room I felt detached, empty. Nothing had changed in the forty-five years my father had known me. He'd learned nothing and nothing I'd done to gain his love had changed his behaviour towards me. I felt numb. More than that, I felt disappointed in myself that I'd given him the opportunity to see me again and hurt me.

I had vowed I'd never let him get to me again but here I was clutching the sides of the chair in the police interview room feeling no different than I had as a child after one of his outbursts, trying to hide the fact that my body was shivering, trying to process the stress hormones rushing through my veins. I fucking hated him.

*

The next day, I sat on the back step of my brother's house, looking at the gum trees as the sun set. Inside, the constant roster of well-meaning condolences and the smell of lilies was starting to make me feel nauseous. I couldn't breathe with the amount of sadness in the room. Suddenly, beams of light shone through the trees in such a cinematic way, it looked like a special effect, like something created on a film set when an aircraft was landing in a forest at night or a spaceship was passing overhead. It seemed otherworldly and supernatural. For a moment I took solace in the thought that maybe this was a sign from Ben, to let me know he was at peace.

At the funeral, I was charged with standing with his casket, to watch over him, before the service began. My brother couldn't bear to leave his son alone and I understood that impulse. As my brother went outside to meet with the minister and greet the hundreds of people who had come to pay their respects, I was left standing next to the cold box that could in no way convey the warmth and joy of the soul it contained. It was a stark reminder of the horror of suicide and the permanence of death.

Later on, after the funeral, although my father thankfully didn't attend, he parked his truck at the end of my brother's street every day, morning and night, and just sat there, so my brother and his wife and daughter would have to see him as they left for work each day and came home each night. It was a classic intimidation tactic, meant to make them afraid. It was stalking.

But this time, we weren't putting up with my father's nonsense. The family went to court and with my Aunty Jenny's help, put together a historic picture of the abuse and torment this man had put our family through, right up to the current stalking. We received a restraining order and although this was little comfort during such a time of grief, it was at least one less thing to worry about.

Call Me By Your Name

After Benny's funeral I returned to Santa Monica and life continued on, seemingly without purpose, for a few years. While I enjoyed my time at the Groundlings, and loved my new friends and new creative challenges, the gnawing feeling in my stomach that something was wrong in my personal life would not go away. I adored my time co-parenting my goddaughter, but that was coming to an end. She was starting school and I started to experience empty nest syndrome.

The more time I spent in therapy, the more my therapist urged me to try couples therapy. Richard wasn't keen. I slowly lost confidence in myself as a sexual being and slowly gained weight, year by year becoming a non-entity. One day everything changed. I went to see the film adaptation of *Call Me By Your Name* by André Aciman – a gay love story set in the 1980s. I saw it with Richard and my reaction was over the top. I couldn't stop crying and I didn't know why. I soon became obsessed with it, and would go see it, again and again, on my own. There was something in the story that released a feeling of grief within me, a sense of lost youth.

I bought the novel, read it, and my reaction only solidified. I realised that I had never celebrated or truly felt loved for who I was, when I was, if that makes sense. When I was the most famous and most adored publicly in my career, I was completely confused about my sexuality and I probably hated myself. My internalised homophobia was so great that I often felt like an imposter, having all the applause and adulation pointed my way, often by women, when the reality was I felt like I held this deep, dirty secret about myself.

Years later of course I came out and got married to a man, but my public life was very quiet by then and when I think about it, I sort of 'buried the lede'. I didn't start with declaring and owning my sexuality. I made all the focus about getting married to a man. I didn't focus on 'coming out'. Deep down inside I was still ashamed of who I was. It's disappointing because I can honestly say that the day I married Richard was one of the happiest days of my life. I was surrounded by family and friends, and it was a very simple, beautiful ceremony. We wrote vows, which were in fact lines, like a script, for the attendees to speak. Each one veered from either wildly funny to deeply emotional or absolutely, wickedly, humorously inappropriate. Even though gay marriage wasn't legal then, it felt incredible to have the love, support and acceptance of our community. I honestly thought we'd be married forever.

Somewhere along the way, our delicate thing got broken.

That's why, years later, a film about a young gay teenager, with parents so accepting and loving of who he was, made me so deeply sad. I was grieving an adolescence I never had. I was grieving a freedom and sense of self-love that wasn't possible for gay men of my generation. I was probably also grieving a sense of closeness in a relationship I saw unfolding on screen that had been missing in my relationship for a long, long time.

The sense of loss was so great it quickly turned into anger and then that anger turned into passion. A passion for music that was *extremely* gay. I had never really addressed my sexuality or been 100 per cent honest, stylistically, about who I was. Suddenly I felt an urge to be emancipated from this and to do everything I was forbidden to do in my career previously. The first step was to do it all myself. I didn't want any collaborators, any co-writers, any producers – nothing. I wanted to make music all by myself. The second step was I wanted it to be unapologetically gay and sexual. And that began with the title: *Homosexual*. As soon as I had the name everything fell into the place. The colours, the packaging, the hair styling; basically the entire visual representation of the music became crystal clear. I was already in control of the sound of the record and now I knew how it would look too.

Along the way to making the music, I started caring about my body again, working out, eating healthier food and seeing myself as a sexually viable person and not just a husk waiting to die. If that sounds dramatic, it's supposed to. I really was just sitting around waiting to drop dead until I felt inspired to make this music. By making the record, something inside me awakened that had been dormant for decades. I compare it to the flowers I often see growing through cracks in concrete footpaths. There was something buried deep within me that refused to die and desperately wanted to be heard.

In the music industry, it's a given that it's always been misogynistic. But misogyny is, at its root, a hatred of the feminine. You can see how being a gay man in a predominantly male, straight industry proved challenging for me to garner the respect and credit for the contributions I made to my songwriting and recordings. With *Homosexual* I was determined to remove all collaborators and to answer the question, once and for all, of what exactly my contributions were. I was not just a lyricist. I was not just somebody who wrote melodies. Maybe in the beginning of my career, but as I was about to turn fifty, I had studied engineering, I had studied sound production and chord progressions and I was able to not only compose my music entirely on my own, but play it, program it, engineer it, record it and do rough mixes of it. I was not just a songwriter. I was not just a performer. I was a producer now.

My latest solo album is my proudest achievement because it is the result of me not quitting a band. Me sticking with the process, success and failures alike, not being afraid to make mistakes along the way or have commercial failures. It's the sound of somebody who did not give up. I never gave up on my fans and I never gave up on myself and the end result is an album that is 100 per cent my vision with the post-production help of just two people: my dear friend and the incredible mix engineer Trevor Yasuda, who did the final mixes, and then the Grammy Award-winning mastering engineer Mike Bozzi.

With songs averaging over six minutes in length, *Homosexual* is the antithesis of 'commercial'. Yet upon release it got the best review of my career. The esteemed British newspaper *The Independent* gave it five out of five stars and called it a 'triumph'. I cried tears of joy when I read that. I was astonished that I believed in myself and it paid off.

When the record was finished, I found out that my dear mentor, Gary Beitzel from Woody's, was a mere week away from dying of melanoma. He initially had oral cancer, a fact that had been kept from all but his closest family for as long as possible. It was suggested to me that if I could somehow get the record to Gary to listen to, it might brighten his spirits.

I was absolutely gutted to hear this news. I'd known Gary was sick, and I had spoken to him after one of his surgeries earlier in the year, but I had no idea he was going to leave us. His name had been in the liner notes of my 'thank you's for all my albums. He had heard each record before it was released. He was at every gig, every record release party and at some of the most important moments of my life. I simply adored him and couldn't conceive the thought of him leaving us. Still, Claire arranged for me to get a link of the music to

Gary and a time for us to talk on the phone, even though his speech was severely restricted.

Soon after, he passed away. I wasn't able to attend his funeral but I watched a live stream of it and I cried my eyes out, along with everyone else.

A few days later, I was sitting at home one afternoon in Santa Monica and heard the most familiar but strange sound. A cacophony of rainbow lorikeets outside my window. I walked outside and sure enough, beyond all explanation, a flock of the Australian birds was chattering and flirting with each other above me. No sooner did I say, 'Gary?' than they flew off towards the sunset. The boy king may have returned to Logan a few years before, but the true king, my mentor, my father from another mother? He returned to stardust that day. I miss him so.

Returning to the Stage After a Decade

The promotion for the new album was intense. It began with head-lining the Sydney Gay and Lesbian Mardi Gras in March of 2022, a few days before the Do You Remember? tour tickets were to go on sale and a full seven months before *Homosexual* was due to drop.

It had been a long time since I first performed at Mardi Gras. I was first invited to perform in 2005, but I wasn't 'out' yet. The experience then was a strangely sad one for me because I was surrounded by a community of people who were so full of self-love and self-acceptance, and yet I was still deeply rooted in my own shame. I was so excited to be able to return to this experience some seventeen years later as a fully out, loud and proud gay man.

The Mardi Gras rehearsals were exhilarating. I worked with the team at New Ground Collective who assembled not just a crew of dancers and three stages on a cricket field, but a narrative and choreography set to the seventeen-minute medley that Trevor Yasuda and I had worked on meticulously. We pulled no self-indulgent punches. We would give the audience exactly what they wanted: classics. It was mostly Savage Garden classics, with my new single 'Let's Try Being In Love' at the very end.

The rehearsals were one thing, but standing on the hallowed grounds of the SCG, I felt my contact lenses almost permanently glue to my eyes when the massive flames of fire shot up in the air. I was not prepared for the sheer heat they generated as we did not rehearse this during the rainy soundcheck. My heart was in my throat when I started 'The Animal Song' and made my way to the stage via a row of line drummers. I knew the audience was with me when the first bars of 'I Want You' rang out and the entire stadium rose to its feet and cheered. The rest was a blur of sweat, glitter and tears of joy.

After that, it was a thrill to go out on tour and reunite with fans around the world in 2023, giving them what they wanted by performing Savage Garden songs alongside my solo material. With the help of Willie Williams, Claire Marshall, Trevor Yasuda and Maddy Coghlan, we designed a pop show that we took all over Australia, the US, Canada, the UK and Scotland. I got to work with Lee Novak and Karl Lewis again, the core of Savage Garden live, plus extraordinary new voices, Sharon Muscat and Virna Sanzone. The show, although not intended to be, ended up being a parallel narrative for what was going on in my private life.

Through telling the songs of the *Affirmation* album, many of which were about my divorce from Colby, I was going through real-life experiences each night on stage, acting out theatrical scenarios and telling anecdotes about leaving and the shame of having to hurt someone you love in order to survive. I cried most nights before I sang 'I Don't Know You Anymore' and during the deeply personal 'Poison Blood', where I thought about my own depression and my beautiful nephew.

If I'm honest, the show was a little too close to home. Thank goodness the loyal and ever-loving audiences, some of whom had waited twenty years to see me in concert, were so supportive. I looked out and saw tears of joy and it hit me that just singing these songs was all the fans wanted. It felt great to be able to make people's lives happier just by being on tour. I feel privileged to be a guardian of the memories that fans have attached to these classic songs and it will always be my intention to give fans what they want, as long as I can.

Clutching at Straws

INTERIOR: Santa Monica, 2023

I'm attending a Zoom session with a psychotherapist who specialises something called EMDR – Eye Movement Desensitising and Reprocessing – a form of therapy for people experiencing PTSD. In my case, I have multiple experiences and memories of trauma. So many, in fact, that my current psychiatrist says he believes this treatment might be my only hope.

For two years prior to filing for divorce, I'd been depressed but kept afloat by the idea that by finally addressing my marriage and leaving, the freedom of starting fresh would solve my problems. In terms of feeling unfulfilled and lonely, yes, filing for divorce was a courageous thing to do, but it also uncovered a deep childhood wound: the fear of abandonment and the reality that I had never processed the traumatic events in a way that my mind and body could put them to rest. For most of my adult life, I'd been a walking time bomb, using whatever skills I used as a child to survive.

The way my therapist explained it to me, sometimes with trauma, especially when it occurs to young people, the experience is simply too much for the brain to process – so we don't. We take the experience and remain locked in fight or flight mode, exactly as we were in that childhood moment. Since fight or flight is a survival response to danger, the brain decides, presumably to keep us alive, that what we are experiencing and witnessing is so horrific and so painful it cannot be processed and must remain tightly packed up, like a zipped computer file stored in an area of the brain that says 'do not open'.

Two things happen when we do this.

Firstly, although our conscious mind is aware the event took place, our subconscious mind, which is where we make sense of our experiences and process emotions, usually in our deep REM sleep, doesn't get a chance to extract, feel, or make sense of any aspect of the trauma. Secondly, any time anything in our daily lives remotely reminds us of the memory marked 'do not open', we respond as though we are back in that moment. Even if we're not consciously aware that a real-life experience is triggering a reminder of a past trau-matic incident, our subconscious mind will commence a sequence of events that start with the fight or flight response. This means, for someone like me, intense anxiety which is often inexplicable and illogical. Imagine how painful this is to experience, repeatedly over extended periods of time and how, after five decades of triggering, this could make being alive feel like periods of suffering occasionally interrupted by brief moments of joy.

I was abandoned several times as a child. I imagine some of those occasions were pre-verbal but of the times I remember, I was not immediately comforted or saved or soothed. I had to take care of my emotional state, my mood, by myself. I made an assumption which then became a belief that I was all alone in this world. Nobody was coming to save me.

How this turned up in my real life is simple: I found it impossible to trust or rely on anyone. Or to believe that anyone could be my 'safe place'. How this might turn up in a routine daily experience is best described by a trip to a mall. I could be with a significant other, happily enjoying a regular retail experience until they turn a corner and disappear momentarily. This happens to many couples. You go shopping. One person's eyes are drawn to a sweater or a piece of jewellery while the other is looking at a book and in a split second they are separated. For most people, this is a completely normal thing. Resolved by maybe looking up, looking around, or texting to see where the other person went.

For me? My hands sweat. My heart races. My stomach ties itself in knots. In the real world, I know my partner has simply wandered off somewhere. But my body is reacting as though I'm a five year old, I've been left alone and nobody is coming to save me. It sounds ludicrous but it's real. The body reacts, in real time, as though an old memory is happening. All frontal lobe logic goes out the window. I have a panic attack.

It can turn up in other ways too. Say I can't sleep at night and my partner has long since drifted off. Suddenly, I'm lying awake staring at the ceiling and a feeling of profound fear and impending doom comes over me. I don't know what I'm afraid of but somewhere in the deep recesses of my mind, there's a memory of waiting up at night for my father to come home from the pub. The still of the night is terrifying because on a subconscious level I still associate the present moment with my ancient memories when horrific violence was about to follow.

I never knew any of this until I met my EMDR therapist. No amount of antidepressants or talk-therapy had ever scratched the surface of this deep pain and those well-worn grooves of thought patterns until I started working on reprocessing those memories.

Reprocessing involves the use of rapid eye movement, often bilateral tapping on the body and gently being guided back through the memories of trauma, only this time as an observer. The patient is encouraged to simply observe, as though the memory were playing at a drive-in movie theatre, or one is sitting on a train and the memory is flickering past outside the window.

Through breathing, tapping, eye movement and allowing the body to experience the emotions, you're able to reprocess the traumatic event in a safe environment. Sometimes two or three times in a row, until the event becomes a memory, like any other event in life, and not something that is happening in real time. The reaction is like any other event in your life. You still have all the same opinions and for me, often some grief and sadness and compassion for my younger self, but my reaction is no longer the feeling of stepping on a land mine. I'm not flinching at the idea of discussing the event, nor am I nonchalant, eyes glazed, numb and walled off from feeling any emotion. I'm simply able to access the memory like everything else in my life up to that point.

In my first EMDR session, I doubt it'll work. I don't believe anything will work. I'm in so much pain, just talking makes me cry.

The therapist and I start out by going through a pre-admission handbook that I've filled out. Family history, family trauma and of course, traumatic events in my life. We then talk through just one of those traumatic memories. The day my father abducted my mother and brother.

Before we begin any of this work, we've had an intake session, where the therapist has helped me identify and access feelings of safety. Both in the workbook and in our intake session, the therapist learns that as a little boy I had a soft spot for a tree in my front yard. It's tall, full of leaves and I would often sit in its generous branches and hug it like a friend. My safest memory is of sitting in that tree while the rain began but remaining completely dry; sheltered by the branches. I'm encouraged to summon that experience and I see and feel the sense of calm. This is safe. I am safe. Now we can begin.

363

She says, 'I want you to imagine you're sitting on a train. And I want you to recall the day your father abducted your mother. If at any time you need to stop, you know the signals we've developed together so use those. If at any time you feel unsafe, remember, this is just a memory, like an old movie. It's just playing, projected on a wall or flickering outside of the train, frame by frame. It can't hurt you. You're just observing. Are you ready?'

She asks me to take my mind back to New Year's Eve 1980, the night of the storm. As I do this, I watch a blue dot on the computer screen move left, right, left, right. In my headphones I listen to the sound of a heartbeat, panning left, right, left, right. On my chest, my hands crossed like a butterfly, I tap a gentle and reassuring rhythm, left, right, left, right. It's intense, I can't sugarcoat it. I feel my pulse race, I feel tears come. I cry. But it passes. It passes! And then there's this feeling of relief. Like a cool breeze on a hot summer's day. Remembering the abduction didn't kill me. It didn't permanently harm me. I'm okay.

Afterwards, we check how effective the work has been by giving the memory a number on a scale of one to ten. The first time I told her about it, I could barely get the words out, I was so choked up. It was a ten. After some work, it's about a seven. We're going to go back in.

In my toolbox, as we call it, I have a whole array of images and places I can conjure in my mind that can bring me back to a feeling of safety. One of them is the old tree I used to sit in. Another is imagining I'm inside the mud hut that Yoda, from *Star Wars*, lives in. I've always been fascinated with sleeping in places that are hidden, like under a desk or under a pillow fort. Yoda's hut is the perfect safe place fantasy for me. In the movies, it's depicted as a cosy adobe structure with carved-out spaces for sleeping. Woven blankets, hot soup and a slow-burning fireplace keep its occupants warm while outside the rain is endless. I imagine I'm inside Yoda's hut now, curled up in a blanket, listening to the fireplace crackle and pop. In my own home, I've got the fireplace going and a woollen blanket over my legs. I have headphones on to listen to the heartbeat noise pan left to right, and I'm watching the blue dot move in the same direction as I gently do the butterfly tap on my chest. We take my mind back to the moment I'm sitting in the bathtub and I hear the disruption outside. Instantly tears fill my eyes.

'It's okay,' Cynthia says, 'you're safe. Just notice the feeling, allow the feeling.'

The feeling is overwhelming dread. But I allow it to fill my chest. Now I follow the memory and let it unfold, like I'm watching an old movie projected at a drive-in theatre.

The rain slashes hard against the high beams of his truck.

The men run around the vehicle.

My father's fists, slamming into my Uncle Colin's face.

The screams of his children.

Then he picks up my mother like she's a sack of potatoes and throws her in the truck.

They're driving away and I'm shivering with cold.

I'm upstairs and I'm sitting on the couch; the television is playing something happy, but I feel so sad. I feel so . . .

'What do you feel?' Cynthia asks.

I stutter, 'I f-f-f feel s-s-s soooo ashamed.'

'Okay, can we spend a little time with that feeling. Can you tell me where, in your body, that feeling sits?'

I wipe my eyes. I point to my chest.

'Okay, can we send a little bit of compassion to that little boy who had nothing to feel ashamed about?'

'Y-y-y yes,' I stutter through tears.

We start the blue dot exercise again and this time, I repeat a mantra in my mind. I imagine adult me, today, holding that little kid shivering on the couch and telling him I love him. 'I got you, kid. I got you,' I say over and over again, imagining holding him and loving him the way I wished I could have been loved. Slowly a smile comes across my face and my breathing eases. I feel the tension in my chest dissipate; what used to feel like black sludge is now disappearing like ink into water. The feeling of shame just . . . fades.

'What do you feel?' Cynthia asks.

'Peace,' I say.

'Do you feel ashamed anymore?'

'No!' I say, surprised.

'And do you understand now, why your aunt and uncle were busy taking care of their children?'

'Yes, of course,' I say.

'Do you think they thought any less of you in that moment?'

'No.' I start to cry. 'I know my Aunty Jenny loved me. She adored me.'

'When you bring this memory up now, what number does it have?' Cynthia asks.

I think for a minute and am surprised to admit, 'Like, a two or a three.'

'Great. That's great.'

INTERIOR: Malibu, Christmas, 2015

Mum has come to visit and it's been wonderful. She's been sleeping in the spare room in our place in Santa Monica and I get to wake up early and sneak into bed with her and give her cuddles like I did when I was a kid. We talk about the old times and she reminds me of innocent happy memories of my childhood I've forgotten. She also tells me about some of the more graphic and horrific things that happened to her at the hands of my father. Things I'd never known.

I cry hearing these burdens she's carried all these years, partly from shame, partly because she somehow wanted to protect his image. I'm glad she feels she can share this pain with me now.

Tonight we're going to Nobu, Malibu, to have a real fancy dinner. It's me, Mum, Richard and two friends of ours.

In the middle of the dinner, my mother and I excuse ourselves from the table to use the bathroom. My mother stops me, one glass of wine in, and she's this adorable cuddle-monkey, full of love and wanting to confess. She starts to apologise about not leaving my father sooner and I stop her dead in her tracks. 'Don't you dare,' I tell her. 'You were a victim too. Don't you ever forget that. We were *all* victims and you don't even realise how grateful I am to you for how you parented me.'

She starts to thank me for the life she's had. She says she's this little girl from Werris Creek who never would have left Australia but thanks to me she's seen the world.

'But don't you understand?' I ask her. 'It's because of *you* that all of this happened. I am the person I am today, because of *you*. Mamma, we won. We made it. Look at us. We're in Malibu at some restaurant way too fancy for us and you're so happy!'

And with the giddiest, childlike voice, she says, 'We did win! I *am* happy!' and I know she means it. Her innocence is intact. Her voice is that of a fifteen-year-old girl. Maybe the fifteen year old she was, so full of life, before she lost her sister, before she met my father, before she lost her mother. She's full of wonder. She is still the happiest, most positive and life-affirming person I know. After everything she's been through. I hold her and she's so tiny, I feel her frail body sink into mine in what she calls a 'Darren hug'. I cry with happiness.

We made it. We really did make it out alive.

INTERIOR: Living room, Santa Monica, 2024. A fifty-one-year-old man sits in front of a laptop having a Zoom session with a female psychologist

I don't want to have therapy today. Every time I sit with Cynthia, it's like peeling the scab off a wound. We've gone through so many of my early life traumatic events and revisited them using EMDR, or, as my therapist likes to refer to it, memory reprocessing. So far, the results have been consistent and positive even though I have to drag myself to the laptop each week. My body does everything it possibly can to resist feeling the emotions associated with the memories. But once my brain is able to sit with the memory, I am able to release a pent-up emotion, usually through tears, that I didn't know I was even holding. The relief is enormous but the work to get there is taxing on my nervous system.

Many of the experiences I revisited in this book leave me depressed afterwards. It's like I'd forgotten how much of an impact some them had upon me, but my job, every day, has been to take a salvage crew down to the bottom of the ocean and dig up my sunken heart. It's a lot and it's starting to give me anxiety about writing. I don't want to revisit anything anymore.

Almost every time I feel like this, we are able to identify a core belief, or some fear I have about myself that is ruling my subconscious mind. Today is a strange one. I've been sad for a few weeks. Yes, it's normal to feel like this going through a divorce after seventeen years of knowing someone, but there's a larger emotion, a bit like being in a helicopter and seeing a whale just beneath the surface. It evades detection and I just can't name it. Something new has happened. For the first time in my life I was able to watch a television show that depicted violence against women and it didn't leave me stricken with fear.

In the past, I couldn't watch anything like that. I remember sitting in a cinema in London sometime in 2011 watching *The Girl with the Dragon Tattoo* and I had to physically leave for parts of the film. Even though my conscious mind was completely aware that what I was watching was a work of fiction, my body reacted to a violent scene as though I was having a panic attack.

At the time, I knew it was because I was very sensitive to my childhood experiences. I didn't realise how the nervous system worked in someone who has been exposed to repeated trauma. In simplistic terms, the body can't differentiate between a perceived threat or a real one and essentially travels back in time and reacts exactly the way it did to the original trauma. The brain of a traumatised person exhausts itself in the process of threat detection. This disables more rational and logical thinking.

In a particularly disturbing scene in an episode of the television show *The Handmaid's Tale* I watched the other night, I realised that I was able to observe the images objectively. I was invested in the story and I had a normal reaction to watching something awful happen to a female character, but it didn't feel like it was happening to me or my mother.

'This is huge, Darren,' Cynthia said.

And she was right. Slowly, but surely, this therapy was rewiring my brain.

I had begun to notice other parts of my life were changing as well. I was no longer seeking validation that things were 'okay'.

A common habit of people with PTSD or children who grew up with abuse is that they feel responsible for other people's moods. They're constantly in fear of being abandoned and therefore read into every micro-expression on a partner or friend's face. If their friend is upset or disconnected, they feel an urge to seek reassurance. This is often a reaction to a fear of abandonment that happened long before the person was even able to speak.

Through speaking with my sister and my mother, I realised I had witnessed horrific acts of violence from about the age of three. In previous talk-therapy, whenever a psychologist wanted to discuss my very early memories, I would begin to stutter. My family used to joke that when I was a child, I had a stutter before I went to school. Well, it was no joke when my therapist would try to take my memories back to a time before first grade. I'd stutter and then shut down all conversation.

Cynthia and I had been working through a lot of this early trauma. Giving a scream or a voice to the early child in me that had no power.

Today was different. I was feeling something more akin to guilt. I explained how even though I knew that it was the right decision to leave Richard, it had taken me years to come to that conclusion. Part of the struggle was that I felt like I was abandoning someone, something that felt antithetical to the way I wanted to live my life. Through therapy we uncovered a bigger feeling: I was ashamed. I felt like a failure.

We were able to get to the root of this feeling and it went all the way back to my earliest memories of keeping up appearances to hide the fact that my father beat my mother. I was so used to keeping secrets and putting on a brave face for teachers, neighbours and relatives, that it had become ingrained in me that it was more important to project the image of happiness than it was to be happy.

The truth is I felt an enormous amount of grief and sadness about the end of my marriage and a huge shadow of shame about the fact that I was not able to make it work for all eternity.

It was time to start letting that go.

INTERIOR: Mexico City, January 2024

I'm sitting in a hotel room in Mexico City, thinking back on the last twelve months. To say I feel traumatised would be an understatement.

This is meant to be my 'vacation'. I haven't had one of those since I went to Norway in 2012. Back then, I sat in a restaurant, deeply unsure about my future, with all of my earthly possessions boxed up and already on their way via ship to Los Angeles. I vowed to never make music again. Retiring was the only thing I was certain about. I had no idea what the next decade would bring but I naïvely thought if I could move us to another country, I could fix everything.

That, clearly, did not work.

But I learned a lot along the way.

I learned no matter how deeply I buried the pain of my childhood, the trauma would find a way to poke its claws up through the dirt and tap me on the shoulder until I acknowledged it. I learned that it's okay to try really hard at a relationship and love and care about somebody and for it still not to work out. The years you spend together aren't erased; they're a triumph. I learned, sitting in a lace shirt in a 2017 Porsche Macan, that although I desperately wanted to die, I'm so lucky that I didn't follow through with that desire. Instead of killing myself, I decided to break the cycles of abuse and trauma, and was able to sit in the discomfort of the pain of my marriage ending and my life and career coming to a massive intersection. And I learned that I'd been using survival skills that had served me well as the child of an abusive father, and had fuelled the ambition of a young man who built an entire career running away from demons.

However, everyone, even a popstar, has to heal.

Sitting in this hotel room now, I still believe in love. I still believe in marriage. I want to have children one day. I want to make music again. I want to tour and I want to be creative. Most importantly, I want to live.

I want to live. Wow. I never thought I'd say those words.

And for that, I'm truly grateful.

*

That evening I go to a concert by a Spanish artist by the name of Mónica Naranjo. I feel completely anonymous. Nobody could possibly know who I am. Except they do. This one man stops me. He is beside himself with excitement, the kind of star-struck excitement I reserve for Madonna. He turns to my male companion and says, in Spanish, 'Is that Darren Hayes?'

What follows is the sweetest request for a photo, hugs, and both of us walking away feeling electric. I can't believe I still have the power, no, the privilege of making a stranger's day better just by saying hello. What an incredible gift that is. On social media and sometimes in the streets I'll often meet fans who tell me that the song 'Affirmation' saved their lives. The one lyric about my belief that we can't control our sexuality in 1999 reached so many questioning queer kids over the past quarter of a decade.

And for that, I'm truly proud.

Epilogue

EXTERIOR: Santa Monica street, sunset, 2024

I'm walking my dog, Huxley, down the street and he's even more stubborn to lead the way than usual. I'm several blocks from where I live, in a part of the neighbourhood I don't often visit, but my friend has just started managing a cool, hip café so I'm going to check it out and say hello.

Huxley seems determined to walk up to someone ahead. I don't see so well with my contacts in, but I make out the shape of a tall, dark and broad-shouldered man. Oh my God. Huxley pulls away from me and the leash leaves my hand like a lost finishing line over a trawler. Up he jumps in slow motion, his Muppet-like fur twisting and turning in all directions, as he hugs this total stranger.

I see the man clearly now. He's seems so . . . kind. That's the word. Kind.

I think of the George Michael song, 'Jesus to a Child'. The man smiles at me just like that.

'Sorry!' I say. 'He's friendly!'

'No, no, it's okay, he's adorable. What's his name?' The man has the most beautiful Latin-tinged accent. I'm not oblivious to the fact that he's also gorgeous.

'Huxley,' I blurt out.

Our eyes lock and it's like we've known each other for a lifetime.

We talk about my dog but we're really just looking at each other. There's a clear connection. With zero trepidation and no evidence this man is gay, I say, 'We should grab lunch sometime.'

He smiles and says, 'I'd love that.'

We exchange numbers and I walk away, pulling Huxley, who definitely does not want to leave.

I'm smiling as I walk down the street. I haven't smiled in a long time.

I get to my house and realise, 'Oh shit! I forgot to say hi to my friend!'

Oh well. Just another reason to lurk around that part of the neighbourhood again.

As I sit down in the living room I hear the most beautiful and familiar sound. The rainbow lorikeets are back hanging out in the tree outside my window. It's been far too long since I've heard their wonderful cacophony of chaos and joy and I could use some of that right now.

I wonder what's going to happen next?

Acknowledgements

Thank you Alison Urquhart for giving me the opportunity to tell my story, especially at Penguin. Your passion, sensitivity and enthusiasm made this dream a reality. Thank you for matching me with Kalhari Jayaweera, the perfect editor, someone so patient and brilliant, who was able to assemble the chaos of my mind and keep all of my intentions intact and legible while providing respectful guidance. Thanks to Rod Morrison for his diligent copyediting. Thanks to Jessica Malpass for arranging publicity for this book. Claire Marshall, we'd all be lost without you, but especially me.

Thank you to my mother, Judy, and my sister, Tracey, for being so brave and venturing into the vast darkness of our past to find the light. Thanks Aunty Jenny, Uncle Col, Matthew, Kim, Daniel and Todd. Thanks Benny. Thanks Colby, Nathalia Rayfield, Lee Novak, Karl Lewis, Willie Williams, Doug Krantz, Monica and Carli Beitzel and those listed in additional photo credits. Thank you to my San Francisco based therapist, Dr David. You changed my life for the better. Thank you to Tracey Turner, who has been a part of my career for twenty years through thick and thin. To Willie Williams who gets thanked twice for never giving up on me. To John and Christine Woodruff for being the most generous and trustworthy people in the music industry and for discovering 'Savage Garden'.

Rosie O'Donnell you are my cutie patootie.

Maggz ♥

Thanks to Larry and Rebecca, Susie Steadman, Clayton Doughty, Kate Hudspeth, Grant Marshall, Justin Shave, Will King, Anna-Maria La Spina, Nicole McIntyre, Elisa Fiorillo, Angie Bekker, Ben Carey, Maddy Coghlan, Trevor Yasuda, Virna Sanzone, Sharon Muscat, Walter Afanasieff, Charles Fisher, Mark 'Spike' Stent, Mike Bozzi, Joan Lader, Carol Tingle, Aimee Macauley, Jade Gould, Emma Powell, Lauren Hales, Myrna Suarez, Troy Brennan, Chris Chard, Andrew Putschoegl, Andrew Huebscher, Stacy Bisel and Brad Walker. Thanks to my first high school music teacher, Susan Landsdown. May you rest in peace. Thanks to Mrs Doust for taking things from there. Guy Stevenson. Johnny & Katie Menke and their beautiful daughter. Thanks Alex Murphy. Thanks Coops, Dickens, Eli, Ollie, Nathan, Matt Whitehead, Fintan and all my new crew.

To H.C., I'm grateful for everything ♥

Special thanks to Gary Beitzel, and everyone who ever worked or shopped at Woody's. Finally, thank you to anyone who ever listened to a song, came to a show, bought an album or supported my dreams in any way. You're the reason I'm here and I'll never forget it.

Credits

Photographs

Page 1 – Judy Hayes, Jenny

Page 2 – Tracey Hayes, Judy Hayes

Page 3 – Tracey Hayes, Rachel Smith, Dawn McMillan

Page 4 – Nathalia Rayfield, Gary Beitzel

Page 5 – Nathalia Rayfield, Colby Hayes, Peita Collard

Page 6 – Paul Webb, Tracey Hayes, Colby Hayes

Page 7 – Colby Hayes

Page 8 – Grant Marshall, Michelle Matthews

Page 9 – Lee Novak, Larry Tollin

Page 10 – Gary Beitzel, Colby Hayes, Leonie Messer, Steven

Page 11 – Gary Beitzel, Angie Bekker

Page 12 – Leonie Messer

Page 13 – Karl Lewis, Gary Beitzel

Page 14 – David Anderson

Page 15 – Grant Marshall

Page 16 – Marisa Cuzzolaro, Grant Marshall

Page 17 – Grant Marshall, Jeff Riedel

Page 18 – Willie Williams, Grant Marshall

Page 19 – Willie Williams

Page 20 – Willie Williams, Daniel Bunker

Page 22 – Willie Williams, Doug Krantz

Page 23 – Alex Murphy, Emily Gibb, Johnny Menke

Page 24 – Andrew Huebscher